# THE FORMULATION OF LOCAL HOUSING STRATEGIES
A CRITICAL EVALUATION

# The Formulation of Local Housing Strategies

A critical evaluation

CHRIS NICOL

LONDON AND NEW YORK

First published 2002 by Ashgate Publishing

Published 2017 by Routledge
2 Park Square, Milton Park, Abingdon, Oxfordshire OX14 4RN
711 Third Avenue, New York, NY 10017, USA

First issued in paperback 2017

*Routledge is an imprint of the Taylor & Francis Group, an informa business*

Copyright © Chris Nicol 2002

All rights reserved. No part of this book may be reprinted or reproduced or utilised in any form or by any electronic, mechanical, or other means, now known or hereafter invented, including photocopying and recording, or in any information storage or retrieval system, without permission in writing from the publishers.

Notice:
Product or corporate names may be trademarks or registered trademarks, and are used only for identification and explanation without intent to infringe.

**British Library Cataloguing in Publication Data**
Nicol, Chris
　　The formulation of local housing strategies
　　1. Housing - Great Britain  2. Housing policy - Great Britain
　　I. Title
　　363.5'0941

**Library of Congress Control Number:** 2001095887

ISBN 13: 978-1-138-26387-1 (pbk)
ISBN 13: 978-0-7546-1692-4 (hbk)

# Contents

| | | |
|---|---|---|
| *List of Figures* | | *vi* |
| *List of Tables* | | *viii* |
| 1 | Introduction | 1 |
| 2 | Housing Supply and the Housing Market | 22 |
| 3 | Demand for Housing | 38 |
| 4 | The Development of Local Authority Housing Strategies and Joint Housing Studies | 72 |
| 5 | Indicators of Housing Demand | 103 |
| 6 | The Use of Data by Local Authorities in England and Wales | 161 |
| 7 | Housing Strategy Development at the Local Level | 210 |
| 8 | Concluding Comments | 230 |
| *Bibliography* | | *247* |

# List of Figures

| | | |
|---|---|---|
| 1.1 | House Prices in the UK | 7 |
| 1.2 | Comparison of the East Midlands' and the UK's House Price Movements | 17 |
| 1.3 | Affordability Index | 19 |
| 2.1 | Changes in Tenure Patterns: Great Britain | 32 |
| 2.2 | Supply of Housing to the Market | 35 |
| 3.1 | Demand for Housing | 44 |
| 3.2 | House Prices in Selected Regions (1980-1996) | 47 |
| 3.3 | Terraced House Prices (Comparison of the Two Case Study Areas) | 66 |
| 4.1 | The Connections in Housing Strategy Formulation | 74 |
| 4.2 | Total Housebuilding Completions: Great Britain (1945-1999) | 76 |
| 4.3 | Housing Completions in Terms of Developer | 78 |
| 4.4 | Are Combined Housing Strategy Statements Prepared? | 93 |
| 4.5 | Current Existence of Housing Liaison Groups | 99 |
| 4.6 | Membership of Housing Liaison Groups | 99 |
| 5.1 | Total Private Sector Housing Completions: Great Britain (1980-1998) | 105 |
| 5.2 | Planning Applications in the 1980s | 107 |
| 5.3 | Empty Dwellings in Great Britain | 119 |
| 5.4 | Planning Decisions and Planning Applications in England | 123 |
| 5.5 | Planning Decisions in the Case Study Districts | 125 |
| 5.6 | Planning Appeals in England | 127 |
| 5.7 | Net Starts in the Case Study Districts | 133 |
| 5.8 | Quarter on Quarter Percent Change in Property Transactions | 139 |
| 5.9 | Branch Distribution of the Nationwide and Halifax Compared to the Regional Distribution of the Population | 148 |
| 5.10 | Comparison of House Prices in the Case Study Areas | 151 |

| | | |
|---|---|---|
| 7.1 | Comparison of Terraced House Prices in the Case Study Areas | 223 |
| 7.2 | Semi-Detached House Prices in the Case Study Areas | 224 |

# List of Tables

| | | |
|---|---|---|
| 1.1 | Response Rates for Questionnaire Surveys | 9 |
| 1.2 | Housing Transactions in England and Wales | 14 |
| 1.3 | Housing Satisfaction | 15 |
| 1.4 | Comparison of the Case Study Districts | 20 |
| 2.1 | Housebuilding Completions in the United Kingdom: 1980-1999 | 28 |
| 3.1 | Average Income of Head of Household by Tenure (£s per week) | 46 |
| 3.2 | Breakdown of the Housing Stock (GB) ('000s) | 50 |
| 3.3 | Household Projections | 55 |
| 3.4 | Do the Authority Use Household Forecasts/Population Projections Prepared by… | 56 |
| 3.5 | Economic Development Policies as an Indicator of Market Demand (%) | 57 |
| 3.6 | Comparison of Regional Guidance Figures and Structure Plan Figures | 59 |
| 3.7 | Comparison of Structure Plan Provision and Build Rates | 61 |
| 3.8 | Structure Plan Population Projections | 64 |
| 3.9 | Comparisons of Housing Figures for Leicestershire | 67 |
| 3.10 | Forecast Population in North West Leicestershire | 68 |
| 4.1 | Use of Housing Strategy Documents | 86 |
| 5.1 | Unemployment in the Case Study Areas, March 1996 (%) | 109 |
| 5.2 | Average Gross Earnings in the East Midlands 1994 (£s per week) | 112 |
| 5.3 | Housing Waiting Lists (1995) | 117 |
| 5.4 | Vacancy Rates in the Case Study Districts (%) | 120 |
| 5.5 | Starts and Completions in the Case Study Districts | 130 |
| 5.6 | Comparison of House Price Series Characteristics | 146 |
| 5.7 | Summary of Indicators Discussed in this Chapter | 159 |

| | | |
|---|---|---|
| 6.1 | Number of Counties Defining a Housing Market Area Based Upon | 165 |
| 6.2 | Make Up of Housing Liaison Groups | 166 |
| 6.3 | Authorities with Integrated Housing Strategies | 167 |
| 6.4 | Waiting Lists - Employment and Usefulness | 169 |
| 6.5 | Waiting Lists - Ease of Use | 169 |
| 6.6 | Housing Association Waiting Lists - Employment and Usefulness | 170 |
| 6.7 | Housing Association Waiting Lists - Ease of Use | 170 |
| 6.8 | Housing Needs Surveys - Employment | 173 |
| 6.9 | Housing Needs Surveys - Ease of Use | 173 |
| 6.10 | Vacancy Rates - Employment and Usefulness (%) | 175 |
| 6.11 | Vacancy Rates - Ease of Use | 175 |
| 6.12 | New Dwelling Starts - Employment and Usefulness (%) | 176 |
| 6.13 | New Dwelling Starts - Ease of Use | 176 |
| 6.14 | Planning Applications - Employment and Usefulness | 178 |
| 6.15 | Planning Applications - Ease of Use | 178 |
| 6.16 | Planning Appeals - Employment and Usefulness | 179 |
| 6.17 | Planning Appeals - Ease of Use | 179 |
| 6.18 | Amendment of Planning Applications - Employment and Usefulness | 181 |
| 6.19 | Density of Applications - Employment and Usefulness | 181 |
| 6.20 | Density of Applications - Ease of Use | 181 |
| 6.21 | Depletion Rates for Allocated Sites - Employment and Usefulness | 182 |
| 6.22 | Depletion Rates for Allocated Sites - Ease of Use | 182 |
| 6.23 | Planning Permission 'Take-Up' - Employment and Usefulness | 184 |
| 6.24 | Planning Permission 'Take-Up' - Ease of Use | 184 |
| 6.25 | Land Prices - Employment and Usefulness | 186 |
| 6.26 | Land Prices - Ease of Use | 186 |
| 6.27 | House Prices - Employment and Usefulness | 187 |
| 6.28 | House Prices - Ease of Use | 187 |
| 6.29 | Volume of Sales by House Type and Area - Employment and Usefulness | 189 |
| 6.30 | Volume of Sales by House Type and Area - Ease of Use | 189 |
| 6.31 | Use of Estate Agent Indicators | 191 |
| 6.32 | Usefulness of Estate Agent Indicators | 191 |
| 6.33 | The Use of Housebuilder Indicators | 194 |
| 6.34 | Housebuilder Indicators | 194 |

x   *The Formulation of Local Housing Strategies*

| | | |
|---|---|---|
| 6.35 | Housebuilders Prepared to Allow Access to their Data | 196 |
| 6.36 | Use of Surveys | 197 |
| 6.37 | Usefulness of the Surveys | 198 |
| 6.38 | Difficulties with the Surveys | 198 |
| 6.39 | Affordability Ratios - Employment and Usefulness | 200 |
| 6.40 | Affordability Ratios - Ease of Use | 200 |
| 6.41 | Income Estimates - Employment and Usefulness | 202 |
| 6.42 | Income Estimates - Ease of Use | 202 |
| 6.43 | Reflection of Economic Policies Within Housing Policies | 202 |
| 6.44 | Use and Usefulness of Indicators | 204 |
| | | |
| 7.1 | Housing Sites of Over 10 Units Built in the Ashby Area 1991-1995 | 214 |
| 7.2 | Tenure of the Case Study Districts | 218 |
| 7.3 | Breakdown of the Dwelling Stock | 219 |
| 7.4 | Dwelling Types in the Case Study Areas | 221 |

# 1 Introduction

**Context**

This study comprehensively examines the housing market as it existed in the 1990s, with a particular focus upon the manner in which local authorities both formulated housing strategies and monitored housing needs and demands. The 1990s provided an interesting period for such an examination. Not only were housing pressures becoming more complex with uncertain demographic projections and changes in household formation, but there was also a return to integrated housing strategies, a policy that had first developed in the 1970s.

This research arises from a general question as to whether or not the provision of housing efficiently and effectively meets the demands and needs of the population. At the time there existed significant debate regarding this issue (Ball, 1996) and the related area of housing needs estimation. (National Housing Forum, 1989; DoE, 1991a; 1995a; Whitehead and Kleinman, 1992; Holmans, 1995) and is still an issue now as we enter a new decade (Bramley, Pawson and Parker, 2000; Holmans, Kiddle and Whitehead, 2000).

One question, examined hitherto to only a limited degree, is the extent to which local authorities can facilitate and contribute to the structure of more integrated and responsive housing provision through housing strategies (Audit Commission, 1992; Cole and Goodchild, 1993; DoE, 1995c). As housing strategies are central to this discussion, it is necessary to focus upon what is meant by this descriptive term (Chapter Four contains a fuller discussion) and a housing strategy is seen as an approach by a local authority to achieve three related objectives;

- To develop housing polices which reflect all tenures.
- To reflect the views of the diversity of different participants in the housing market.

## 2    The Formulation of Local Housing Strategies

- To ensure that policy and implementation are better co-ordinated.

It is this notion of strategy that has been advocated in government advice, and which may be seen as being a return to the initial concepts of Housing Investment Programmes (HIPs), which will be discussed later.

To achieve these objectives, the manner in which local authorities develop links with private housebuilding companies is clearly relevant, as is the degree to which authorities overcome departmentalism in the preparation of polices which direct housing provision. To clarify these issues, it is worthwhile briefly discussing housing provision, stressing why it is necessary for private housebuilders to be included in the formulation of housing strategies.

Currently and throughout much of the last decade, over 80% of all new homes are constructed by the private sector and public sector completions rarely rise above 35,000 homes per annum (see Table 2.1). In this situation, it is perhaps necessary for housing strategists to take a pragmatic view, acknowledging that the speculative housebuilder is the main instrument of implementation. A recognition of the need to work with private speculative housebuilders as an agency of implementation is not recent. In 1977, for instance, the introduction of a form of local housing strategy, the Housing Investment Programme (see Chapter Four) explicitly referred to the need for a local authority to examine the contribution to the supply of housing that could be made by the speculative housebuilding industry.

It has to be stressed that new housing supply is relatively limited in relation to the overall housing market. For instance, in 1994 less than 1% of the housing stock was newly built properties (CML/BSA,1996). By the end of the 1990s this had reduced to around 0.75% (Wilcox, 2000, Table 17c). One alternative to new build may be the conversion of existing properties, either from other uses into housing or from an extensive housing use to one which is more intensive. Both of these options have been discussed in recent years by amongst other Lord Rogers in the publication *Towards an Urban Renaissance* (Urban Task Force, 1999) and then more practically the DETR report *Conversion and Redevelopment: Processes and Potential* (DETR, 2000).

Even in respect of social housing, private housebuilding companies are important. For instance, as direct social housing provision by local authorities has declined (see Table 2.1), there has been an increasing expectation that the shortfall will need to be met by private housebuilders.

The form that this type of social housing will take varies greatly, ranging from low-cost sale, through cross-subsidy developments, to homes for rent in co-operation with housing associations (Dunmore, 1992). Affordable housing provision by the private sector has been supported by central government through a number of different Planning Policy Guidance Notes and policy circulars and this continued to develop throughout the late 1990s (DoE, 1991f; DoE, 1992a; DETR, 1998; DETR, 2000).

Before moving on to examine the implications for housing provision, it is necessary to point out one further factor that complicated the housing market of the 1990s. Of the 35,000 social housing units annually completed, an increasing proportion are provided by housing associations. Table 2.1 indicates that, in 1990, housing association and public sector housing completions were almost equal. This situation altered considerably, in the early 1990s so that by 1994 housing associations completed 12 units to every 1 completed by the public sector. By the end of the 1990s the situation was even more pronounced with 1 local authority home being constructed for every 50 housing association units (Wilcox, 2000, Table 19k).

Clearly, the situation that existed in the 1990s, and one would argue continues to exist presently, is one where the development of housing policy is disconnected from its implementation. For instance, a local authority produces policies which attempt to direct housing investment, yet it is left to the strategies of other agencies (private housebuilders and housing associations)[1] to put these policies into practice, resulting in policy being seen as a means of 'enabling'. As indicated, the supply of housing is presently fragmented, creating a situation where co-ordination is required to ensure supply meets overall demand. Similarly co-ordination is required as the focus has changed so that no longer is traditional housing development on greenfield sites the best option. Policy reflects that higher densities may be expected close to transport nodes, whilst conversions of redundant industrial buildings may be best placed to meet housing shortfalls. Traditionally, a range of agencies have worked with specific local authority departments: planning departments with private housebuilders; housing departments with housing associations; private old persons homes with social services. This has produced a complex network of working

---

[1] Since the research for this work was carried out, the situation regarding the integration with housing associations appears to have improved, with the publication of various guidance notes and best practice manuals.

relationships, which may create a situation of poor integration in terms of policy and implementation.

Of crucial importance for housing strategies is the accurate determination of housing demand and need, particularly the manner in which this can be determined at a 'local' level (see Chapters Two and Three). This can be seen at two separate levels. The first is in terms of overall housing requirements. The second level is the determination of the degree to which these households will require certain house types, certain locations, and certain tenures. Whilst the issue of global housing need has been comprehensively examined (Dorling, 1991; King, 1991; Shaw, 1993; Champion, 1993; Holmans, 1995) in recent years, the latter issue has been somewhat neglected. This work develops the debate regarding co-operation and collaboration through the inclusion of a field of study which has been the focus of limited research, namely methods by which local authorities can effectively monitor housing markets at the local level (Coopers and Lybrand 1985c; Coopers and Lybrand, 1987; Guillou, 1990; Scottish Homes 1993; Maclennan et al., 1998).

**Objectives**

Having established the general context of this research, it is necessary to focus more directly on the objectives of the study and this is achieved through stating three research questions;

1. To what degree do local authorities operate in a fashion that allows policies to be integrated and co-ordinated?
2. To what extent are private housebuilding companies, as the main implementers of housing policy, involved in the development of housing strategies?
3. To what extent do local authorities employ relevant data as a means of monitoring the housing market?

Before moving on to the methodological issues, it may be useful to expand these research questions in terms of the themes in which they relate.

- **Interdepartmental Working.** The first theme to be examined is the manner in which local authorities work interdepartmentally to create housing policies which reflect the views of both the housing and planning departments. This has been examined and promoted by both academic researchers and the government over recent years (Carter and Brown, 1990; Carter, Brown and Abbot, 1991a, 1991b; Audit Commission, 1992; Cole and Goodchild, 1993; DoE, 1995c).

- **Interagency Working.** As highlighted above, most new housing is provided by agencies other than the local authority. This creates a situation where the local authorities housing strategy has to be implemented by a third party. It is important, therefore, for the authority preparing the strategy to have a strong relationship with the agencies which are responsible for implementing the polices.

- **Monitoring.** An informed knowledge of the housing market through monitoring changes in demand and need will enable housing strategies to be responsive. Part of this study will examine the degree to which the data was employed by local authorities.

**Methodology**

*General Approach*

The research objectives stated above require the research to undertake both new empirical work and critical analysis of existing literature. Reference has already been to important relevant research related to the field of housing strategies, and the literature will be examined further in later chapters.

The literature review indicated which areas had been well covered (house prices for instance), which areas had been the focus of less attention (joint agency and joint department working) and where past research had been almost completely lacking (the data which local authorities actually monitor). The depth of material that examines house prices (for instance Evans, 1978; Fleming and Nellis, 1987; Holmans, 1990; Muellbauer, 1990) was found to be considerable.

Whilst examining 'housing markets', the research indicated that this generic definition contained numerous different conceptual research areas. For instance housing and its influence on expenditure patterns and savings behaviour (Gentle et al., 1994; Maclennan et al., 1994) or the change in government support for housing (Wilcox, 1994, Table 13b; Kearns and Maclennan, 1991). Although this study focuses upon one area of research, it is clear that a detailed examination of certain supplementary 'themes' was necessary to fully understand the issues involved. To retain this focus upon the core issue of housing market monitoring and policy integration, the literature reviewed has been integrated into the individual chapters. It is hoped that employing this methodology allows the discussion to develop logically.

Since both Coopers and Lybrand and Gulliou examined the field in the 1980s conditions have changed significantly. With the adoption of the Town and Country Planning Act 1990 and the Planning and Compensation Act 1991, the local authority has found itself in a position where the development plan has become increasingly important. The adoption of section 54a,[2] has placed an added responsibility upon planning authorities. Development plans have become policy documents of increasing consequence, and increasing importance is being placed upon formally adopted policies, so that planning authorities now have greater responsibility to ensure that the policies adopted will work with housing providers, as opposed to ones that are in conflict with the pressures of the housing market. It is prudent to reassess integrated housing strategies in light of this change in emphasis. In addition to the change in the legislation governing development planning, conditions in the housing market have changed. Coopers and Lybrand examined a housing market that was growing in confidence and expectations (their research was set in period 1 in Figure 1.1). Between 1987 and 1990 (the period when Guillou was conducting his research) the market peaked and fell (period 2). The period that has been the focus of this study (1990-1995) is one that has seen the housing market continue to slowly weaken, stabilising, then 'bumping along the bottom' (Hooper, 1992), until 1996.

The differences in these three periods could be illustrated by simply examining some standard data, such as house prices, or perhaps transactions. However, if this is done it becomes clear that the data can still present conflicting information, highlighting a need for further analysis.

---

[2] It should be noted that the 1991 Planning and Compensation Act introduced a new section to the Town and Country Planning Act (Scotland) 1972, section 18a, which creates the same development plan primacy as section 54a does for England and Wales.

Introduction 7

**Figure 1.1 House Prices in the UK**

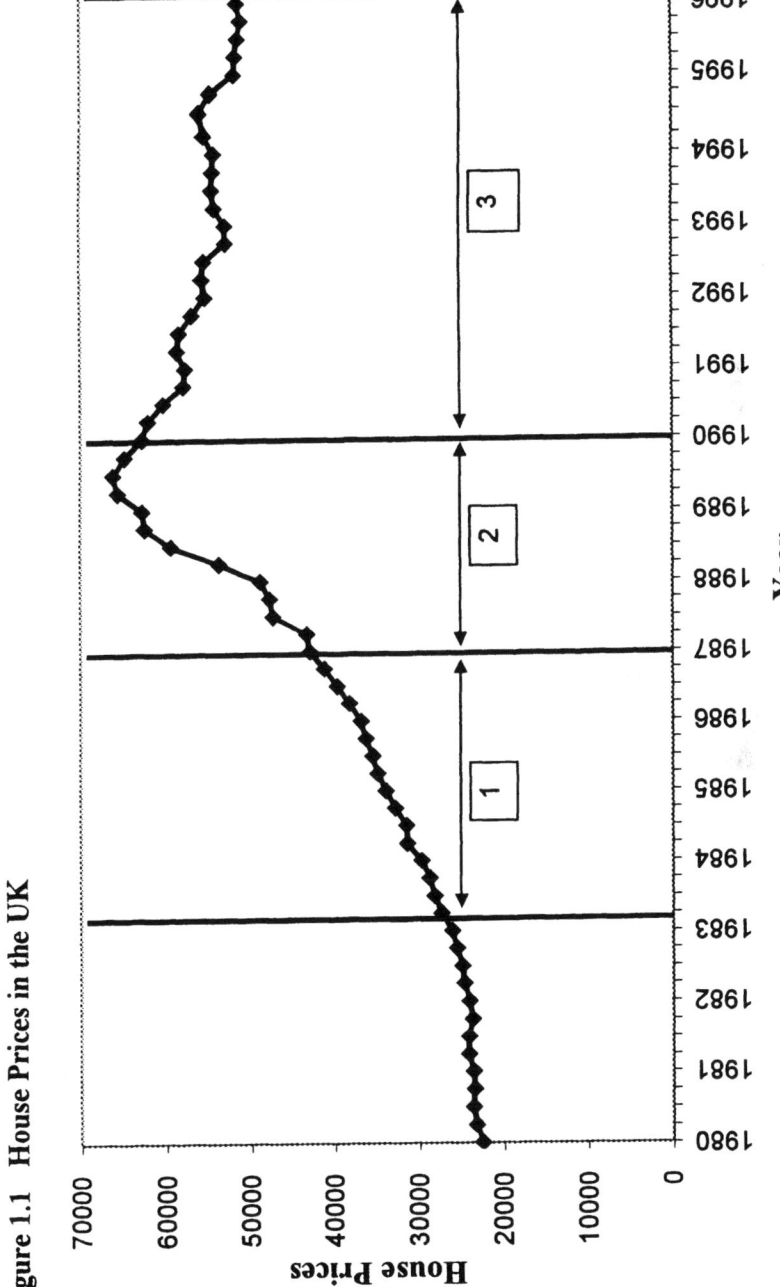

Source: Nationwide Building Society House Price Series

Between 1985 and 1988, housing starts rose by 20%, house prices increased by 65% and property transactions increased by 23%. Between 1987 and 1990, housing starts fell by 28%, property transactions fell by 27%, whilst house prices increased by 47%. Between 1990-1994, housing starts increased by 21%, transactions fell by 9% and house prices increased by 9%. This data is all derived from the same source (from tables in *Housing Finance*, CML/BSA, 1995) and is based on statistics compiled by central government agencies, yet it would appear to present conflicting information. Take, for example, period 3 in Figure 1.1, during which period housing starts increased whilst housing transactions fell. If either of these data sets were to be viewed independently, it would suggest an expanding housing market (housing starts) or a contracting housing market (housing transactions). This data may, if interpreted incorrectly, present wholly inaccurate signals regarding housing markets, but this may not be a problem if authorities do not monitor such movements in data sets.

Returning to the general methodology employed in this research, it could be suggested that housing provision (and, it follows, housing strategy formulation) is essentially a quantitative issue, in which housing allocations are the end product of the process. However, it may be useful to approach the issue of housing strategy formulation and provision in terms of a qualitative evaluation of the processes and procedures adopted by Local Authorities, and the extent to which different sets of data are utilised in the preparation and monitoring of a housing strategy. This approach was taken deliberately, as it was seen that the debate over housing requirements and housing allocations had given rise to considerable literature and significant debate. What appeared to be lacking was a critical qualitative evaluation of the manner in which certain quantitative targets, e.g. housing allocations, could be developed and disaggregated through better information and co-operation between agencies. Simply, this research should be seen as being placed at the early stages of housing provision, i.e. when housing strategies are formulated, focusing upon why they are necessary and the manner in which practice can be improved. This said, there are areas where certain quantitative analytical techniques may, with hindsight, have been justified, for instance in the critical analysis of the data sets.

## Questionnaire and Interviews

Much of the empirical evidence presented in this study is a result of questionnaire surveys. In the summer of 1994, 122 questionnaires were sent to county councils, metropolitan authorities and districts in the East Midlands region (the East Midlands was chosen as a case study region for reasons that will be discussed below). In the past, questionnaires have often been criticised for failing to achieve adequate response rates (Moser and Kalton, 1985). However, as can be seen in Table 1.1, attained high response rates. This response rate may have been due to two factors. Firstly, reminder notices, a standard questionnaire procedure (Bramley and Watkin, 1996), were sent to the county councils and the metropolitan authorities. This was not undertaken in respect of the district authorities as it was felt that this may have created some degree of 'ill-feeling', possibly limiting the success of the case studies that were to be examined later in the research. The reminder notices appear to have been successful in achieving the better response rates recorded for the county and metropolitan authorities.

**Table 1.1   Response Rates for Questionnaire Surveys**

|  | Number Sent | Number Returned | Response Rate |
|---|---|---|---|
| County | 47 | 43 | 91.5% |
| Metro-Authority | 36 | 25 | 69.4% |
| E.Midland District | 39 | 20 | 51.3% |

Secondly, the intention was to keep the questions self explanatory in an attempt to achieve high response rates. Although this would appear to be a successful strategy (see Table 1.1), it did result in less detail with respect to certain areas than one may have wished. The questionnaires were designed in such a way that information regarding all three objectives (internal co-ordination, external collaboration and market monitoring) could be obtained in one data collection exercise. The questions were chosen largely to resolve areas that remained unanswered by previous studies. The detailed use of indicator questions was based upon the data that had been examined by Coopers and Lybrand, with additional questions introduced both as a result of discussions with planners, housebuilders and estate agents, and through the literature review.

The primary advantage of using a questionnaire survey in this context was that it offered the opportunity for all counties and all metropolitan authorities, outside London, to answer and express their views.

Once the case study areas were identified (see below), it became clear that a structured approach to data gathering at the local level was necessary. The approach taken was to begin with an examination of regional policy, developed by a consideration of the situation at the county level, before examining the local position. Initially this stage was based upon an examination of policy documents (regional guidance, structure plans, local plans, etc.) but it soon became clear that it would be necessary to interview key participants in housing provision and housing policy formulation. This was to ensure that areas of concern not sufficiently explained in the published material could be examined and to allow the reasoning behind the polices to be understood. A list of interviewees and a guide to the subjects covered is contained in the appendices, but broadly it was thought necessary to discuss the situation with housing and planning officers at the county and district councils, representatives of the HBF, individual private housebuilding companies, and local estate agents. To this localised focus, individual interviews with specific agencies of a more national relevance were organised if it transpired that the available literature did not fully explain the areas of concern for this thesis.

The 'focused interview' or 'standardised open ended interview' technique was the most appropriate method of conducting this section of the research. This recognised approach (Bell, 1993; Greenfield, 1996) allowed respondents to talk freely around specific themes, allowing elaboration on certain issues if this is what the interviewees wished. The major problem with this approach concerned the possible preclusion of consolidation and comparability of results, as the interviews may progress in different directions. However, focusing the interview on certain areas has ensured that the information gathered at the interview stage was comparable. The interviews were requested through initial letters to the chief planning and housing officers, so again the introductory contacts were at similar levels. From this the authorities responded and there was a degree of comparability, in terms of position, for most of the interviewees.

## Why the East Midlands?

This study employs case studies at two levels. Firstly the East Midland region can be seen, in aggregate, to be a case study of the regional context. Secondly, case studies of particular districts have been employed in the research to allow the detailed discussion regarding co-ordination, collaboration and monitoring to be illustrated by specific empirical data. This section will discuss why case studies are useful in principle and then indicate why the case studies utilised in this research have been chosen.

The employment of case studies allows the research to concentrate upon specific areas, examining, at one point in time, the processes that operate in the chosen location. Bell (1993) suggests that interviews and observations are the most frequently employed methods for case study research, yet she does indicate that no method should be excluded. The localised case studies (i.e. the focus on Mansfield and North West Leicestershire) have been undertaken to introduce more detail to the original survey work. Clearly, the limitation of the localised approach, focusing upon two districts, may be that the results are so specific that generalisations can only be made with difficulty. However, as the case study choice is justified in detail, and the conclusions are made on the evidence gathered, one would argue that this approach contributes a level of detail that is largely absent from the current research literature.

### *Choice of Region*

The choice of both the East Midlands (the regional case study) and North West Leicestershire/Mansfield (the localised studies) is based upon economic criteria (for instance employment figures, industrial growth, spending patterns, growth forecasts, etc.). With respect to the East Midlands, this was supplemented by the fact that it can be seen as a region which is disparate in outlook, straddling as it does the traditional North-South divide. The physical barrier of the Peak District results in the region's north-western fringe having stronger connections with the conurbation of Greater Manchester, whilst the northern parts of Nottinghamshire are essentially part of the South Yorkshire conurbation. At the southern extremes of the region, Northamptonshire can be seen as having strong links with the South East. In other respects, the region is similarly divided, geographically it includes the upland areas of the Peak District and the fenland areas of Lincolnshire. Choosing a region with such differences would ensure that the survey delivered to authorities in the region should include 'rural' and 'urban' areas; agricultural and industrial; economically growing and economically declining; innovative and traditional (in terms of policy formulation). There is, therefore, an assumption that the information gathered from the East Midland districts would represent the methods by which districts, in general, co-ordinate, collaborate and monitor as part of the housing strategy formulation process.

It is necessary to highlight, in rather more detail the economic factors that existed in the early to mid 1990s when the field work was being undertaken and to illustrate the suitability of the region as a focus for research. This will be supplemented by an overview of the region's housing market, to indicate the context within which housing strategies would be formulated.

- Economy

Analysts (Cambridge Econometrics, 1994, 1995 and 1996) suggest that the East Midlands is a region with several strengths; a diverse economic structure; a flexible work-force; a strong base of existing companies, and a competitive relocation option to existing UK companies, particularly those in the South East. In addition, over 250 overseas companies have set up in the region (Henley Centre, 1994). Of these, Toyota in Derbyshire is one of the largest inward investments in Western Europe, worth over £650 million and expects to spend £110 million annually with local component manufacturers. Cambridge Econometrics suggested that;

> The fastest output growth is forecast for the East Midlands, East Anglia and Wales. All three regions are expected to benefit from manufacturing growth much faster than the UK average (Cambridge Econometrics, 1995, p.11).

Cambridge Econometrics perceives the East Midlands to be the second fastest growing region in terms of employment, and only 0.1% per annum behind East Anglia. This characteristic is borne out by other indicators. The region is forecast to have an annual growth, in terms of gross domestic product, of around 3.0% between 1996-2005. For the future, Cambridge Econometrics (1996) forecasts that between 1997-2005 there will be a growth in employment in the region of 1.4% per annum, placing the East

Midlands well above the UK average. It must be stressed that any positive aspects for the East Midlands as a region will have to be placed in perspective, as within the region there are pockets of stagnation and economic decline. The most obviously declining industry is that of coal. In 1980, in Nottinghamshire alone, there were 30 pits employing 40,000 people. By 1994, this had fallen so that only four pits remained operational, employing around 3,000 people.

One of the factors which makes the region attractive for manufacturing output is the fact that it is a relatively low-waged economy. Comparing the relative wage rates for the regions places the East Midlands as the fourth lowest wage rate region in the UK (Cambridge Econometrics, 1995, Table B1.1). This makes the region attractive for employers, but low wages will not support income growth, increases in consumer spending, and rising house prices. In the Cambridge Economic Review (Chapter 3), counties were ranked in terms of disposable income per capita. Lincolnshire and Leicestershire were 30th and 31st respectively, whilst Nottinghamshire and Derbyshire were 36th and 38th respectively (Mansley et al., 1992). The cost of house purchase is significant, often being the largest single purchase many households may make. Therefore, the higher the income, the greater the value of the house that can be afforded. One would argue that disposable income is often seen as a proxy of the propensity to consume owner occupied housing. If this is the case, the East Midlands does not have the most encouraging economic profile for housing market expansion.

However, in the longer term, the East Midlands as a whole is seen as having slightly above the national average consumer expenditure growth. Cambridge Econometrics (1994, p.10) forecast a growth of 2.4% per annum for the region between 1995 and 2005, whilst the UK as a whole is projected to increase by 2.3% per annum. This was borne out by their 1995 survey which forecast consumer expenditure growing by 2.7% per annum, the second highest growth rate in the UK. The most recent survey (Cambridge Econometrics, 1996) appears to retract such a positive expenditure prospects by placing the East Midlands as a region with only 'average' prospects. This suggests that there is potential for the expenditure of the population to increase, which may support increased in owner occupation. Yet the region has a high level of owner occupation at present and any expansion of the tenure may result in it reaching levels which are unsupportable in the long term (see below).

14   *The Formulation of Local Housing Strategies*

- Housing

In 1992, the East Midlands region had a housing stock of 1,660,000 dwellings (DoE, 1993a, Table 9.1). When the data for the East Midlands is compared with the national tenure profile, it is clear that the region has a higher rate of owner-occupation than the national average and also a lower level of socially rented housing. It would appear that as the housing market of the region is largely dependant upon owner occupied housing, it is therefore ideally placed to be a case study in a discussion which seeks to examine the manner in which the interagency production of housing units is integrated in a general housing strategy. Table 1.2 illustrates how, over recent years, the number of property transactions in England and Wales has fallen from the high levels recorded in the late 1980s. Between 1992 and 1994 transaction numbers increased by 6.5%, only to fall back. The East Midlands region suffered a fall in residential property transactions of 31.8%, in the six years between 1987 and 1992. When compared with the average for England and Wales (where a drop of 40.8% has been experienced (CML/BSA, 1994)) it becomes clear that the region's owner-occupied housing market has not been affected as badly as other areas, although in terms of 'trends' it is similar to the national situation.

**Table 1.2   Housing Transactions in England and Wales**

| Year | 1988 | 1989 | 1990 | 1991 | 1992 | 1993 | 1994 | 1995 |
|---|---|---|---|---|---|---|---|---|
| Actual number of transactions ('000) | 2148 | 1580 | 1398 | 1306 | 1136 | 1196 | 1274 | 1135 |

**Source:** HBF, 1996, *Housing Market Report* Table 4, April

A survey conducted in the early 1990s (Coles, 1991, Table A6) indicated that in the East Midlands, 84% of respondents viewed owner-occupation as the tenure that they would be occupying in two years time. Obviously, such a positive view of the tenure may have been affected by the continued slump in the housing market, but it is clear that households in the region aspire to owner occupation. Housing market strategies will therefore have to be aware both of the traditional strength of owner occupation in the region, and the positive attitude would-be householders have to the tenure. The expectation is that private housebuilders will play a significant role in the provision of housing in the East Midlands, as this is what has happened in the past and what many households wish to see in the future.

However a similar survey carried out in 1993 presented the tenure aspiration responses in a different way. Here the difference between those aspiring to owner occupation and those who are already owner occupiers was measured. This 'aspiration gap' was low for the East Midlands, third lowest in the short term (two years) and second lowest in the longer term (ten years) (Eldridge, 1994). She suggests for the high 'gap' regions:

> ...that the underlying demand exceeds current tenure by a substantial margin. (p.17)

The implication is that in the East Midlands such high demand does not exist. One could surmise that this presents the argument that the region is approaching an equilibrium in tenure faster than many of the other regions, suggesting that it may be one of the first to reach the maturity suggested by Fulton (Fulton, 1993). This could, of course, be due to a transient disenchantment with owner occupation. Yet, as the long term aspiration for owner occupation is also relatively low, it highlights that the region may be approaching tenure saturation for owner occupation. If this is the case (and it is possible to draw too many conclusions from this one survey) it highlights a greater need for market identification on the part of the region's housebuilders and a need for social housing to become recognised as the tenure that between 10-20% of the region's population will require. One would argue that this greater market identification and housing provision direction (in terms of market or social) is exactly the role an integrated housing strategy could fulfil, further illustrating the suitability of the region as a case study.

**Table 1.3  Housing Satisfaction**

|  | Very Satisfied | Quite Satisfied | Neither Satisfied nor Dissatisfied | Quite Dissatisfied | Very Dissatisfied |
| --- | --- | --- | --- | --- | --- |
| East Midlands | 55% | 36% | 5% | 1% | 4% |
| G.B. | 57% | 33% | 5% | 3% | 2% |

**Source:** Coles, 1991, Table A9

As can be seen in the table, the region had a higher-than-average percent of respondents showing dissatisfaction with their present accommodation, although it is unclear whether this dissatisfaction was with the tenure, the location or the accommodation itself. Only Greater London had a higher percentage of very dissatisfied respondents, and Scotland, West Midlands and Greater London had fewer very satisfied householders. What this data seems to indicate is that the East Midlands has the potential to be a dynamic housing market, as a number of households may well be prepared move, in an attempt to gain greater satisfaction from their housing.

As can be seen in Figure 1.2, house prices in the East Midlands appear to closely reflect movements in national house price series, a trend that has become particularly noticeable in recent years. Although this figure has utilised Halifax house price data, a similar trend could be seen if Nationwide or DoE house price data was utilised. The East Midlands housing market may therefore reflect trends in the national housing market, and it could therefore provide a useful case study area.

Throughout the 1980s the East Midlands experienced a housing starts to population relationship consistently above the UK average (DoE, 1995d, Fig. 2.27). This situation peaked in 1988, when approximately 5.5 housing units were started in the region for every 1000 people. On average in the UK only 4.5 units per 1000 persons were being completed at this time. Perhaps most important for the region's housing market, was the fact that the region continues into the 1990s as one of the most 'affordable' for owner-occupied house purchase. This assertion is based upon the Housing Market Report (HMR) regional affordability index (HBF, 1995a), which estimates the first year mortgage interest payments as a percentage of average take home earnings of the regions households. As can be seen in Figure 1.3, households in the East Midlands have to use less of their income when purchasing a home than the UK in general. Yet this may not be the case at the local level (see Chapter Seven).

Although the criteria for choosing the East Midlands relate to its economic circumstances, the East Midlands housing market appears to have a number of factors that may make it a useful case study region. It reflects changes in general house prices, illustrating a degree of connection with the national housing market; the region's housing market could be described as mature and particularly strongly connected with owner occupation; and it is forecast to be one of the strongest growing regions in the UK, which may create an expanding housing market.

Introduction 17

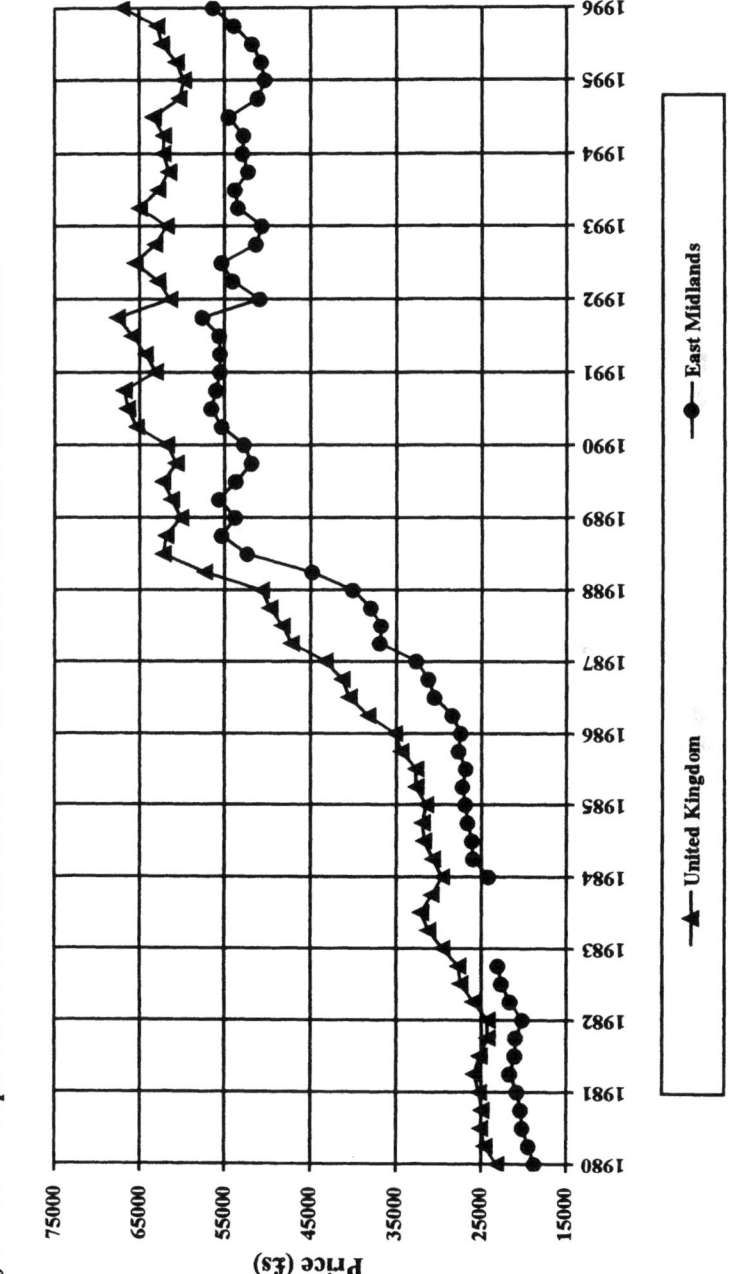

Figure 1.2 Comparison of the East Midlands' and the UK's House Price Movements

Source: Halifax

18  *The Formulation of Local Housing Strategies*

Notwithstanding these positive points, the region has a number of factors which may be sufficiently negative to create problems for the expansion of the housing market: patches of employment and prosperity alongside unemployment; low forecast disposable income growth; and the possibility that the housing market has become 'mature' with limited prospect of expansion in terms of owner occupation. This suggests a housing market that could develop towards greater levels of owner occupation or remain at a similar division, in terms of tenure, to that experienced currently. Either way, it presents a complex housing market (whether it is more complex than any other is debatable) which would make it well suited for a case study of housing strategy formulation.

*North West Leicestershire and Mansfield*

As the case studies are an attempt to ascertain the degree of housing strategy development at the local level, it is necessary to focus more directly on the choice of localised case studies. As highlighted previously, the case studies are two contrasting housing markets (Ashby and Mansfield) within two contrasting districts (North West Leicestershire and Mansfield).

The population of North West Leicestershire, the district of which Ashby is part, had a growth in population more than twice as high as Mansfield (Table 1.4). In terms of the economy in each area, Mansfield has higher rates of unemployment (Table 1.4) and problems of urban regeneration, whilst North West Leicestershire, and Ashby in particular, have benefited from the close proximity of the A42/M42 and the M1. Such a methodology for a case study (examining contrasting areas) is not new. Barrett and Healey (1985), for instance, looked at economically buoyant and economically declining areas. It should be stressed at this stage that it is very difficult to arrive at a precise definition of a geographical housing market area.

It is clear that there is a difference between a housing market in a theoretical context and a definition that could be developed in practical terms and operationalised by those involved in housing provision and household choices. This difficulty is exacerbated when it is considered that different agencies may well have different ideas as to what a housing market is. Examining the field from a purely theoretical standpoint may offer the greatest compatibility, possibly suggesting a common view of the housing

Introduction 19

**Figure 1.3 Affordability Index**

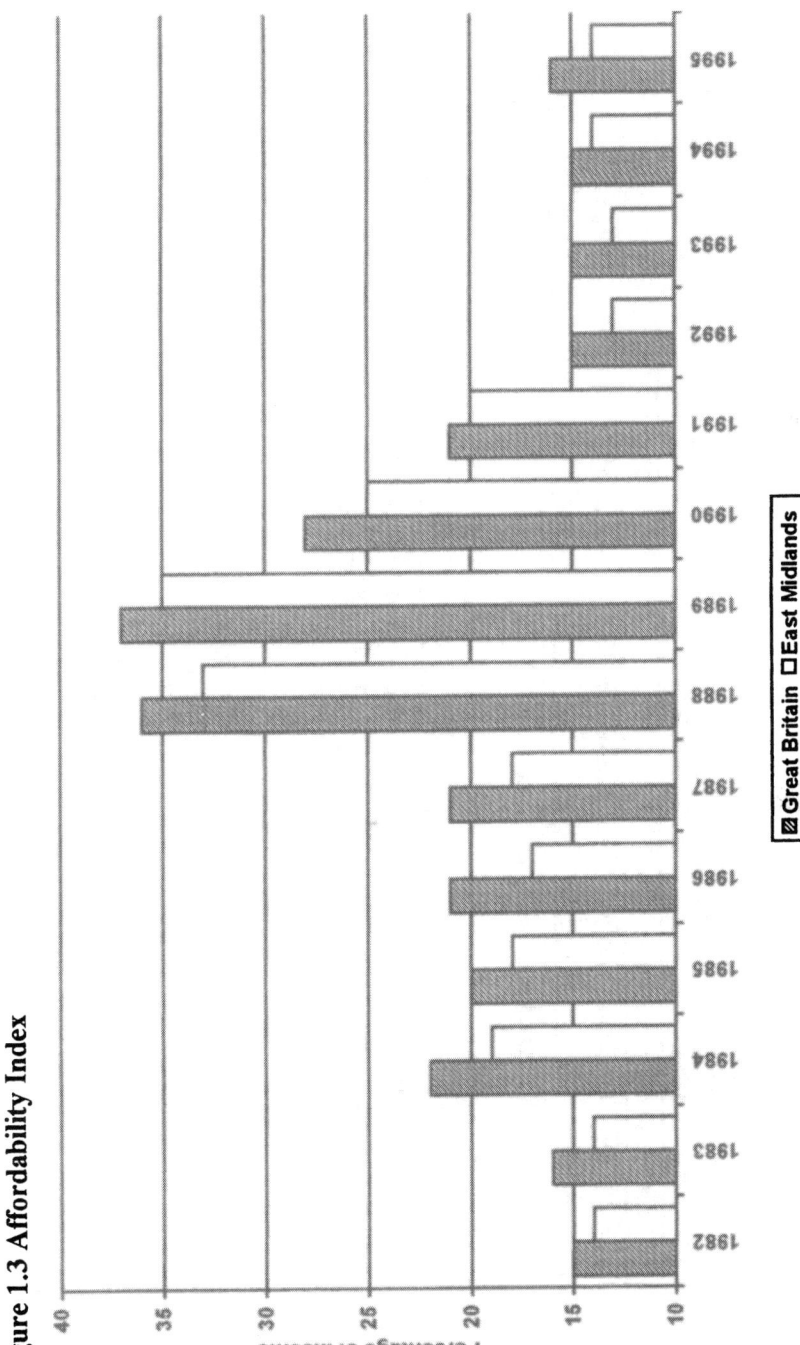

**Source:** HBF, 1995a, Table 2, p. 12

**Table 1.4  Comparison of the Case Study Districts**

|  | Mansfield District | NW Leicestershire |
|---|---|---|
| Population Change 1981-1991 λ | 1.03% | 2.72% |
| Area (hectares) # | 7,770 | 29,700 |
| Unemployment May 1995 q | 14.8% | 7.4% |
| Number of Households * | 39,816 | 31,142 |
| Level of Owner Occupation w | 69.2% | 73.5% |
| Level of Car Ownership e (% of households with no car) | 25.2% | 35.0% |
| Forecast Growth Rates* | 10.5-14% | 14.5-16% |

**Sources:**

λ 1991 Census County Reports for Nottinghamshire and Leicestershire (Part 1), Table C
# Mansfield Local Plan, December 1993 (Consultative Draft) and Table 8.1; OPCS, 1991 Census Report: Leicestershire Part 1 (Table D).
q Mansfield and Burton on Trent Travel To Work Areas, data from both counties Employment Bulletins
* 1991 Census County Reports for Nottinghamshire and Leicestershire (Part 1), Table G
w 1991 Census County Reports for Nottinghamshire and Leicestershire (Part 1), Table G
e 1991 Census County Reports for Nottinghamshire and Leicestershire (Part 1), Table G
* Henley Centre 1994 'Local Futures', Table 11.9, p. 240

market as a place where housing choices and housing exchanges are facilitated. There is, however, a significant difference between theoretical definitions and those that occur in practice, where the geographical definition of housing markets becomes important. In this discussion, both the economic, theoretical view of a housing market and the more practical, geographical view are examined.

As this research seeks to examine local housing strategies it will focus, where appropriate, on local housing markets geographically. Although this concept is discussed in greater detail in the next chapter, it is appropriate at this stage to discuss the implications of a housing market definition for these case study areas in broad terms. The primary focus will be upon the towns of Ashby de la Zouch and Mansfield and, where available, data will be discussed which reflects these definitions. However, data is not always readily available and in some instances a wider geographical definition will have to be employed, for instance Travel to Work Areas (these are often used as a definition of a housing market area, see Chapter Two). As this research examines the manner in which a local authority formulates housing strategies, it is clear that in some cases the district will be viewed as the 'housing market area'. This suggests imprecision, yet it reflects what occurs in the housing market in practice. In practical terms, it is the only way of approaching the issue. For instance, the situation at the district level has to be discussed, but this would not accurately reflect a housing market, which would only be appropriate through a more focused case study.

Although this discussion examines the local case study areas as a result of their differences, both have a number of similarities. The major similarity between the two areas is that both are centred on towns which have, at one time in their history, been dominated by deep coal mining. Both districts are on the fringes of what is described as the Leicester/Derby/Nottingham triangle (DoE, 1994). In planning terms, both districts (at the time of the case study research) had a structure plan which is either adopted (Leicestershire) or close to adoption (Spring 1996, the Nottinghamshire plan was on deposit), with the result that these districts had the most developed and up-to-date strategic policies in the East Midlands.

# 2 Housing Supply and the Housing Market

**Introduction**

As the previous chapter indicated, housing supply and the housing market are complex, with housing supply being implemented largely by agencies outside the direct control of local authorities. It is difficult to provide a summary view of the housing market, but one possible approach may be of a lattice of different 'sub-areas' (such as tenure; house type; geographical location) linking with one another.

This chapter will illustrate where supply fits into the wider housing market and try to illustrate the fluidity of housing supply. In addition, it will show the extent to which the various agencies which supply housing interact to meet demand. This chapter will highlight why there is a need for integrated working and co-ordination between authorities and housing providers, by indicating how important private housebuilding companies are as suppliers of new homes. Chapter Three will develop these themes through an examination of housing demand and the relationship between the economic concepts of effective demand and housing need.

**The Housing Market**

Before an agency can successfully develop a housing market strategy, it must attempt to understand the concept of the housing market. A definition of markets found in many economic models is that of an 'exchange process', with supply and demand reaching an equilibrium where price is determined (Maclennan, 1982; Harvey, 1993; Bramley, 1996). Applied to housing, this basic concept suggests that, as housing costs fall, more people should be able to afford homes, so demand increases. Yet this is simplistic in the extreme and, as with most economic models, requires the support of many assumptions, assumptions which distance it from the real world. Needleman (1965) highlights the economic idiosyncrasies of the housing market and the degree of association between different markets with the result that the housing markets 'price' is determined by more than a simple supply and demand equation. In recent years researchers (Bramley et al., 1995) have presented a number of economic models which have attempted to reconcile housing and land supply with economic theory.

The housing market is unusual in three respects. Firstly, the degree of fragmentation should be noted, with the housing market existing as a collection of various submarkets, disaggregated in terms of tenure, house type and geographical location (these will be looked at in more detail below). Secondly, not only is the housing market disaggregated, it is a market in which the good is locationally fixed i.e. once constructed it can only be sold in that geographical location, so that it cannot be placed on different markets, depending on conditions. The third, and perhaps in economic terms the most unusual factor, is the degree to which prices are determined by sales of existing properties. In essence, the establishment of value in residential property is through comparison, i.e. the market price/rent of similar properties. Due in part to the comparison valuation methodology, coupled with the small number of new properties entering the market, new supply is largely priced by comparison with existing properties. For example, in the early 1990s, new building added less than 1% to the housing stock each year (Malpass and Murie, 1994) and in 1988 of all building society advances, only 9.6% were for new properties. This proportion has remained similar in recent years with the figure in 1993 being 10.6% (CML/BSA, 1994, Table 5). This small rise in recent years may be due to the fact that existing homeowners have not been as active in the market.

There are a number of analytical divisions which separate the 'overall' housing market (i.e. that which encompasses all housing) into distinct smaller markets. At the margins, the distinction becomes blurred, but generally the submarkets are autonomous (Black and Stafford, 1988). These submarkets may be disaggregated in terms of:

- House Type

House type is a loose term, used in this context to define the categorisation of dwellings in terms of 'building form'. Houses are available in a number of different forms, ranging from small Victorian terraces to modern executive homes. Widely accepted definitions are those used by the Department of the Environment (DoE, 1991b, DoE, 1993a ) and its successor the Department of the Environment Transport and the Regions:

> Detached House
> Semi-detached House
> Terrace House
> Flat or Maisonette
> Bungalow

All of these categorisations may be further separated through the addition of the age of the dwelling and the size of the property. Maclennan (Maclennan, 1982) developed the notion of defining housing submarkets in terms of how would-be households' search patterns effectively filter housing opportunities, taking into account acceptable tenures, types and locations, whilst discounting those which are unacceptable. Every household consists of one or more individuals, with slightly differing preferences. Therefore, submarkets evolving from search patterns can only be an amalgamation of similar household preferences. Prior to beginning a search for a house, would-be householders will establish parameters of house types that will be of interest e.g. a large garden for children; a flat for easy maintenance, etc. The result is that the housing market is once again subdivided into submarkets, which are quasi-autonomous.

- Housing Tenure

The markets for different housing tenures tend to contain different types of household, income groups, etc. Households on the margin of each tenure will consider 'neighbouring' tenures, if the relative costs, benefits and choices are both comparable and available. The market for different tenures is therefore complex, with demand for one tenure depending, to some extent, on the availability of other tenures (Murie et al., 1976). For example, a household which may view a rented house from a local authority as an acceptable tenure may find themselves examining other tenures, due to the fact that local authority homes are unavailable. This unavailability could be due (amongst other factors) to a lack of supply, exacerbated by an allocation system which 'rations' those units that remain, favouring households which meet certain criteria. It has been argued that the use of tenure as a label is little more than a consumption definition, only illustrating the terms on which households occupy their homes whilst neglecting to show how homes are supplied and the financial situation of the households (Malpass and Murie, 1994). This may be true, yet it does allow the different patterns of housing search to be defined in broad terms, highlighting a method of sub-market delineation.

- Location

Similar house types are often found in similar areas, with the result that, in some respects geography is the practical reflection of both tenure and type delineation. As housing is fixed in one location geography is an important, some would say crucial, criterion for delineating housing markets. Much discussion has taken place regarding the extent to which housing may be divided into a number of small geographical submarkets (Ball and Kirwan, 1977; Munro, 1986; Maclennan et al., 1987; Bramley et al., 1995; Wylie, 1994) and this will be discussed in more detail later in this chapter. These geographical differences exist because of the fixed nature of housing which presents households with different geographical choices. Survey work carried out by the author has found that 58% of county council planning departments took some notice of the geographical make-up of housing markets, when determining housing policies.[1] For instance, since the 1970s, Nottingham County Council (NCC) has employed labour markets, as demonstrated by travel-to-work areas (Coombes, 1995), to reflect housing market areas. As a result, instead of preparing housing allocations for eight districts, the County Planners have prepared the allocations for five 'sub-areas', referring to the travel-to-work areas of the eight districts. The net result is that a District's housing allocation consists of a collection of travel-to-work areas. For example, the South Nottingham sub-area comprises all or part of six districts (NCC, 1994). Such attempts at reflecting the actual housing market has been suggested and encouraged by the DoE (DoE, 1991c). and more recently and more directly by Scottish Homes (Maclennan et al., 2000).

One would suggest that fully developed housing strategies will provide a useful function 'portioning' housing supply into these different

---

[1] In the summer of 1994 the author carried out a questionnaire survey of all the County Councils in England and Wales, to ascertain the extent to which housing market indicators are utilised. Of the 47 delivered, 43 were returned (a response rate of 91%) One of the questions concerned the definition of market areas. This is discussed more fully in Chapter Six.

parts of the housing market. The data gathering and co-ordinating role of the housing strategy examined in this research would logically allow for a better understanding of how the demand for housing can be better met by more 'focused' supply.

Although, to a degree, such market definitions exist in all tenures, the nature of the present housing supply system is such that it is the most economically-secure owner-occupiers (and to a lesser extent those considering private renting) who can effectively realise their aspirations as regards house type and location. In the case of social housing for need there is greater 'demand' than supply, illustrated by the fact that local authority housing waiting lists far out-number the available supply of housing units. In addition the supply of units is often disproportionately made up of the less attractive stock, including the so called 'difficult-to-let estates'. The choices available to households requiring social housing is therefore limited to what the housing providers can offer.

These three possible ways of viewing housing markets, namely in terms of house tenure, house type and geographical location are purely illustrative. They are descriptive of the way individual householders search patterns may create a means by which the UK housing stock becomes delineated and fragmented into various markets. Yet a housing market that is currently viewed as falling within one type of definition may not always remain so. Over time, the housing in one geographical area can be included in a different housing market either through tenure change (owner occupation to private renting; local authority renting to owner occupation) or through redevelopment and a change of house types. This geographical definition of a housing market is important and it is worth expanding on this theme.

*Geographical Definitions of Housing Markets and the Relationship to Local Housing Strategies*

In Scotland research has been conducted for a number of years examining the manner in which a housing market can be defined. For instance Maclennan, examining the Glasgow housing market, suggested that sub-markets exist, both in terms of housing categories and geographical locations, confounding the argument that the housing market represents a competitive equilibrium model (Maclennan, Munro and Wood, 1987). Earlier statistical modelling work on the same city by the same research centre had come to the conclusion that population characteristics, income and employment groupings of households are the most important factor in determining sub-markets (Munro, 1986). This work appears to suggest that simplistic definitions of a geographical housing market will at best only partly be reliable, and are more likely to be unhelpful. This is an issue for housing strategy formulation, as strategies will have to be based upon geographical local authority boundaries. Wylie's work on the Scottish housing market was highly critical of Strathclyde Regional Council's definitions of housing market areas as being purely arbitrary, a conclusion she shares with Maclennan (Maclennan et al., 1987; Wylie, 1994).

Although much of this Scottish work would appear to be critical of the concept of defining geographically housing markets and housing strategies, other research has been supportive. For instance in 1993 Scottish Homes published a best practice guide for their local offices, determining housing needs and producing a strategy for achieving these in terms of local housing markets. The 'Best Practice Guide' defines a Housing Market Area as;

> ...a relatively self contained (independent) area. (Scottish Homes, 1993, p. 20)

Scottish Homes recommend their district offices to identify these self contained areas through an analysis of migration patterns and commuting flows. Further work for Scottish Homes by Maclennan et al. resulted in the publication of another 'best practice guide' in 1998 which developed from its predecessor. This indicates that a functional housing market area should be seen as one which may be defined as;

> ...the geographical housing market area in which a substantial majority of the employed population both live and work and where those moving house without changing employment choose to stay. (Maclennan, More, O'Sullivan and Young, 1998, p. 30)

They go onto discuss the pros and cons of various different approaches that can be used ranging from structure plan housing market areas, travel-to-work-areas, computer modelling of housing market areas and defining an area based on local knowledge or instinct. It is left to the users of the manual to determine which definition they will use.

The data for commuting flows is obtained from the Department of Employment's travel-to-work areas or alternatively the local labour market areas

## Table 2.1 Housebuilding Completions in the United Kingdom: 1980-1999 (Number in brackets refer to percentage of total completions)

| Year | Private Sector | Housing Associations | Public Sector | Total Completions |
|---|---|---|---|---|
| 1980 | 131,974 *(54.5)* | 21,422 *(8.9)* | 88,590 *(36.6)* | 241,986 |
| 1981 | 118,579 *(57.4)* | 19,420 *(9.4)* | 68,567 *(33.2)* | 206,566 |
| 1982 | 129,022 *(70.5)* | 13,532 *(7.4)* | 40,309 *(22.0)* | 182,863 |
| 1983 | 153,038 *(73.2)* | 16,777 *(8.0)* | 39,218 *(18.8)* | 209,033 |
| 1984 | 165,606 *(75.1)* | 17,308 *(7.8)* | 37,647 *(17.1)* | 220,561 |
| 1985 | 163,470 *(78.7)* | 13,734 *(6.6)* | 30,452 *(14.7)* | 207,656 |
| 1986 | 177,647 *(82.2)* | 13,068 *(6.1)* | 25,417 *(11.8)* | 216,132 |
| 1987 | 191,187 *(84.5)* | 13,117 *(5.8)* | 21,853 *(9.7)* | 226,157 |
| 1988 | 206,996 *(85.6)* | 13,479 *(5.6)* | 21,456 *(8.9)* | 241,931 |
| 1989 | 187,504 *(84.7)* | 14,598 *(6.6)* | 19,323 *(8.7)* | 221,425 |
| 1990 | 165,197 *(82.5)* | 17,221 *(8.6)* | 17,854 *(8.9)* | 200,272 |
| 1991 | 156,859 *(83.2)* | 20,500 *(10.9)* | 11,225 *(5.9)* | 188,584 |
| 1992 | 145,877 *(82.3)* | 25,652 *(14.5)* | 5,696 *(3.2)* | 177,225 |
| 1993 | 146,235 *(79.3)* | 34,782 *(18.8)* | 3,349 *(1.8)* | 184,366 |
| 1994 | 151,493 *(80.1)* | 34,820 *(18.4)* | 2,814 *(1.5)* | 189,127 |
| 1995 | 150,100 | 38,500 | 1,900 | 190,500 |
| 1996 | 146,500 | 31,500 | 800 | 178,800 |
| 1997 | 150,600 | 27,400 | 200 | 178,200 |
| 1998 | 145,200 | 25,100 |  | 170,300 |
| 1999 | 148,600 | 22,200 |  | 170,800 |

**Source:** Table 6.1 of *Housing and Construction Statistics 1980-1990 and 1982-1992* and Table 1.2 of *Housing and Construction Statistics December Quarter 1995. Part 1*, DoE, HMSO.
1995 onwards is seasonally adjusted from the DETR via *Housing Finance*

developed at Newcastle University (Champion and Green, 1975 and 1987; Champion and Brunsdon, 1988). A definition of a housing market could therefore follow the Scottish Homes Best Practice Guide, and be based upon some type of travel-to-work area, although the latest version suggests that these should be developed locally and not be reliant on Department of Employment published definitions.

As highlighted in Chapter One, the case study areas represent different definitions of travel-to-work area. Mansfield has its own travel-to-work area (Nottinghamshire County Council, Employment Bulletin 6/96) whilst Ashby forms part of a travel-to-work area based upon a settlement, Burton on Trent, not only in a different District but also in a different region (Leicestershire County Council, Unemployment Bulletin, May 1996). This indicates that even if we use travel-to-work areas, problems remain, in so far as these definitions still do not respect local authority administrative boundaries. However simply due to the fact that the data is available, travel-to-work areas may be employed in the formulation of housing strategies as a means of establishing the commuting flow component of a housing market. This would allow the strategy to be prepared reflecting the fact that the housing that is provided within one local authority boundary may well be utilised by individuals commuting and being employed in other local authority areas (see later chapters which discuss this issue with reference to the case studies).

## Housing Supply

As can be seen in Table 2.1, the largest supplier of housing in the UK is the private sector. Although the proportion of homes supplied by the private sector has generally increased throughout the 1980s, the actual number of units has fluctuated, in response to differing levels of demand. Gillen (1994b) divides the 1980s and 1990s housing production, i.e. both starts and completions, into six separate phases which can be seen in Table 2.2. Since the early 1980s, owner-occupation has been promoted by political and economic policies which, when coupled to a decline in alternative tenures (Muellbauer 1990; Maclennan, Gibb and More, 1993; Malpass and Murie 1994), has meant that housebuilders have found increasing demand, in general terms, for their product.

The speculative housebuilder 'gambles' that conditions prevalent at site conception will remain the same, or become more favourable (for the seller) in the period between conception and completion. Clearly, this can backfire if the conditions envisaged do not materialise. This has been the case recently with supply outstripping demand and many housebuilders have found themselves owning expensive sites which cannot be developed in the short term due to the fact that the land was purchased on the assumption of a rising market. Other housebuilders have found themselves constructing units to be placed on a market which is rapidly contracting.

One of the demand indicators mentioned in a later chapter concerns the use of the time between start and completion. Monk, commenting on the average time between start and completion of a dwelling in the 1980s, indicated that it took around 6-18 months. Malpass and Murie, examining the situation in the early 1990s, stated that the time period was between 15-20 months (Monk, 1991; Malpass and Murie, 1994). This data would appear to indicate a fall in market demand as the time from start to completion has increased. This concurs with what has occurred in the market, suggesting time between start and completion may be a useful indicator of housing supply and, by implication, housebuilders perceptions of demand (see below).

Throughout the 1980s and 1990s, controls on all forms of public spending, in particular local authority spending, has resulted in a reduction in public sector housing provision, a fact that can be clearly seen in Table 2.1. An examination of the housing and construction statistics clearly demonstrate that, throughout the 1980s, in the order of 30% of social housing provision has been for special needs, the elderly, the sick and the disabled (DoE, 1993c), i.e. those groups that the private sector do not specifically cater for. This has meant that only two-thirds of the units provided have been for general needs housing, reducing even further new social housing provision for households in which the main constraint is the inability to compete for housing effectively in the private sector.

Government policy has allowed many social housing tenants to purchase their home at a discount, the discount being greater the longer the individual has been a tenant. Throughout the 1980s it would appear that supply to the owner occupied sector was significantly increased by the inclusion of 'right-to-buys', with the result that the increase in this tenure has been due (in part) to tenure shifts, rather than just new production. It is estimated that 80% of the growth in homeownership between 1981-1991 was attributable to council house sales so that by 1991, 9% of owner occupied stock was former council houses (Forest et al., 1995). The success of these 'right-to-buy' policies has removed from the tenure the most attractive dwellings and the most affluent tenants. As Holmans states;

> ...sales to local authority sitting tenants were primarily to households with heads in full-time paid employment, whose characteristics resembled those of other owner occupiers much more than those of households that remained tenants. (Holmans, 1995, p.49)

The 'attrition' from such widespread tenure transfer and the lack of new general needs housing construction has in effect residualised the tenure (Morris and Winn, 1990; Forest et al., 1990; Malpass, 1990). As can be seen in Table 2.1, the actual contribution to new supply from public sector construction has fallen to below 4% (in the early 1980s, the public sector were providing between 70-80% of all new social housing). To a significant degree, this shortfall has been compensated for by the re-emergence of housing association provision. Combining both housing association and public sector completion's indicates that social housing new-build has remained at around 15% of all completions between 1986 and 1994, when it peaked at around 20%. Since then however the share has fallen back further to around 12%, further indicating the importance of the private sector in housing provision.

Other commentators (Dunmore, 1992) reflect that there is a growing move towards subsidising the end user through the benefit system, rather than a subsidy for unit construction or the tenure as a whole. This problem has been discussed extensively in a number of studies e.g. Hills (1991). The problem would appear to be worst for those households who are earning too much to qualify for benefits but are earning too little to meet housing costs effortlessly.

Another source of housing for rent is from the private sector, renting homes for profit. This subsection was once the largest of the housing providers, but is now responsible for a very small proportion (see Figure 2.1). This decline has been due to a variety of factors, ranging from legislation and political expediency to alternative investment opportunities (Hamnett and Randolph, 1988). Private building of homes for rent has been minimal over recent years (Kearns and Maclennan, 1991) and as a result new supply of homes to this tenure is rather unusual, founded on properties transferring from other sections of the housing market. Interestingly, over recent years the number and proportion of privately rented properties has

32   *The Formulation of Local Housing Strategies*

**Figure 2.1   Changes in Tenure Patterns: Great Britain**

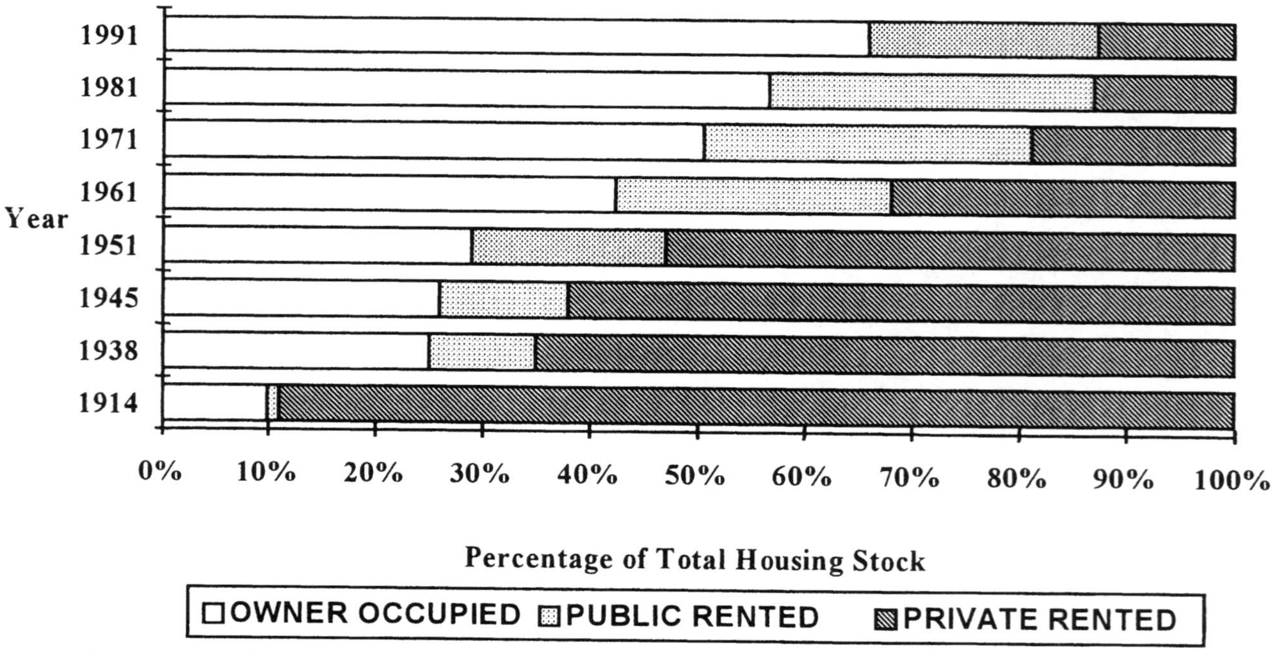

**Source**: Forrest, et al. (1990), Table 3.1, and Table 1, *Housing Finance*, No. 22

increased. In 1988, 9.2% (2,077,000) of the housing stock was privately rented, by 1993 this had increased to 9.9% (2,333,000) and by 1998 this had risen to 10.6% (2,581,000) (Council of Mortgage Lenders, 2001). This increase could be due to incentives (Crook et al., 1991; Merrett, 1992), yet it may be more likely to be a result of stagnation in owner occupied housing (Crook et al., 1995). Households may have found themselves becoming landlords, as they find their properties difficult to sell. It could be argued that the number of privately rented properties is actually greater than appears in the published data. This might arise from the way mortgage lenders increase repayments when a mortgage is granted on a home which is being let, as well as additional administration costs, and there is, therefore, an argument that a substantial amount of 'informal' renting might be taking place. There is a case for research to be undertaken investigating the importance of this 'informal' rented sector.

As can be seen in Table 2.1 the supply of new housing association dwellings has been gradually increasing since the mid 1980s, both in real terms and in terms of the proportion of all housing supplied. A problem exists in that many of these units have been purchased from private speculative housebuilders. There may, therefore, be a degree of double counting. This rather unusual 'run off' effect is discussed in more detail below. Table 2.1 illustrates how dominant the private sector is as a housing supplier. Even during the recent property slump, this form of housing provision has been responsible for around 80% of all new housing.

**Pipeline Model of Housing Supply**

The pipeline analogy, a notion predominantly envisaged as a description of land availability (Hooper, 1985; DoE, 1993b) can be seen as a useful representation of the supply of housing to the market. A model using this analogy is shown in Figure 2.2. The aggregate (all tenure) level of housing supply is represented in Figure 2.2 by a large 'header tank'. This is then separated into different 'pipes' satisfying different demands or needs. The volume of housing flowing along each 'pipe' alters primarily as a result of government policy, but will also be affected by the way the providers perceive demand (see below). Changes by government in both their economic and housing policy, will result in changes in the pipeline which has to accommodate the greatest volume of housing. The degree to which there has been economic and political influence upon specific pipelines has been discussed in detail, with debates highlighting the various subsidies that home ownership has received compared to other housing tenures (Pearce and Wilcox, 1991; Hills, 1991; Foster, 1993).

As the model demonstrates, the flow can be checked at various stages, but if it is not then housing production will have to flow from the end of the pipeline as residential units. To illustrate this, examine the owner occupied pipeline in Figure 2.2. If the housebuilder, after an initial appraisal, believes a market does not exist, then the valve can be closed at this first stage. The work carried out to appraise sites does not require any formal commitment, only expenditure of resources, a cost which is averaged out and met by the overall profits from units constructed and sold. The next stage is the first where financial commitment in an actual or legal sense will have occurred, through the acquisition of land. This varies from holding the land on option (the situation where the housebuilder pays the landowner some form of premium for an assurance that the land will not be sold to another developer) through to outright ownership. Even if the land is bought it can be 'moth-balled' (Smyth, 1982; Hooper, 1994) or held back by closing the next 'valve'.

The final valve is controlled by a third party, the planning authority, and concerns the gaining of planning permission. Once the housing supply has passed this final 'valve' there is only one economic outcome for the builders and that is production and sale. Any other option would be impractical, as the builder will be left with the costs incurred to reach this stage. As can be seen, at the very end of this pipeline, the unit can be purchased by an organisation (a housing association for instance), or even an individual who perceives an opportunity to rent the unit. During the 1990s, particularly around 1992-93, there was a flow from the private sector to housing associations. This is due to the fact that builders have found difficulty in selling completed units to private owner-occupiers during the recession. The 1992 Autumn statement resulted in housing associations receiving a 'one-off' cash injection of £750 million. This was a result of government policy seeking to stabilise the housing market whilst boosting the provision of social housing. And allowed a significant number of new build units aimed at private market sale to be transferred into Housing Association ownership, providing social rented units.

*Housing Supply and the Housing Market* 35

**Figure 2.2 Supply of Housing to the Market
(Data from *Housing Finance*, 1996)**

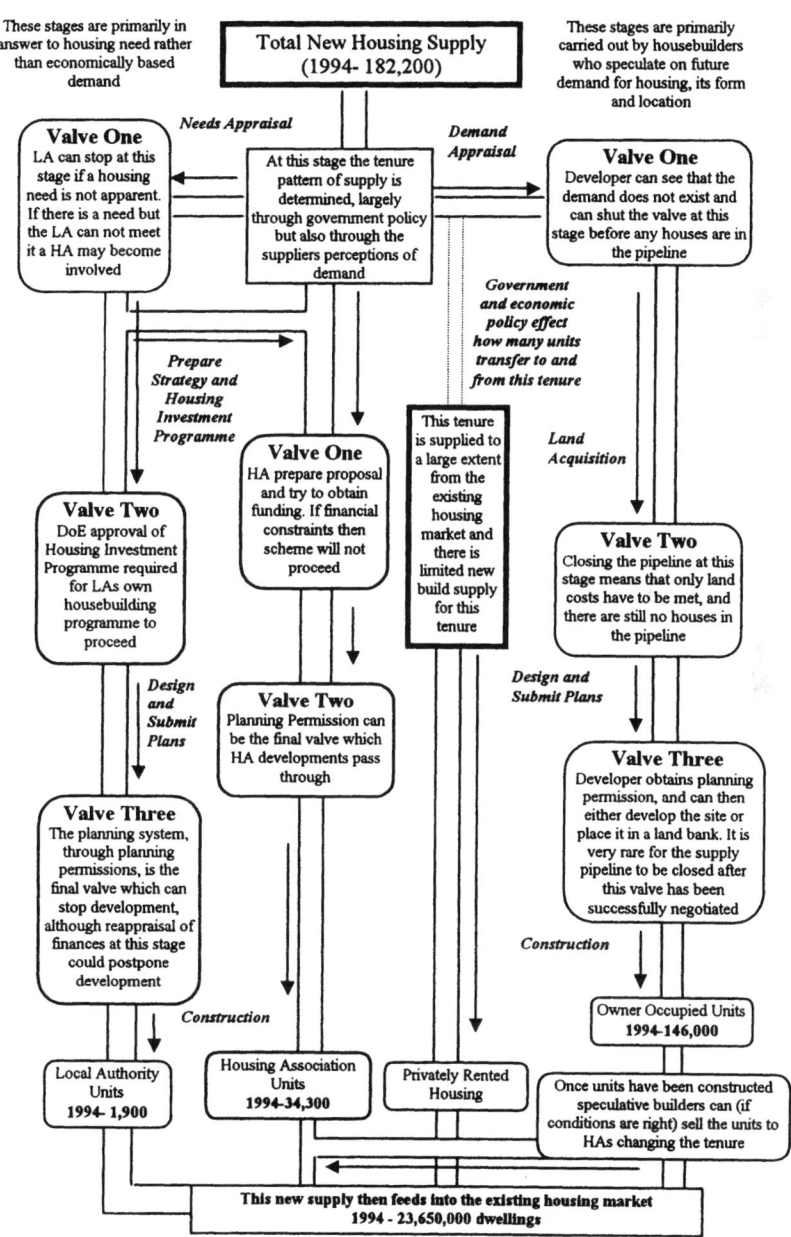

36   *The Formulation of Local Housing Strategies*

Comparing the figures from Table 2.1, with the diagrammatic representation in Figure 2.2, it becomes clear that the 'pipeline' which has been responsible for most of the housing supply over the last twenty years is that of private housebuilding, the vast majority of which has been speculative building for owner occupation. Clearly local authority provision has been effectively curtailed at the second 'control valve' (where funding, through Housing Investment Programmes (HIPs), has to be approved by the DoE). The data in the figure is simply to illustrate the balance, both the balance in terms of tenure and also the balance in terms of new supply versus existing housing units.

Housing supply is often divided into two parts: social, needs-based housing and that of demand-based speculative housing for owner occupation. As can be seen from the model, there is a point where speculative housing can be transferred into the housing association supply. It could be argued that this has only occurred because of the downturn in the housing market experienced in the late 1980s early 1990s, and the cash input which the Treasury gave to housing associations in the 1992 Autumn Statement. However, the need for an integrated strategy is already apparent, as this would facilitate the supply to the whole housing market, be it at a local, regional or national level, to be examined. Once the trends in supply can be discerned, it would be easier for policies to be developed which could direct the flow of housing units along one or more 'pipelines', then into the housing types required.


**Conclusion**

This chapter has highlighted that a precise definition of a housing market is difficult to achieve, as the term can often be used interchangeably. 'Housing market' can be used to define a geographical area; it can be a term used to reflect all homes, regardless of tenure, or simply one specific tenure; the term could refer to the economic process through which homes are exchanged; all of these definitions may be seen as being the housing market. This chapter has also demonstrated that private housebuilding companies are the largest provider of new homes to meet estimated housing requirements. In addition to this discussion the pipeline model visually illustrated that far from housing supply being exclusively provided for one sector of

*Housing Supply and the Housing Market* 37

the housing market there can be circumstances when homes are 'diverted' from one pipeline to another.

In terms of the specific discussion that is the focus of this book this chapter has served an important function. It has highlighted in more detail the need for greater co-ordination, in two respects in particular.

- This chapter has shown that housing production has little co-ordination, with houses being produced for different sectors of the housing market by different agencies. The discussion and the pipeline model indicated that there are avenues through which homes intended for one housing requirement, have in effect been supplied for another (for instance public homes and the Right-to-Buy). This clearly shows that there is a need for an examination of housing policy and the manner in which it can direct housing production, in the direction through which housing requirements are effectively met.
- It has indicated the dominance of private housebuilding companies in the production of new homes. This supports the need for greater co-ordination between the agencies of implementation (housebuilders) and the policy formulators (in this case the local authority).

Of all the practical definitions of a housing market, the one which this chapter has shown to be the most problematic for housing strategy formulation, is that of geography. It has become apparent that the geographical delineation of a housing market will have to be robust, as it cannot be taken for granted that a district boundary is also that of a housing market. However, as the housing strategy, as a document, is prepared by a local authority with a administrative boundary, false (in the practical sense) boundaries will have to be utilised. However, this is not to say that the local authority has to examine the issue in this context. It has been shown from empirical work that many authorities already examine housing markets in terms of a geographical delineation other than administrative boundaries. This is to be commended and one technique utilised in practice, that of travel to work areas as a means of determining a self contained housing market, will be employed for the case study areas later in this thesis. The next chapter will develop this contextual and background analysis through an examination of housing demand.

# 3  Demand for Housing

**Introduction**

This chapter will focus upon one of the core themes that underpin the housing market, namely the concept of housing demand (housing supply was examined in Chapter Two). This discussion is important, as it is the manner in which housing demand is monitored and assessed by local authorities that will underpin much of the formulation and development of local housing strategies. It should be stressed that that household forecasts and allocations will not be a significant part of the discussion in this chapter, as it is felt that this area has been examined is sufficient detail elsewhere.

Before commencing upon the substantive discussion, it is important to indicate that this chapter will examine data from the case study areas as well as employing the results of the empirical research work undertaken for this study.

Initially it is important to examine what is meant by the term 'housing demand' and what different definitions can be employed to explain the term. Although elsewhere in this book, research definitions are not given as 'stand alone' sections in the discussion, in the case of housing demand, and its meaning in terms of this the arguments put forward, it was felt necessary to do so.

The term 'housing demand' can often be enough to imply that a study will only examine homes provided by the open market, through speculative housebuilding or private sector renting. This is largely a result of the economic based view of supply and demand. This is compounded by the fact that traditional studies of the housing market have tended to divide discussion of demand for housing into two sub-areas namely:

- Effective housing demand, the homes required by households who have the ability to pay market price for housing. This

demand is met by commercial housebuilding companies or other bodies making a profit from housing demand.
- The alternative is to examine housing need, which is met by social housing agencies or local government, as a social welfare objective.

Although evidence can be found to argue the economic viewpoint, the earlier discussion has indicated the complex and fractured nature of the housing provision, and as a result a 'pigeonhole' approach may be misleading. For instance the precise point at which effective demand stops and need begins is difficult to determine, as there may be a significant area of uncertainty at these margins. This 'grey area' is sufficient justification for an examination of the housing market as a single entity. However, as this book examines the formulation of *integrated* housing strategies, which are seen as documents which reflect the whole housing market, it is appropriate to mirror this 'global' view in terms of the treatment of demand. Therefore in the context of this research 'global demand' will be seen to be the overall housing requirement, encompassing effective (economic) demand and subsidised housing need. It is appreciated that this approach, although necessary, may be seen to be rather unusual. Therefore it is necessary to examine this 'division' in housing requirements in rather more detail, simply to ensure that the reasoning behind the choice of 'global housing demand' is fully appreciated.

**Demand and Need**

The concept of housing demand/need should be viewed at two levels. At one level there is an all embracing 'global housing provision', formulated by agencies such as the Department of the Environment Transport and the Regions (DETR), into a prediction of the number of households that will require housing in the future, regardless of their ability to pay. This is based upon population projections which are then employed within more specific population modelling methods to arrive at household projections. This forms a guide for both local and central government policy formulation. This concept is very different from that identified by authors such as Watson et al. (1973), Bramley (1989) and van Zijl (1993a; 1993b), who have predominantly approached the issue from the social objective of defining households in need.

This alternative concept, that of housing need, is a means of identifying the number of households who will not have their housing requirements met by the private sector. It is this group of households that governments and the public sector are most concerned with. This concern is a result of the gradual evolution of the welfare state and the general acceptance that governments should at the very least support or provide a 'safety net'. This has created a situation where successive governments have been responsible for housing certain households, through local authority housing and more recently through providing financial assistance to Housing Associations.

The Housing Services Advisory Group defined this social approach to need as including those households which;

> (a) lack and require separate (but not necessarily self contained) accommodation for their well being; and
> (b) live in accommodation which is not up to socially acceptable standards of
>   i) Fitness
>   ii) Availability of the five basic amenities
>   iii) Space
> (Housing Services Advisory Group, 1977, p. 27)

This category of housing need currently refers to households which, primarily for economic reasons, find themselves unable to obtain housing offered by the market (Holmans, 1995). However, in its early years local authority housing (still the major supplier of housing for need) was not viewed in such a way. As Berry (1974) put it:

> ...local authorities should cater for general needs and not only for the poorest families. (Berry, 1974, p. 90)

Local authority housing has historically been seen as a solution for households in the greatest *housing* need, not necessarily *economic* need. Yet, over recent years, local authority housing has gradually become residualised, with the result that it is now the tenure of the poorest households in society (Murie, 1983; Forest and Murie, 1983; Malpass, 1990).

The definition of 'global housing demand' used in this discussion will add to the social view of housing need, would-be households which can effectively demand private sector housing for owner occupation, provided by either speculative housebuilders or the sale of properties by existing owner occupiers (i.e. the second hand market). The word 'effective' used in conjunction with demand could be seen as the key difference between the 'demand' for social housing and that for homes provided by the market. Effective demand has been defined as occurring when households not only require something, but have the economic resources to acquire it (Chiddick and Dobson, 1986; Chiddick, 1987; Field and MacGregor, 1987).

As can be seen from the discussion in Chapter 2 the current housing needs of the majority of the population are met by owner occupation and the expectation is that the future needs of the population will continue to be met by this tenure (Forrest et al., 1995; Holmans, 1995; HoC, 1996). This assumption is sustained both by government policy, which continues to encourage owner occupation, the financial services industry which offers lower rates of interest on loans secured on property and public opinion, with many households viewing owner occupation as their eventual housing destination (Saunders, 1990; Kleinman, 1991; Cairncross, 1992; Ford and Wilcox, 1992; Maclennan and Gibb, 1993c; Coles and Taylor, 1993; Forest and Murie, 1994; Clapham, 1996).

Estimating effective demand is an uncertain science. In the report to the House of Commons Environment Committee a number of expert witnesses indicated the methodology employed when estimating effective demand (HoC, 1996). The commonest technique is the 'net stock' approach. This method first estimates the net increase in household stocks based upon an analysis of the forecast number of households. From this base it assumes that demand from owner occupiers will develop in the future, in the same way as it has in the past, whilst the remaining households are assumed to require social housing. Clearly this technique is uncertain and a number of assumptions have to be made, not least the fact that future levels of effective demand will reflect those that have occurred in the past. As it is so uncertain it would appear to benefit from improved information on local housing situations, a role that would be achieved through the development of housing strategies.

At a local level, if a would-be householder can purchase a dwelling at a current market price, then demand is effectively met. However, if an external factor were to raise the price, then householders who, in the past had sufficient income and assets to effectively demand housing, will no longer be able to do so. If Bramley's assertions regarding the openness of housing markets is correct (Bramley, 1993) this would then result in an increase in demand in alternative areas, where these displaced households may find that their demand becomes more effective. Similarly, if a local authority pursues constraint polices, whilst neighbouring areas do not, would-be householders in the constrained area may find that they cannot demand effectively. In the terminology of economists this 'latent demand' will then create demand in neighbouring housing markets as households have to alter housing search patterns and examine other housing markets.

With regard to the monitoring of housing markets, this 'diversion' of demand can be problematic. As demand is forced away from its intended market area, becoming demand in another housing market, it will create complications for any methods employed by the local authority to monitor demand, as it will be illustrating a 'second choice' location. It is extremely difficult to overcome this and it may be artificial to even try. If effective demand is what the indicators are attempting to measure, then any conclusions drawn from the data monitored will have to be based upon the conditions prevalent in the housing market at one particular period in time. Yet housing policy makers will have to realise the implications of changes in conditions, in this respect influencing the number of households effectively demanding housing. This would appear to be the case in rural areas in the late 1980s, when resident villagers found that within their housing market they could not afford housing on the open market, i.e. they are unable to effectively demand homes. Instead villagers would often have to find housing away from their friends, family and often jobs, their place in the local community being taken by second home owners, retiring households, or even commuters from the urban areas (Constable, 1987; Lee-Steere, 1989; Clark, 1990; Nicol, 1991).

This indistinctiveness is not confined to the margins between effective household demand and household need. Examining house type choice, for instance, illustrates similar lack of clarity. For instance, a household may be searching the market for a property with two bedrooms, yet if a three bedroom property is offered for the same price (it may, for example, require renovation) then the household will consider this as an option. This illustrates that on a personal level, housing demand is a series of compromises, with households evaluating the 'plus and minus' points of each property until a balance is achieved.

The argument that effective demand in one area could be seen as housing need in another, gives a clear indication that the margin between effective housing demand and housing need (in practical terms the border between tenures) is fluid and changes with time. This argument is just as appropriate for the differences between house types and the geographical view of housing markets. There is, therefore, a need for a cross-tenure strategy which attempts to marry households' residential ambitions with the various housing types and tenures on offer in the local housing market. This illustrates why housing strategies which comprehensively assess the housing situation, and are then employed to develop housing policies, are essential in the provision of an equitable and implementable housing supply.

**Global Housing Demand in the UK**

Throughout the 1980s and 1990s, the primary regulators of demand operated in such a way that owner occupation was the favoured tenure. Demand favoured owner occupation due to a mixture of economic circumstances (real wage rises, access to finance, etc.), favourable government policies and a growth in the number of households coupled with a lack of alternative housing tenures. Problems only started to become apparent when one of the 'valves' described in Figure 2.2 (namely that of economic control and cost of borrowing) influenced demand away from owner occupation, whilst other factors continued to promote the tenure. Forrest and Leather estimate that, by the year 2006, home ownership levels nationally may reach 77% (Forrest and Leather, 1995). They realise that this assumption is not without substantial uncertainty, yet it illustrates that in the longer term owner occupied housing will continue to be the dominant tenure.

Figure 3.1 gives a representation of the demand for housing. It can be seen that both demand by newly forming households and demand from existing households who change house or tenure compete with each other for the available supply. The supply of new homes is boosted in this model by the recycling of second hand homes. This is particularly important in the private rented and owner occupied sectors, where household moves are dominated by transfers within the existing stock. In 1991, only 10.8% of mortgages were granted on newly built properties (DoE, 1993a, Tables 1.9, 1.10 and 1.11). This shows the dominance of the existing housing stock in the market. Although it has been suggested that current input from new

44   *The Formulation of Local Housing Strategies*

**Figure 3.1   Demand for Housing**

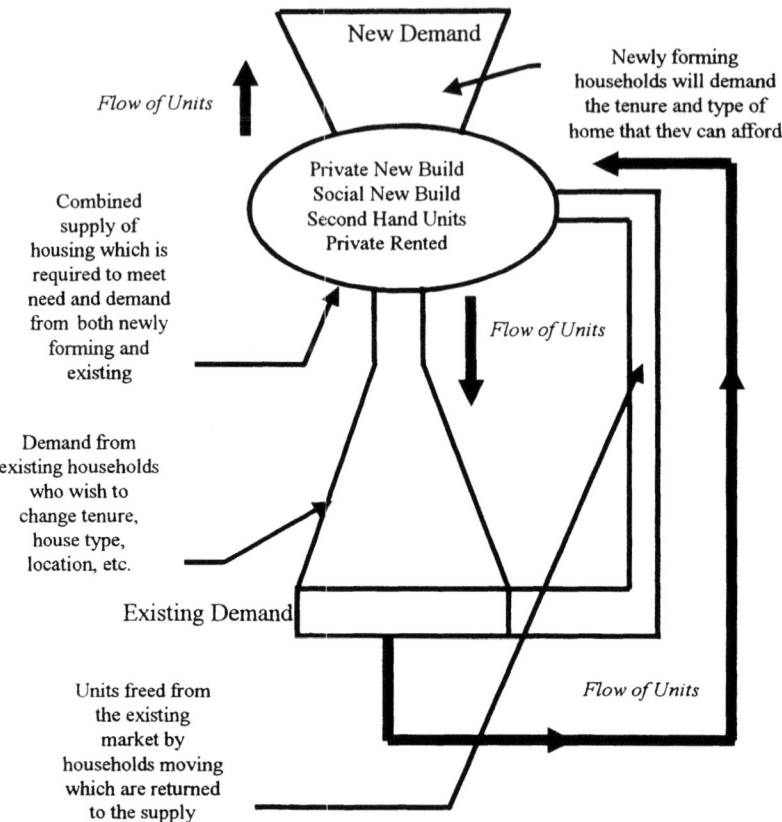

home construction has increased (Stewart, 1994), available statistics do little to suggest this is having a major effect on the make-up of supply. The situation within the rented sector is even more marked, as limited new supply results in the existing stock monopolising the market. Take, for example, the position of public housing. Between 1$^{st}$ April 1991 and 31$^{st}$ March 1992, 399,419 units were available to let and it is estimated that, of this, only approximately 3% were new construction. (Author's analysis of unpublished Chartered Institute of Housing Data).

Figure 3.1 illustrates diagrammatically the complex set of 'flows' that operate in the demand for housing. It is clear from this and Figure 2.2 that supply and demand in the housing market consists of a number of different 'connections' and stages where choices on the part of buyers and sellers, households and housebuilders, can alter the manner in which the housing market operates. This is presented to indicate the need for housing strategies to be comprehensive, monitoring the housing market as a whole.

**The Situation at the Tenure Margins**

If it were simply a choice between public rented and owner occupation there would be a relatively straightforward tenure selection process largely determined by an ability to pay. However, between these two opposite extremes there are a number of different 'tenures', which complicate demand choices. Examining each of these in turn.

*Renting From a Housing Association*

As the Conservative government eroded the powers of local authorities, housing associations became the providers of social housing on an unprecedented scale. This trend continued with the Labour government returned in 1997 (see Table 3.2). The question is, does the existence of housing association renting add further choice to the housing market? There are two initial assumptions that could be made as to whether or not this is the case. Firstly as housing association provision has grown as local authorities has declined (see Table 2.1), an initial assumption would be that housing associations have supplanted, rather than supplemented, local authority supply.

The alternative view is that increased housing association provision will add an alternative housing choice. If this view is to be supported one would expect housing associations to offer something different to households, than that available through the local authority stock. One possible method for determining if this is the case is to examine whether the households occupying housing association homes are different from those who occupy local authority homes. In economic terms, if this were to be the case one would expect the more wealthy households to be housing association tenants whilst the less affluent would rent from the local authorities 'residualised stock' (Morris and Winn, 1990; Forest, et al., 1990; Malpass, 1990). Kleinman (1991) argues that housing association growth is dependent on private finance which results in higher rents, increased risks and a drift up-market from traditional groups. As can be seen in Table 3.1, the average income of housing association tenants, in 1992 was lower than for those renting from the local authority. By 1996 this situation had changed so that the tenants income balance was in favour of the housing association.

**Table 3.1  Average Income of Head of Household by Tenure (£s per week)**

|      | Owners | | Tenants | | | |
|------|--------|--------|--------|--------|--------|--------|
|      | Outright | With Mortgage | Local Authority | Housing Association | Private: Unfurnished | Private: Furnished |
| 1992 | 194 | 320 | 110 | 102 | 149 | 170 |
| 1996 | 225 | 380 | 131 | 145 | 223 | 222 |

**Source:** Wilcox, 1998, Table 34, p.124

The 1990s saw social housing rents rise faster than average earnings, with the result that there has been an increase in housing benefit payments to tenants to help pay for these higher rents (Page, 1993; Wilcox, 1994). This can be seen in the case study area of the East Midlands, where one housing association (East Midlands Housing Association) has 60% of its tenants qualifying for housing benefit. It would appear that, far from providing a housing service at the margins between Local Authority renting and other tenures, housing association renting has supplanted the local authority sector. Yet, up until 1987, housing association provision was not at a sufficiently high level to act as a substitute for the decline in social housing provision (Kleinman and Roberts, 1991).

Demand for Housing 47

**Figure 3.2 House Prices in Selected Regions (1980-1996)**

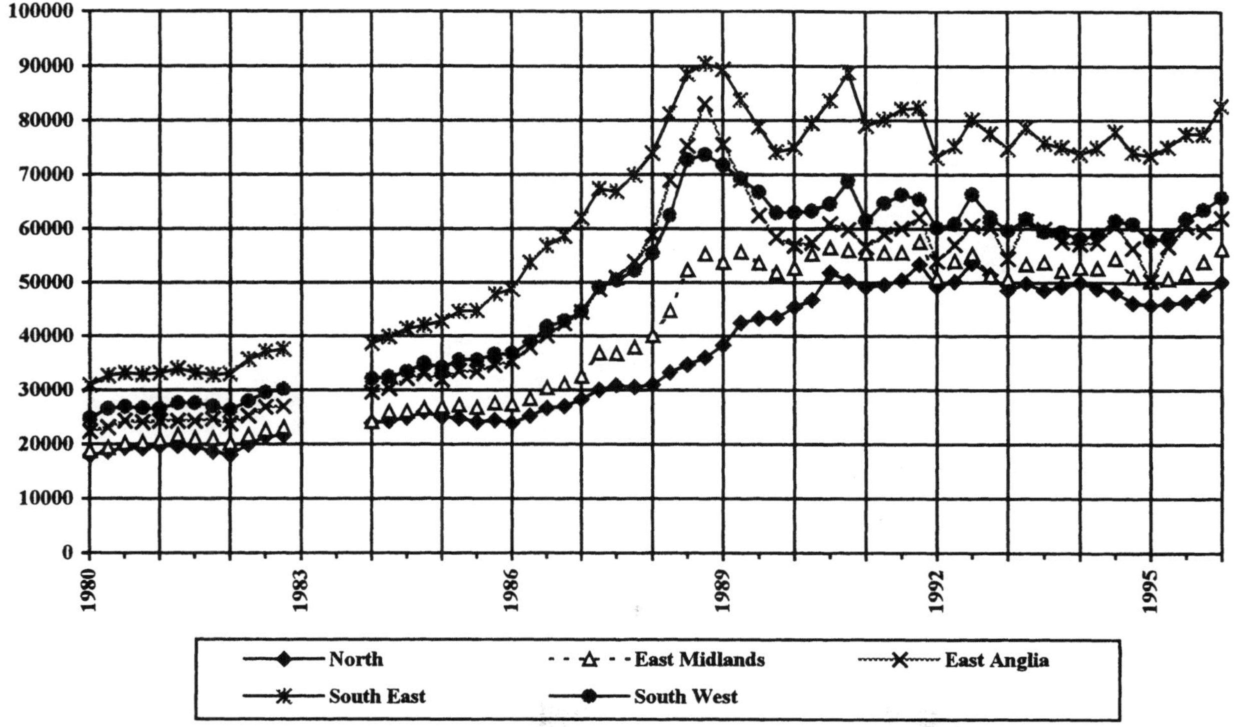

**Source:** Halifax (The data for 1983 is unavailable)

## Shared Ownership

This is probably the only truly 'hybrid' tenure, in-so-far as it contains attributes of both owner occupation and rental housing. Introduced by the 1980 Housing Act, shared ownership occurs when the purchaser buys a share of a dwelling (between 25-75%), renting the remainder. Usually this is from a housing association, although this does not have to be the case. Householders often have the option to 'staircase' the level of ownership, until they own the property outright. In some cases the tenancy agreement precludes such stair-casing, or sets a limit on the share of the property that can be purchased. Such a 'cap' on stair-casing is an attempt to ensure that the property remains, to some extent, within the social housing sector (NFHA, 1991). The fact that householders can purchase different percentages of a properties equity, means that this tenure is one of the most flexible. Housing associations currently manage 60,000 shared ownership units in the UK, and output has grown by over 250% since 1989 (Randolph, 1995).

A household considering shared ownership will have to be prepared to purchase a minimum of 25% of the property, and therefore certain households will be precluded from access to this 'hybrid' tenure. One would anticipate that households with incomes that are either uncertain or low, may find difficulty in obtaining a mortgage to support the purchase of even a 25% share. Due to the fact that house prices differ regionally (see Figure 3.2), one would anticipate that the economic attributes of households entering shared ownership may differ throughout the country. If the assumption were made that incomes for households on the margins of shared ownership were broadly similar throughout the UK, one would anticipate that, in regions with lower house prices, households would be able to purchase a greater percentage of equity than in the more expensive regions.

Shared ownership would therefore benefit marginal households to different degrees, dependent upon the area of the country in which they are based. Generally the household types who benefit from shared ownership are those in the:

> Middle market of social housing...the wide range of households who can afford more than a fully subsidised rent but cannot afford full owner occupation. (NFHA, 1991, p. 21)

This tenure, therefore, crosses the margins of renting and owner occupation and, whilst housing association renting appears to simply mirror the social renting function of local authorities, this tenure does increase choice in this 'middle market'. Not only can shared ownership be seen as meeting a 'gap' in the housing market, it also fits well between the objectives of the political parties, which should ensure that it will continue to grow if there is a change in government. Randolph (1995) suggests the tenure has yet to attain a 'critical mass' where demand can become self perpetuating. He argues that the tenure should not only be publicised more, but further research should be conducted regarding the way households move in and out of shared ownership and the affects of stair-casing to 100% ownership. This later detail is a particular issue that concerns rural planning authorities, which see shared ownership housing as being a means of providing low cost home ownership, and often use 'exceptions' policies to provide this housing. If rural planning authorities do allow shared ownership housing as an 'exception', then they are entitled to limit 'stair-casing' to 80% of ownership (DoE, 1991e; DoE, 1992a).

The provision of new rented housing through the social sector will primarily meet the needs of the weakest households (economically), although marginal households' demands can be met by the 'hybrid' tenures, such as shared ownership. The major factor operating in both these markets is that they are, to all intents and purposes, 'closed', so that households have to fulfil certain eligibility criteria before a local authority or housing association will consider housing them. Private renting is a tenure which acts as a 'buffer', housing both some of the poorest households in society whilst also providing homes for those seen as being relatively affluent individuals. Although it is an important tenure in the way that it caters for persons and households moving from location to location, supporting labour mobility, in terms of new production it is relatively insignificant. As will be highlighted later, an increase in the demand for privately rented homes is most often met by properties which transfer from the owner occupied housing market.

*Private Renting*

After years of decline efforts have been made to revive this sector of the housing market (the Business Expansion Scheme for instance (Merrett, 1992)). These have had a degree of success increasing the number of

## Table 3.2  Breakdown of the Housing Stock (GB) ('000s)

| | Owner occupied | | Privately rented | | Rented from HAs | | Rented from LAs or new town corporations | | All dwellings |
|---|---|---|---|---|---|---|---|---|---|
| 1969 | 9063 | 49% | 3877 | 21% | | 0% | 5548 | 30% | 18488 |
| 1970 | 9356 | 50% | 3677 | 20% | | 0% | 5698 | 30% | 18731 |
| 1971 | 9612 | 51% | 3578 | 19% | | 0% | 5810 | 31% | 19000 |
| 1972 | 9926 | 52% | 3443 | 18% | | 0% | 5854 | 30% | 19223 |
| 1973 | 10212 | 50% | 3318 | 16% | | 0% | 6906 | 34% | 20436 |
| 1974 | 10408 | 53% | 3200 | 16% | | 0% | 6029 | 31% | 19637 |
| 1975 | 10610 | 53% | 3076 | 15% | | 0% | 6185 | 31% | 19871 |
| 1976 | 10818 | 54% | 2978 | 15% | | 0% | 6322 | 31% | 20118 |
| 1977 | 11026 | 54% | 2894 | 14% | | 0% | 6447 | 32% | 20367 |
| 1978 | 11120 | 54% | 2936 | 14% | | 0% | 6487 | 32% | 20543 |
| 1979 | 11348 | 55% | 2870 | 14% | | 0% | 6521 | 31% | 20739 |
| 1980 | 11618 | 56% | 2811 | 13% | | 0% | 6499 | 31% | 20928 |
| 1981 | 11898 | 56% | 2337 | 11% | 469 | 2% | 6380 | 30% | 21084 |
| 1982 | 12270 | 58% | 2318 | 11% | 483 | 2% | 6180 | 29% | 21251 |
| 1983 | 12604 | 59% | 2304 | 11% | 504 | 2% | 6035 | 28% | 21447 |
| 1984 | 12913 | 60% | 2290 | 11% | 525 | 2% | 5924 | 27% | 21652 |
| 1985 | 13223 | 61% | 2258 | 10% | 548 | 3% | 5820 | 27% | 21849 |
| 1986 | 13575 | 62% | 2198 | 10% | 565 | 3% | 5723 | 26% | 22061 |
| 1987 | 13962 | 63% | 2134 | 10% | 586 | 3% | 5600 | 25% | 22282 |
| 1988 | 14418 | 64% | 2072 | 9% | 614 | 3% | 5412 | 24% | 22516 |
| 1989 | 14826 | 65% | 2064 | 9% | 651 | 3% | 5190 | 23% | 22731 |
| 1990 | 15094 | 66% | 2112 | 9% | 706 | 3% | 5015 | 22% | 22927 |
| 1991 | 15267 | 66% | 2218 | 10% | 737 | 3% | 4916 | 21% | 23138 |
| 1992 | 15421 | 66% | 2270 | 10% | 801 | 3% | 4811 | 21% | 23303 |
| 1993 | 15605 | 66% | 2289 | 10% | 870 | 4% | 4710 | 20% | 23474 |
| 1994 | 15809 | 67% | 2290 | 10% | 944 | 4% | 4605 | 19% | 23650 |
| 1995 | 15947 | 67% | 2476 | 10% | 1036 | 4% | 4401 | 18% | 23860 |
| 1996 | 16095 | 67% | 2536 | 11% | 1104 | 5% | 4301 | 18% | 24037 |
| 1997 | 16274 | 67% | 2566 | 11% | 1191 | 5% | 4185 | 17% | 24216 |

**Source:** Housing and Data Statistics Division, DoE, Bristol; DoE, 1993a; CML/BSA,1996, CML 2000

*Demand for Housing* 51

privately rented homes from just on two million in 1989 to two and a half million in 1998 (Wilcox, 2000) but the tenure has remained, relatively small (see Table 3.2). There is a plausible argument that an informal and unofficial private rented sector exists, formed from homeowners who have, for one reason or another, found themselves with two homes. This could be due to an individual working abroad who lets his/her home for 6 months or, the property is let due to the fact that the owner cannot sell. As mortgage lenders attach an additional interest charge if a home is let, plus the fact that tax would have to be paid on any rent received, many 'landlords' may not admit to letting properties so the scale of such a market is very difficult to establish, and further work is necessary in this area. It could be argued that if this is the case this sector will diminish if the housing market recovers, as this would allow individuals to sell their properties (Wilcox, 1994).

As can be seen from Table 3.2, owner occupation is the dominant tenure in the housing market. New supply is primarily provided by private speculative housebuilders and, as mentioned previously, even housing association provision often involves private speculative housebuilders, through the use of affordable housing 'quotas' (Barlow, Cocks and Parker, 1994). It is therefore crucial for a housing strategy to be aware of the housing market within which private housebuilders operate.

## Population Projections and the Future Need for Housing at the National Level

If the research questions indicated in Chapter One are re-examined, it is clear that an examination of quantitative issues, such as population and household projections are not of central importance to this thesis, where the focus is directed towards qualitative issues and collaboration. This quantitative, numerical discussion has been the focus of other research (Guillou, 1990; Field and MacGregor, 1993; Holmans, 1995) and therefore this section will not examine this area in great detail. Yet it is necessary to examine the quantitative area, if only to place the research questions and the analysis of 1990s housing strategies in the context of housing 'numbers'. The remainder of this chapter will focus upon population and housing forecasts, what could be described as the future 'demand' for housing. This discussion will commence with an examination of population projections at a national level before focusing upon the local case study areas of Mansfield and Ashby.

The most simple method for the determination of a 'global housing need' is to carry out a form of residual analysis, subtracting from the estimated total of future households the actual number of current households. Leaving aside for a moment the difficulties in estimating households, this approach is still problematic. Although this method will highlight shortfalls it will not demonstrate movements within the housing market. For instance, over any time period there are a number of units which become unfit, are demolished, or otherwise lost from the housing stock. Take, for instance, the work of Holmans. In his research he highlights the existence, in 1991, of a crude surplus of almost 600,000 dwellings (Holmans, 1995, p.12). Yet from this there are always a number of units which are vacant, either due to continued adjustments in the housing market, or because they are second homes. To ensure that any housing needs model is sophisticated enough to be useful, factors such as these have to be reflected.

*Population Projections*

It is not enough to suggest that future population, the base for overall housing demand, is represented simply by existing population plus births minus deaths. There also has to be an opportunity to take account of both immigration and emigration. At a national level in the UK population, change is primarily a result of natural growth or decline (the balance of births versus deaths). The birth rate will give an indication of the household formation rates that will affect the household projections 'x' years into the future. Although the actual age at which the population begins to form households and, in practical terms, when this will be apparent in the household forecasts is uncertain, the greatest uncertainty is seen to be in terms of migration assumptions.

Migration is the greatest contributory factor to sub-national population growth patterns (Champion, 1993). As a result, much change in population is due to migration, and it is assumptions in this area which are responsible for the majority of forecast debates. Inter-regional differences in population growth are noticeable in the UK (King, 1993) and this tendency can even be seen at more local levels where enumeration districts reflect different levels of population growth, and therefore housing demand. One would suggest that a developed housing strategy, one which is based upon sound data and surveys, may enable migration to be better monitored (see later chapters on the monitoring methods).

Figure 3.4 indicates population projections for the UK up until 2051. It should be borne in mind that the longer the timescale for projections, the more uncertain they become. Since projections are published regularly by both central government agencies and independent forecasting units (every 2-5 years appears to be the norm) the longer term projections can be continually monitored and updated. Yet it is the short term projections, the most useful for policy makers and indicating the likely movements and pressures in housing markets, that have to be robust. These projections can already be in place and working through development plans by the time re-assessment is carried out.

Looking at the shorter-term in more detail, the OPCS have projected the UKs population for every individual year of the 1990s. Although this does not give the household data required for a determination of 'global' housing demand, it does suggest that there will be around 3% more people living in the UK in 2001, an assertion that will only be tested when the 2001 census is completed and published.

*Household Projections*

From the base population data, it is necessary to adapt the statistics to form household forecasts, the data that will indicate the degree of future 'global' household demand. According to the Office of Population Census and Surveys/General Register Office for Scotland (1992), a household is either,

(a) One person living alone; or
(b) A group of people (who may or may not be related) living, or staying temporarily at the same address, with common housekeeping. (OPCS/GRO (S), 1992, p. 10)

The Environment Committee stated that a household can be either a person living alone or a group of individuals who share housekeeping arrangements or a living room (HoC, 1996). Although these definitions are clearly intended to enumerate the types of households in existence in 1990s Britain, they still suffer from problems identified in the 1960s. Equations of actual household numbers still neglect to fully reflect the concept of potential

## 54  The Formulation of Local Housing Strategies

households, i.e. persons living as part of a household, who would wish to form their own household. The definitions used currently for household projections only reflect concealed married couples and concealed lone parents (DoE, 1991a), and this limited definition of concealed demand suggests a need for 110,000 homes (Holmans, 1995). The Environment Committee, calling for the continued publication of regular household projections, recommended that the government should carefully examine areas such as household formation factors with a possibility of the projections becoming more responsive to the way households form (HoC, 1996). In the response to the Environment Committee, the Government stated that it intends to publish a discussion document examining household estimates (DoE, 1996).

The latest set of household projections (DoE, 1995a) differ significantly from those prepared in 1991 (DoE, 1991a). This difference can be seen in Table 3.3. The latest set of forecasts have been examined by the Environment Committee of the House of Commons (HoC, 1996) and the consensus is that, if they are inaccurate, it will be through an underestimation rather than overestimation. In the Government's response to the Select Committee's report it was stressed that it (the Government) was fully committed to improving the underlying data and projection methodologies (DoE, 1996). In the 1996 report (HoC, 1996), it was suggested that there will be a further 4.4 million households in England by 2016. Yet this is simply one set of projections and may offer only one *possible* direction for future household growth. As Shaw (1993) states;

> Perhaps the only thing that can be said with confidence about this or any other set of population projections is that they will turn out to be wrong! (Shaw, 1993, p. 50)

Tilling highlights why there are considerable differences in household projections, mainly deriving from the methodology employed by forecasters (Tilling, 1994).

Of the forecasts highlighted in Table 3.3 Holmans' figures are the only set which attempts to differentiate between demand for all housing (i.e. the global demand) and effective demand. The Environment Select Committee examined the issue from the perspective of housing need, and heard detailed submissions from a number of agencies, many containing different estimates of housing need (HoC, 1996). In their response to The

*Demand for Housing* 55

Environment Select Committee, the Government indicated that it was attempting (in conjunction with Cambridge University) to develop an improved housing model (DoE, 1996). Updated estimates of housing need will be published once this model has become operational. The uncertainty of this whole area gives further justification for the adoption of a housing strategy which integrates the 'global' demand with all forms of housing supply. One would argue that if this were done at the local level, and regular monitoring were to be carried out, there would be a more responsive housing supply, altering to reflect changing levels of effective demand and housing need.

**Table 3.3 Household Projections**

| Forecaster | Period | Demand Per Annum |
|---|---|---|
| Audit Commission (1992) *Developing Local Authority Housing Strategies* | 1991-2001 | 169,400-200,800 (England) |
| DoE (1991a) *Household Projections 1989 Based* | 1991-2001 | 156,700 (England) |
| DoE (1995a) *Household Projections 1992 Based* | 1991-2001 | 183,100 (England) |
| DoE (1993a) *Housing and Construction Statistics* | 1991-2001 | 147,700 (England) |
| PHRG (Chelmer Model) Unpublished | 1991-2001 | 182,836 (England and Wales) |
| Holmans (1995) Owner Occupied Households | 1991-2001 | 145,100 (England) |
| All Households | 1991-2001 | 183,100 (England) |

*Household Forecasts at the Local Level*

The household projections which develop into policy at a local or county level can often take a different approach. For instance they may be based on OPCS data, decennial census and mid-year population estimates, which are then adapted to account for a number of different variables. Table 3.4, highlights the responses to part of a questionnaire sent to a number of Local Authorities in 1994 (see Chapter Six).

As can be seen from this empirical survey, authorities use more than one source of data, either as base data for their own projection methods or as a comparison for the figures which they produce. It indicates that there is no established method upon which all housing allocation and land release policies are based. As no method is technically incorrect, different techniques result in different figures, providing support to both the pro-development and the conservationist lobbies in the land availability debate (Planning, 1993,1994a, 1994b, 1994c,1995a, 1995b). It is outside the remit of this discussion to account for differences in the figures each method may produce and these questions are discussed more fully elsewhere (Guillou, 1990; Corner, 1994; Gillen et al., 1995).

**Table 3.4 Do the Authority Use Household Forecasts/ Population Projections Prepared by...**

|  | DoE (%) | OPCS (%) | Other (%) |
|---|---|---|---|
| County Councils | 34.9 | 20.9 | 74.4 |
| Metropolitan Authorities | 40 | 68 | 52 |
| East Midlands Authorities | 15 | 30 | 70 |

The preparation of structure plans may take a number of years to proceed through all the stages of preparation (see below), before becoming formally adopted. As population and household projections are produced regularly this may result in one set of projections being superseded by a more recent set whilst the plan is being compiled. Such uncertainty results in the structure planning authorities having to make choices. For instance the plan, or the parts of the plan that deal with housing, can be delayed to ensure that the most up to date projections are contained in the document. This occurred in Nottinghamshire, where the County Council requested the Chair of the Examination in Public to allow certain matters to be postponed to allow the then soon-to-be published 1992-based household projections to be included. Alternatively, the policy-makers can use the latest set of projections from policy conception, whilst being aware that there is a strong possibility that by the time the Plan becomes adopted a new set of projections may be available. This could result in the planning authority having to update the plan to take into account these new projections.

The major implication of this combination of different projections is that data can be found to support almost all views, from those of the Council for the Protection of Rural England to the House Builders Federation (Planning, 1995a). One argument is that, at this stage, the mathematical process, which has produced population and household projections, now encounters political decisions. As strategic planning authorities introduce the effect their own policies will have on the population projections at the local level, there is scope for the figures to be increased or decreased. When housing allocations are devolved to the districts (in the two tier authorities), the process becomes one where the sites that are allocated can become politically significant and the technical process can be hidden behind political choices. Justification for figures and low allocations are often based upon low build rates that have occurred in the past. Clearly this is a circular argument, with the statistics supporting the policies, which support the statistics. It would, therefore, appear that at the local level household allocations can be self-perpetuating. Yet is this the case? It can be seen, from Table 3.7, that the implied build rates of structure plans in the East Midlands differ significantly from that experienced in past years.

Bramley, in his submission to the House of Commons Environment Committee, suggested that one way of producing better forecasts would be to introduce methods which reflect changes in the economic factors of households (HoC, 1996). One would argue that this type of technique should be viewed as more than a means of placing development where employment is. It should also be a means of determining the type and tenure of the housing provided, i.e. estimating the demand for housing. Examining the data which may allow such detailed demand estimates to be made is a central part of this discussion and will be examined in subsequent chapters, yet at this stage it is worthwhile highlighting one of the areas investigated in the questionnaire.

Table 3.5  Economic Development Polices as an Indicator of Market Demand (%)

|  | Yes | No | No Answer |
|---|---|---|---|
| Counties | 48.4 | 32.6 | 18.6 |
| Metro-Authorities | 24.0 | 68.0 | 8.0 |
| E.Midland Districts | 45.0 | 45.0 | 10.0 |

One of the questions addressed to the local authorities (see Chapter Six) examined the degree to which economic policies were seen as an indicator of market demand. (If economic growth were to be examined this should result in a situation where economic growth and the location of housing should be compatible). With sustainability and the debate about reducing car journeys and pollution, one would suggest that there should be strong links between employment and economic growth and housing locations. However, as can be seen in Table 3.5, there are a significant number of authorities which stated that economic development polices were not monitored as potential indicators of housing demand, indicating that economic development and housing policies may be contradicting one another. Why this may be occurring is discussed later in this chapter.

However, one conclusion can already be made from the empirical research underlying this part of this research. Bramley's call for greater co-ordination between economic and housing policies in general may require considerable work before such an integrated approach is implemented. This assertion is due mainly to the fact that many authorities appear to do little in the way of integrating their *own* economic and housing policies. Examining the case study districts indicated that North West Leicestershire DC did not utilise economic development policies as indicators of potential housing demand, whilst Mansfield DC employed economic development policies as indicators of potential housing demand.

**Housing Demand in the Case Study Areas**

*The Regional Level*

In 1991, the East Midlands Regional Planning Forum prepared a regional strategy providing a guide for the future of the region into the 21st century. This strategy was then submitted, as advice, to the East Midlands regional office of the DoE. In July 1993, the DoE published the consultation draft of the Regional Planning Guidance (RPG) which was finally produced in a complete format in March 1994, as RPG 8. The guidance has been criticised as being not so much a regional strategy as a;

> ...shopping list of current proposals, pet projects and pious political expectations. (Gillingwater, 1992, p. 423)

This is perhaps to be expected, given the way guidance formulation is strongly influenced by county councils (Coates, 1996). Yet, even if it does do little more than highlight current policies, formulating regional guidance does bring the various authorities together to 'knit' their own policies into one cross county strategy. If done successfully this should insure compatible policies are pursued. As the regions have no democratically derived powers, as county and district councils do, it would border on autocracy for the regional guidance to impose policies which run contrary to those which develop through public consultation and democratic processes. Currently, there are only two stages in the whole development plan system where there is an opportunity to place regional guidance under scrutiny. One is during the consultation period of the draft regional guidance, whilst the other is after the policies have been placed in structure plans, allowing an opportunity to discuss them at the Examination in Public.

Table 3.6 Comparison of Regional Guidance Figures and Structure Plan Figures

| County | RPG Figure | Structure Plan Figure *(Year of Adoption or Publication in Brackets)* | Current situation in structure Plan 'Updates' |
|---|---|---|---|
| Derbyshire | 3,250 | 3,446 (1990) | Public Consultation Period (May 1996) |
| Leicestershire | 3,500 | 3,533 (1994) | Adopted (January 1994) |
| Lincolnshire | 3,400 | 3,460 (1991) | Public Consultation Period Complete (May 1996) |
| Northamptonshire | 3,500 | 3,466 (1992) | Discussion Document for New Structure Plan (January 1996) |
| Nottinghamshire | 3,250 | 3,025 (1994) | Modification Stage Submitted to Committee (July 1996) |

In terms of housing, RPG 8 gives annual figures for each county from 1991-2011. It is felt that, to meet the predicted demand, structure plans will annually have to make provision for 16,900 homes over that period twenty years. This is to be divided between the counties as shown in Table 3.6, which also highlights the structure plan figures that have been adopted. As can be seen in the Table, the structure plans tend to be at different stages of the adoption process. Leicestershire's plan was placed on deposit in November 1991 and was finally adopted in January 1994. All strategic plans have to undergo a formal consultation and publicity process, allowing all interested parties to become involved in the process (Cullingworth and Nadin, 1994). The consultation period is the democratic section of the adoption process allowing any individual to comment on the proposed policies. The number of respondents to a consultation period can be considerable. For instance Leicestershire, one of the case study counties, received around 1,000 comments, whilst Nottinghamshire received in the region of 720. Before adoption, structure plans have to undergo an Examination In Public (EIP) an exercise that gives an opportunity for the proposed policies to be discussed and debated. In terms of this research, the consultation period and EIP allows the opportunity for different household forecasts and demand estimates to be examined.

At the Leicestershire Structure Plan EIP, vociferous opposition to the County's housing allocation by the HBF led the Panel Chair to recommend a compromise figure of 57,500 new homes. This was 8,500 more than in the original submitted plan, but fell far short of the 63,500 home figure, suggested by the HBF. As can be seen in Table 3.7, Leicestershire chose not to adopt the panels recommendation, instead increasing the figure by 3,800 to 53,000 (Planning,1993a; 1994a).

The structure plans for Leicestershire and Nottinghamshire are the most current strategic plans in the region. Leicestershire has an adopted plan in operation whilst Nottinghamshire hopes to adopt its plan some time in the Autumn of 1996. An examination of specific housing markets in the region should bear this in mind, as focusing upon these two counties will allow an analysis of a housing market that is operating under a recently adopted set of policies. Although there is a case for an examination of housing markets where policy formulation and plan coverage may require a degree of updating, over time all the counties will have to follow the lead of Leicestershire and Nottinghamshire. Perhaps more important is the fact that Nottinghamshire and Leicestershire are counties where the 1989 and 1991 based household projections are not widely divergent, (at least for the life of the structure plan). This is not the case for counties such as Derbyshire

Demand for Housing 61

**Table 3.7 Comparison of Structure Plan Provision and Build Rates**

| County | Leicestershire | Nottinghamshire | Lincolnshire | Northamptonshire | Derbyshire |
|---|---|---|---|---|---|
| Time Period | 1991-2006 | 1991-2006 | 1988-2001 | 1988-2006 | 1987-2001 |
| Housing Provision | 53,000 | 48,100 | 51,900 | 62,400 | 51,700 |
| Structure Plan Implied Annual Build Rate (Dwellings Per Annum) | 3,533 | 3,206 | 3,992 | 3,467 | 3,446 |
| Average Annual Private Build Rates (Completions) 1985-1994 | 2,838 | 3,099 | 2,985 | 2,682 | 2,501 |
| Average Annual Housing Association Build Rate 1990-93 | 484 | 473 | 278 | 162 | 395 |
| Combined Average Annual Build Rate | 3,322 | 3,572 | 3,263 | 2,844 | 2,896 |
| % Change from Past Build Rate to Implied Build Rate | +6.4% | -15.4% | +22.3% | +22% | +19% |

**Source:** Gillen, 1995, Table 5.8

where there is significant difference between the two sets of projections (DoE, 1991a; 1995a).

It could be argued that local authorities in the case study areas employed housing development as part of a broad land use policy, which may be contrary to where economic growth and market demand is occurring. In Leicestershire, for instance, the County inserted policies in the Structure Plan which requires housing land to be allocated:

> ...within and adjoining settlements which offer a realistic choice of transport options. (Leicestershire CC, 1994, Housing Policy 2, p. 12)

This policy seeks to direct all developments along rail/bus corridors. Some districts and housebuilders opposed this policy on the grounds of flexibility, but it was generally accepted through the EIP process. This type of policy owes much of its acceptance to the question of 'sustainability', and at face value it would appear to echo Bramley's economic-based housing demand projections, as one would envisage new employment occurring close to transport links, therefore supporting the household growth. However, in North West Leicestershire this argument appears to collapse. The transport choice corridor in this district is based upon the proposed Ivanhoe Rail Link from Burton, through Ashby to Loughborough. However the districts links with the West Midlands (A42/M42), the Toyota factory in South Derbyshire and, perhaps more importantly, the East Midland airport do not appear to have been reflected in this transport choice corridor. Take, for example, East Midlands Airport. The District Council sought to locate additional development at Castle Donnington, in an attempt to balance housing and employment in the north east of the district. The County was not strongly against such a plan, although it was seen to be outside a transport choice corridor. What halted this proposal was a mixture of local opposition and the proximity of the airport itself.

In Mansfield DC, industrial restructuring has left the area with a considerable amount of derelict land (205ha) of which 61ha has been affected by mining (Mansfield Regeneration Partnership, 1994). The District Council propose to concentrate development in the Mansfield and Mansfield Woodhouse areas, using development as a means of encouraging urban regeneration and the redevelopment of derelict and unused land. This policy has been supported by the District's successful Single Regeneration Bid (SRB) for the Mansfield Woodhouse area. One would suggest that this may not be the type of economic-based housing demand estimation that Bramley envisaged (HoC, 1996). Yet such housing policies do appear to suggest that housing demand will be occurring in areas where the Council's other policies will also support development. Both the situation in Mansfield and North West Leicestershire indicate the additional complications that ensure housing policy cannot simply encourage housing supply to be directed towards areas of demand.

It has been demonstrated in the proceeding sections that estimates of global housing demand at the national, and county level can be uncertain. Looking at both the case study districts in more detail does little to contradict these views.

*Mansfield*

Nottinghamshire County Council apply policies to 'sub-areas' rather than districts, partly a response to the artificiality of administrative boundaries. This divides the county into five sub-areas and Mansfield is included in the West Nottinghamshire sub area, along with parts of the neighbouring Districts of Ashfield and Newark and Sherwood. Table 3.8 illustrates the County's population projections for each of the sub areas. This system is largely based on the population model that the County Council employ, which divides the county into 15 'projection zones', which can be collated to form either the five sub areas; the eight districts; or the area of greater Nottingham. Each of the 15 'projection zones' is based upon whole wards which:

> ...allows the use of the wealth of information collected at ward level. Therefore, for example, the production of local fertility and mortality correction rates, which use ward birth and death information was possible. In addition, future population estimates can be directly related to projection zones. (NCC, 1994b, paragraph 3.36)

The previous Structure Plan, which had a base date of April 1988 and was approved in 1991, provided for 45,300 new dwellings between 1988-2001 in the whole of the County. For the same period, Mansfield had an allocation of 4,700 units. It should be noted that the Draft Local Plan that was on Deposit in the summer of 1996 actually runs from 1988-2003 so that the figure the District use contains an additional 720 dwellings for

64  *The Formulation of Local Housing Strategies*

these extra 2 years. These figures were based upon high migration assumptions, a feature which is not the case in the latest Structure Plan. When preparing its Local Plan, the District Council accepted the earlier Structure Plan's migration assumptions and believed Mansfield's population would rise to just over 104,000 by 1996 (Mansfield DC, 1994, p.11). However, interviews with officers at Mansfield highlighted that the council were of the opinion (summer 1995) that this level of migration may now be too optimistic, a view in line with the lower migration assumptions of the current Structure Plan. This illustrates, once again the uncertainty created by migration figures.

**Table 3.8  Structure Plan Population Projections**

| Sub-Area | 1991 | 2006 | 2011 | Change 1991-2011 | Change % |
|---|---|---|---|---|---|
| South Nott | 646,700 | 665,900 | 666,000 | 19,300 | 3.0 |
| **West Nott** | **217,500** | **226,300** | **228,300** | **10,800** | **5.0** |
| West Bassetlaw | 59,400 | 63,000 | 64,200 | 4,800 | 8.1 |
| East Bassetlaw | 45,900 | 47,700 | 48,100 | 2,200 | 4.8 |
| Newark | 50,700 | 54,800 | 56,600 | 5,900 | 11.6 |
| County | 1,020,200 | 1,057,500 | 1,063,300 | 43,100 | 4.2 |

**Source:** Table 1.1 NCC Structure Plan Deposit Draft, April 1994a

The strategic housing allocation was rolled forward and based upon a different timescale than the figures in the Draft Local Plan. In Mansfield, in the 15 years between 1991 and 2006, the County perceive a demand for around 4,500 dwellings, and a further 1,400 between 2006 and 2011 (Nottinghamshire CC, 1994). It is apparent from an examination of the Mansfield Consultative Draft Local Plan that this figure falls short of that which the District Council allocated (4,700 units between 1988-2001, with an additional 720 dwellings for the extra two years of the Local Plan to 2003, giving a total of 5,420 dwellings, paragraph 6.3.5).

The actual figure that the District have suggested in their Local Plan is neither 5,420, 4,700 nor 4,500, but is in fact 4,000 (Policy H2). This discrepancy is due to the fact that the Structure Plan and Local Plan periods are not the same (the Local Plan is based upon the housing allocations of the earlier Structure Plan) and a number of units had been completed between the Local Plan base date (1988) and its publication date, and therefore have to be discounted from the future allocation.

It can be seen from the Mansfield situation that the development plan system is far removed from its ideal of being a flow model with RPG providing the Structure Planning authorities with regional guidance, and the Structure Plan providing strategic direction for the Local Plan. Instead, a situation has arisen where a mis-match of different time based policy documents suggest different levels of housing demand for the same area. Although problematic, this is to be expected as it indicates how different authorities and tiers of local government have reacted to local circumstances and/ or government guidance.

A main housing objective of the Mansfield Local Plan, is stated in paragraph 6.4.6:

> Provide a range of housing sites where people will want to live and housebuilders will want to build.

Clearly there is a need for the Council to be aware of the housing needs and demands of the population, in an attempt to achieve these objectives. The way the District monitors the housing market and implements its housing policies is therefore important. The District Council prepares annual land availability studies to monitor the trends in the development of housing land. The latest study has been able to employ computer technology using a data base which has monitored the progression of each site. The planning department hope to supplement this system through the introduction of geographical information systems, to allow a locational element to be employed. It would appear that there is scope for computers to be used to log and monitor a number of different data sets, producing summaries, which may prove useful for both the officers and the councillors. The type of data that may be employed is examined in Chapters Five and Six.

Mansfield District Council envisage most of the dwellings being built by the private sector, and there is no policy directly concerned with blanket affordable housing 'quotas' in the district. The type of site allocated in the plan, coupled with the low house prices that already exist in the District (see Figure 3.3), would possibly result in starter or family homes, at the less expensive end of the market being provided. This should ensure that,

66  *The Formulation of Local Housing Strategies*

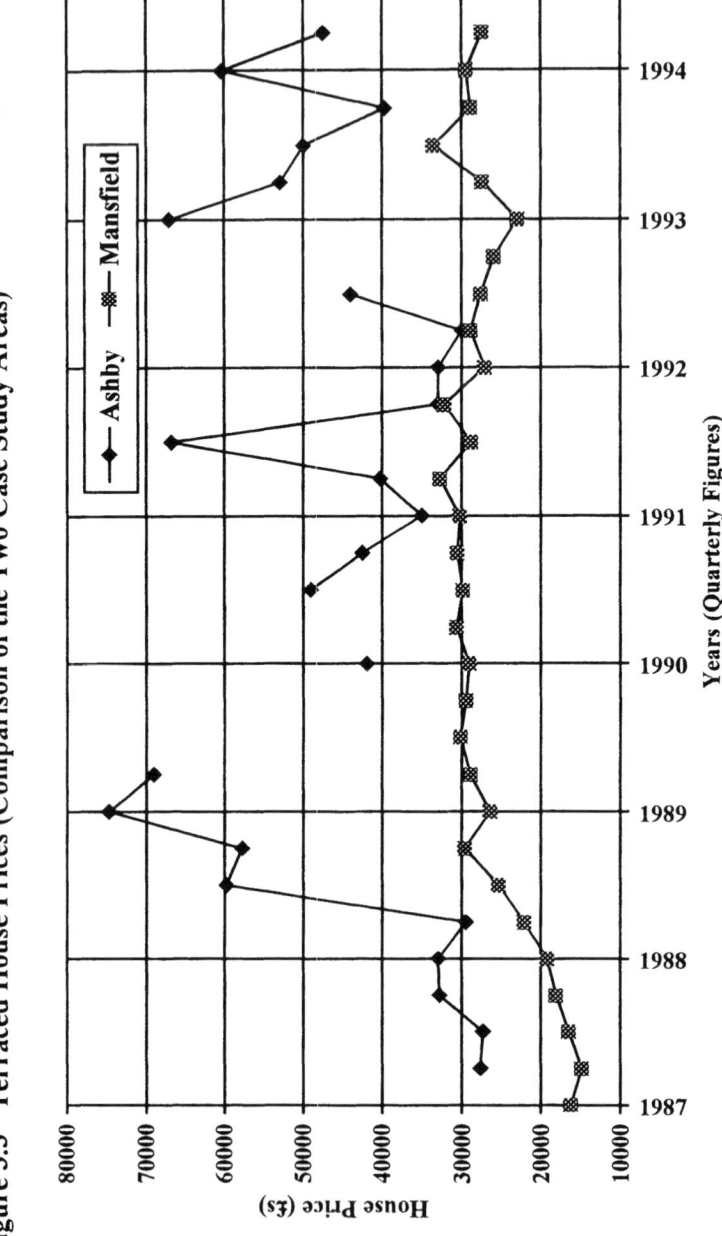

**Figure 3.3**  Terraced House Prices (Comparison of the Two Case Study Areas)

**Source:** Halifax (Missing data is due to insufficient sample size)

for a great number of households, open market housing is affordable and their housing choices can be met by the open market.

The Local Plan comes closest to discussing the issue of private speculative development directly meeting housing needs in Policy H13, which encourages dialogue between the authority and the development agencies as a means of establishing affordable housing. This course of action would be pursued in areas where there is a 'demonstrable' lack of affordable housing. The Local Plan highlights the means by which a situation such as this could be highlighted, through referring to the housing waiting list in addition to more detailed local appraisals, such as housing needs surveys. However, there is a major difference between dialogue and actual implementation, and it is arguable whether or not dialogue will result in housing for need being produced, particularly when housing is being employed for urban regeneration purposes, as this may create a situation where housebuilders profits are already limited through land reclamation, landscaping and more difficult marketing conditions.

**Table 3.9 Comparisons of Housing Figures for Leicestershire**

| Agency | Suggested Housing Allocation |
|---|---|
| Housebuilders Federation | 65,000 |
| Panel Chairman | 57,000 |
| Regional Planning Guidance | 52,500 |
| Leicestershire's Adopted Figure | 53,000 |

**Source:** Planning 21/01/94 'Landmark or black mark for self-approval regime?'

*Ashby (North West Leicestershire)*

In the summer of 1995, Leicestershire was the only county in the East Midlands with a formally adopted Structure Plan, adopted in January 1994. In practical terms, as the County has an adopted Structure Plan, it is in a powerful position regarding the strategy of its neighbours, as it can appear at the Examinations in Public (EIP) of counties such as Nottinghamshire or Derbyshire and argue that the plan under consideration will cause the adopted policies in Leicestershire to be placed under strain. This has already occurred at the EIP for Nottinghamshire's Structure Plan, where Leicestershire argued that the allocation for Rushcliffe was too small, and as a result would place pressure on the north Leicestershire districts.

68  *The Formulation of Local Housing Strategies*

The Leicestershire Structure Plan was one of the first to be self-approved, under provisions introduced by the 1991 Planning and Compensation Act. The Government's intention, when self-certification was introduced was that the process would fit into a hierarchical structure of planning strategy, where regional planning guidance would form the basis in which it would be accepted. However, because Leicestershire adopted its Plan before the guidance was published in its final form, this did not occur. The net result of this is that the adopted figure falls below that advocated by the House Builder's Federation (not particularly surprising), the EIP panel's report (formerly this would have been more likely to have been the figure adopted) and the Regional Guidance itself. The comparisons can be seen in Table 3.9.

The population forecasts prepared by Leicestershire County Council project a growth for the District of 15% over the Plan period, and this can be seen in Table 3.10. This is due to characteristics that are widespread throughout the country, namely an increase in single person households. An analysis of the 1991 census illustrates that the early figures (i.e. 1991) have proved to be exceptionally accurate as the actual number counted in the census was 80,566. This discrepancy may be explained by the Census' possible under-counting (Tilling, 1995). It would be expected that the longer-term figures may be less reliable, but these will be monitored and updated by amended review Structure Plans.

**Table 3.10  Forecast Population in North West Leicestershire**

| Year | 1986 | 1991 | 1996 | 2001 | 2006 |
|---|---|---|---|---|---|
| Number | 78,900 | 81,000 | 83,600 | 87,700 | 90,400 |

**Source:** NW Leicestershire DC, 1993, Draft Local Plan, Paragraph 7.12

Although at the time of writing and carrying out the fieldwork the County possessed an adopted Structure Plan, when NW Leicestershire formulated the Local Plan an earlier replacement Structure Plan was in force. When the Council prepared the Plan, the District provided for 6,900 units for a twenty-year period between 1986-2006, equating to approximately 345 units per annum. The adopted Structure Plan allocates 5,800 units for a fifteen year period, approximately 380 units per annum. This would appear to be a reasonably accurate allocation, given the fact that dwelling completion's during the early 1990s were between 300-400 (DoE, 1994b).

In discussion with the County Council, it transpired that the figure for demand in the County was derived from an essentially technical methodology, using the Chelmer Model. However, a number of different methods were employed to provide additional information on the levels of demand and need in the County. After consideration of a number of factors, including environmental constraints, employment growth and an estate agent survey, the County then decided upon the size of the District allocations. This would suggest that the County had employed economic policies as a means of establishing where housing allocations would be located, even though NW Leicestershire District Council had not.

The estate agent survey was carried out in 1988, when the first stages of Structure Plan preparation were embarked upon. It was an exercise in collecting data on house prices, which supplemented a survey of house prices collected from newspapers. Although welcome in so far as this illustrates the county attempting to monitor the housing market, there are limitations. Firstly there are technical problems with the data collected in such a survey (see Chapters Five and Six). Perhaps more important is the fact that the survey was conducted in 1988. Although one appreciates that the plan was being prepared at this time, the differences in the conditions in the housing market between 1988 and even 1990 are dramatic. Figure 3.3 in this chapter indicate how house prices have fallen between 1988 and the mid-1990s, whilst the discussion in Chapter One highlights other data indicating a housing market collapse. This clearly indicates the fluid nature of the housing market and the importance of monitoring techniques reflecting this fluidity.

**Conclusion**

With the conclusion of this chapter, part one of this book now draws to a close. The discussion has thus far dealt with the context for housing strategies, namely the housing market, housing supply and housing demand. It should be clear that there developed into the 1990s a disjointed approach to housing demand assessment and housing supply, and this should be an indication of the need to develop an approach where the housing market is better analysed and monitored by the local authority; analysis and monitoring that is used to influence the development of housing strategies. The next chapter will indicate that there already exists a framework document that could be revisited to provide the integrated housing strategy that is needed. Before moving on however it is worthwhile recapping the themes discussed in this chapter.

This discussion in this chapter examined the difference between effective demand and housing need highlighting that they can and, in terms of integrated housing strategies, should, be combined to provide an overall 'global' housing demand. Over recent years, housing demand has largely been met by the private sector with new social housing provision being relatively limited. Owner occupation remained until well into the late 1990s the tenure supported fiscally by government and continues to be the 'ideal' tenure of the majority of the population. For this demand to become effective, and allow access to owner occupation it is necessary for households to have sufficient capital and income to purchase a home. Since income is important for this tenure, one would expect income levels to be monitored, to estimate the levels of households that will require owner occupation or social housing need. This is an area that will be examined further in later chapters. Yet demand can not be easily categorised in terms of effective demand and housing need, and the situation at the margins of these definitions is rather complex. This was illustrated through an examination of 'hybrid' tenures such as shared ownership. What this indicates is that there is a need for housing strategies to integrate the departments in a local authority responsible for land release for private development (the planning department) and provision of social housing (the housing department). Further integration with agencies outside the local authority is necessary given that housing is largely provided by private housebuilders or housing associations. To summarise, this indicates a need for integration of the different 'players' in the housing market, to ensure demand is being met in the most effective way.

This chapter has introduced the results of the empirical surveys and the data collected from the case study areas of the East Midlands as a region and the two identified housing markets as they form part of the wider district. This analysis and discussion is contained in what may be seen to be a review based chapter as its treatment here supports the development of this discussion in a more logical manner. The survey work that has been introduced here has indicated that, in terms of housing forecasts, many authorities use sources of data other than those readily published by the DoE or OPCS. This may indicate that the debate on housing numbers at a holistic level is further complicated, when these 'independent' population and household projections are incorporated into the discussion. Although interesting in so far as it gives an indication of the basis for forecasts, it is only an indication.

# 4 The Development of Local Authority Housing Strategies and Joint Housing Studies

## Introduction

Earlier chapters have shown that the 'housing market' is both a complex concept, and in practical terms separated into a number of 'sub types': tenure, type of dwelling, type of household, etc. (Murie, Niner and Watson, 1976; Birchall, 1992; Malpass and Murie, 1994). Within the housing market, this complexity is associated with the different agencies which make provision for different client groups, and where different economic and housing policies affect different sectors of the housing market in different ways.

For a housing strategy to achieve its objectives, a degree of consensus between local authority departments and providers of homes, regardless of tenure, is necessary. The aim of this chapter is to discuss the three main linkages that are crucial to a local authority housing strategy, namely:

- The link between central and local government in terms of housing policy (i.e. the means by which national policy is translated into local housing solutions).
- The link between local authority housing and planning departments (i.e. the manner in which the two functions that are most directly concerned with housing compliment and support one another).

*Local Authority Housing Strategies and Joint Housing Studies* 73

- The link between housing producers and planning authorities (i.e. the relationship between the housing policy makers and policy implementers).

Each of these areas will be examined in turn, to illustrate the way in which linkages between these important participants in the housing market have evolved. As with the previous chapter, the results of primary empirical research will be included in the following analysis, supplementing the review data that is also contained within this chapter.

Figure 4.1, visualises housing strategy formulation as three 'zones' which connect vertically, whilst within these zones there are horizontal links. The main difference between a horizontal and vertical link is that the agencies linked horizontally could be seen as being equal 'partners', all having a role to play, and none being totally dependent on the other. The vertical linkages are altogether different. In this case they are based on hierarchy. Central government, through legislation, circulars, guidance, etc. influence local government policy, but what is perhaps more important is financial control, which can be used to direct local government policy. In Figure 4.1 this is illustrated by the fact that there is a hierarchical link between Central Government, then the County Council and finally the Local Authority (represented by the ellipse in the Figure). There are hierarchical links between the local authority as a whole but there are also links between the two departments primarily concerned with housing strategy formulation (namely planning and housing).

The grey ellipse in the centre of the Figure (Zone 2) illustrates local authorities and the manner in which the departments within such authorities interact and co-ordinate policy development. It should be noted that the county council are outside this ellipse and are in the hierarchical structure. County councils are included in zone 2 due to the fact that the household projections and structure plan land allocations, income profiles and economic forecasts will have to be considered not only by the planning department (in determining land release policies) but also by the housing department (in estimating future levels of housing for low income groups). In the case of metropolitan authorities, the role played by the county council in the figure, will be taken by the councils own 'strategic' planning section (i.e., the officers who prepare part one of the Unitary Development Plan). As this occurs within the council (i.e., within the grey ellipse) one would expect greater co-ordination and interdepartmental working. It can be seen that both

74  *The Formulation of Local Housing Strategies*

**Figure 4.1  The Connections in Housing Strategy Formulation**

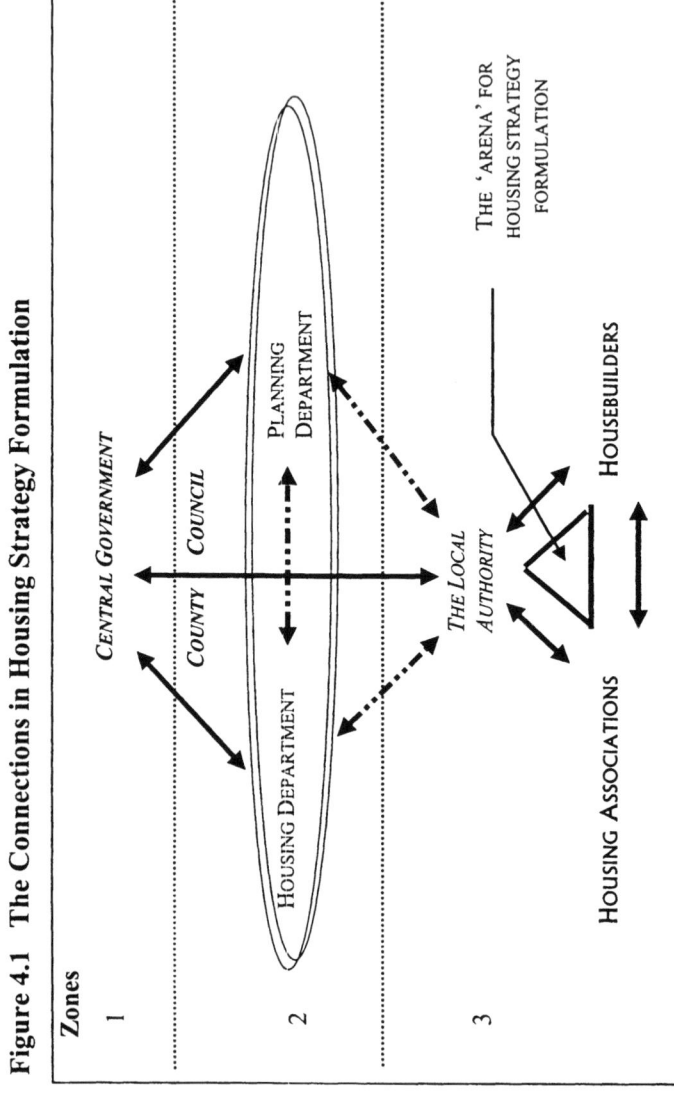

**NB** Please note that this figure is not intended to suggest housing and planning departments exist in county councils.

## Local Authority Housing Strategies and Joint Housing Studies   75

housing and planning departments are directed and controlled by central government and the degree to which this control is exerted may differ between the different departments. In addition the local authority as a whole is part of this hierarchy of control.

Zone 3 is where the enabling authority will have to discuss with the implementing agencies how the housing strategy will reach fruition. In the context of this discussion, zone 3 is the most important, as it is the arena in which links between all participants in housing production, at a local level, will have a chance to discuss and exchange views and information. It is arguable whether the local authority is an 'equal partner', as it retains the ability, within limits, to withhold planning permission, placing it in a position of power over the other agencies in zone 3. However, all the partners in zone 3 have some element of influence over the others, a view that will have to be put to one side whilst strategy is being discussed.

This diagram is simplistic, for instance the inclusion of county councils does not reflect unitary authorities, where such a level of government does not exist (it could be argued that in unitary authorities the situation should be more straightforward, with the strategic and local issues being examined by the one organisation). However one would suggest it does illustrate the manner in which a housing strategy connects to a number of different agencies and governmental tiers. As such an illustration it is useful as a 'guide' for this chapter which will discuss a number of these connections in more detail.

**Central and Local Government Relationships**

It is important to place into perspective the current relationship between Local and Central Government. To successfully achieve this aim it is necessary to examine the historical context of such a relationship. This could go as far back as the establishment of the Royal Commission on Housing of the Working Classes in 1884, and the Housing of the Working Classes Act in 1890, arguing that this indicated the first government 'housing policy'. Alternatively the development of municipal housing (through legislation such as the Housing and Town Planning Act 1919 (The Addison Act), and the subsequent Housing Acts of the 1920s, could be seen as an appropriate start date (Merrett, 1979; 1982). However for this research the end of the Second

76   *The Formulation of Local Housing Strategies*

**Figure 4.2   Total Housebuilding Completions: Great Britain (1945-1999)**

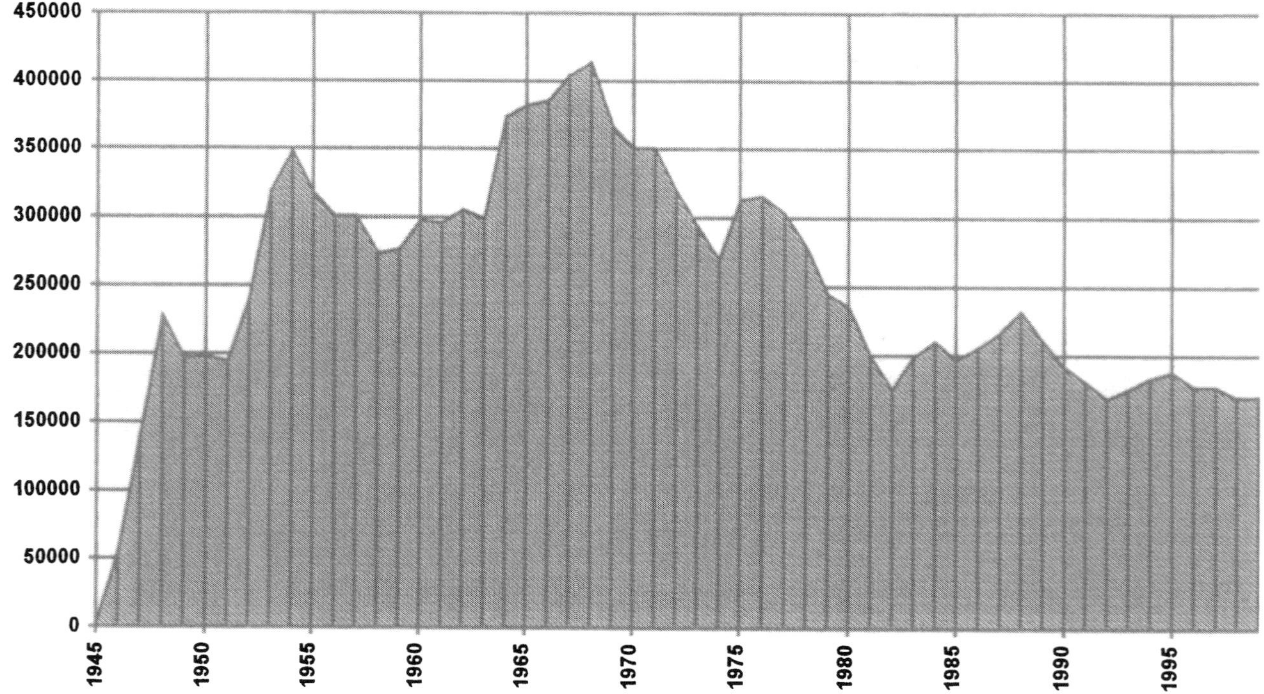

**Source:** Housing and Statistics Division, DoE and DoE, 1993a. Data from 1993 is from *Housing Finance*, Table 3

World War offers a more appropriate introduction to Central Local Government relationships.

Berry (1974) argues that during the Second World War, in an attempt to effectively manage the war effort, the Government introduced national planning for all forms of production. This centralist control, implementing policies in pursuit of an established strategy, was therefore familiar in the immediate post war years. It was generally acceptable in political terms that a real post war housing shortage (created by bottlenecks in the housing supply system in addition to the large numbers of homes destroyed during the war) should be tackled by a government-inspired housebuilding drive (Cullingworth, 1979; Darke and Darke, 1979; Merrett, 1979; Malpass, 1986). As a result, post war policy implementation was viewed and tackled in a similar way to war time industrial management, comprehensively managed from the centre. Donnison suggests that;

> It was the determined attempt to resolve these problems which led governments step by step into increasingly comprehensive housing commitments. (Donnison, 1967, p. 99)

The Housing Subsidies Act 1967 and the Wilson Government's drive to achieve 500,000 completions per annum (Malpass and Murie, 1994, p.70), represents the culmination of this phase of government housing policy. The late 1960s peak can be seen in Figure 4.2.

As can be seen in Figure 4.3, public sector direct provision was crucial to the high levels of construction in the late 1940s and early 1950s. This was achieved because funding was available and both the local authority and central government were pursuing similar objectives. From the late 1950s onwards, local authorities found themselves constructing fewer homes aimed at meeting general housing need, instead becoming more specialised builders, constructing homes for groups of the population seen to be in a certain category of housing need, i.e. those losing their homes through slum clearance programmes (Malpass and Murie, 1994). The residualisation of local authority housing (Morris and Winn, 1990; Forest et al., 1990; Malpass, 1990) may well have started in the 1950s when construction started to focus upon certain types of home.

From the 1950s onwards an implicit national housing strategy developed, whereby the private sector provided the core of homes. From this large scale 'base', public housing providers have been able to develop a

78  *The Formulation of Local Housing Strategies*

**Figure 4.3  Housing Completions in Terms of Developer**

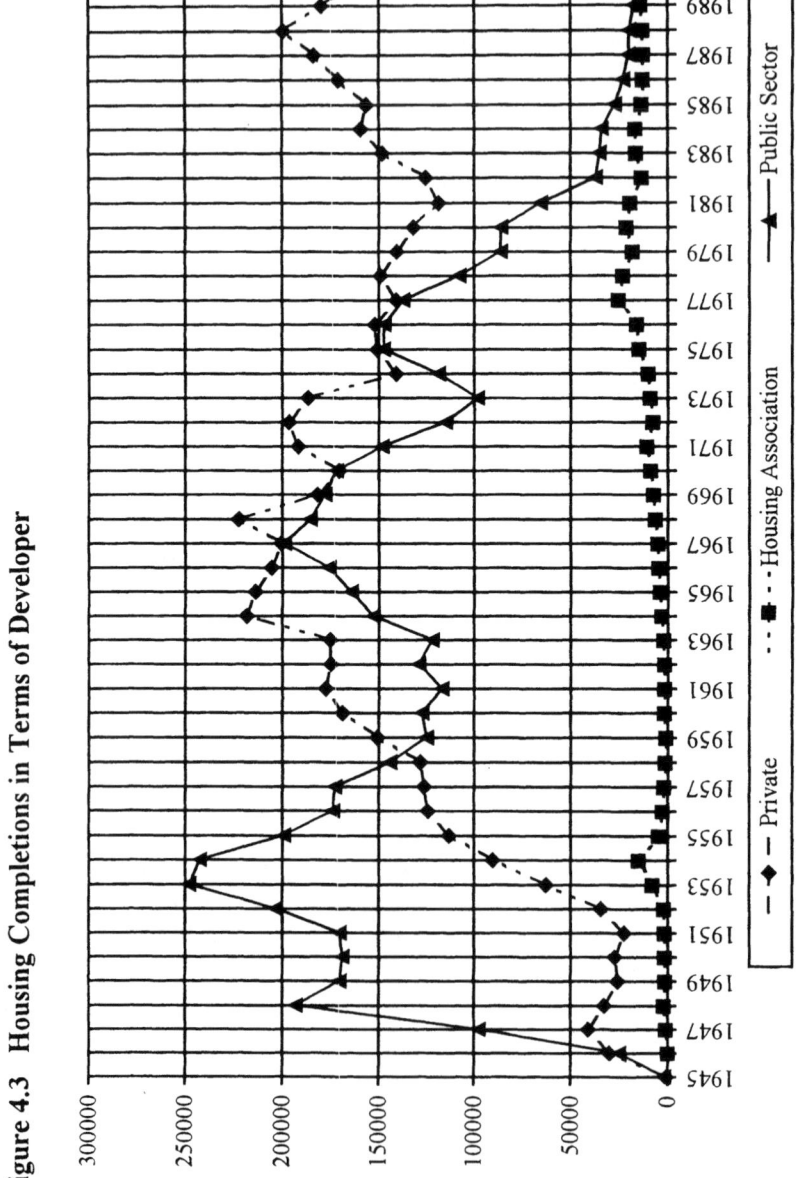

**Source:** Housing Statistics and Data Division of the DoE and DoE, 1993a

housing strategy, through direct construction for groups of the population where the housing needs and demands are not met by the private housebuilders. It was clear that the simplest method of achieving strategic aims was for the public sector to conduct its own implementation. As Aneurin Bevan, the Minister of Health in the first majority labour government said;

> If we are to plan we must have plannable instruments, and the speculative builder, by his very nature, is not a plannable instrument. (Foot, 1973, p.73)

In an attempt to achieve practical policy commitments, housing policy had, possibly by default, evolved into a housing strategy.

In the late 1960s and early 1970s, the situation regarding housing provision started to change. In 1968 a White Paper *Old Houses into New Homes* was published, emphasising the shift away from redevelopment towards rehabilitation. This was mainly due to economic constraints, but public dissatisfaction with the social affects of large scale redevelopment, slum clearance and systems building, also played a part (Cullingworth, 1979; Malpass and Murie, 1994). With housing improvement replacing redevelopment and clearance as the main focus for housing policy, a logical conclusion would be that housing strategies would become more complex, simply because of the number of different avenues through which housing policy could be pursued. In the past a housing strategy could simply be an objective of building 'x' number of homes. In the climate of rehabilitation and economic constraints, targeting and identification of priorities would become far more important, with the result that it would be necessary to take a broader view of an area's housing situation.

The late 1960s early 1970s could be seen as a turning point in both local/central government relations and the perception of housing strategies. Until that time there had been a broad consensus between local and central government, in so far as both had worked towards building homes. The tighter budget constraints introduced in the 1970s meant that local authority housing, traditionally a high capital cost, was a prime target for budget cuts. Until 1976, for instance, there had been no restriction on the number of council houses a local authority could build (Houlihan, 1983). At this point in the discussion it is worth examining the development of Housing Investment Programmes (HIPs), which in 1983 Houlihan suggested as being the then latest attempt at supervision and financial accountability, a procedure that had been developing since 1945 (Malpass and Murie, 1994).

*Housing Investment Programmes*

By the mid-1970s there was a growing feeling that, because the housing situation and needs of different communities differed widely throughout the country, it was no longer necessary to have a centrally-led housing strategy (Morris, 1980). However, there remained a need to ensure that local housing policy continued to relate to national policy. It was seen by some that local housing should have an equivalent to Transport Policy Programmes, which would require housing authorities to produce comprehensive housing strategies (Cullingworth, 1976). The Housing Policy Green Paper, 1977, both formally identified the need for *local* housing strategies and highlighted the issues and topics that they should concentrate on. In summary, each local housing department was called upon to make an assessment of the housing needs in its area. From this survey work, housing officers would prepare a three-part document: a *strategic statement* that would highlight needs and policies; a *numerical statement* examining housing conditions and tenures; and a *bid for allocation* requesting funds to achieve the objectives and priorities in the strategy (Murie and Leather, 1977). Paragraph 6.08 of the Housing Policy Green Paper suggested that:

> The local authorities own investment programme will often lie at the heart of the local housing strategy. But the local housing strategy must go much wider. In many areas public rented sector provision will provide only some of the answers. The right local mix of solutions will involve action by all concerned with rented and owner occupied housing. (DoE, 1977d)

As the Green Paper was introduced by a Labour Government, it can be seen that a growth in the involvement of the private sector was being encouraged before the Conservatives took office in 1979. It would appear that the Thatcher and Major administrations spent much of the 1980s and 1990s developing, for local housing authorities, an enabling role that can trace its ancestry back to the last Labour Government.

The concept behind this Green Paper became clear in DoE circular 63/77, *Housing Strategies and Investment Programmes: Arrangements for*

*1978/79.* This, and subsequent circulars, established the foundations of the HIP process that remains today. Cole and Goodchild suggest that this early stage in Local Housing strategy evolution:

> ...stimulated the growth of research and information services in housing and led, as it was intended to do, to a greater emphasis on inter-departmental and inter-organisational working and a more thorough and systematic approach to the task of planning, implementing and reviewing housing policies. (Cole and Goodchild, 1993, p. 3)

From an early stage problems started to arise. The annual guidelines prepared by the DoE tended to focus on technical issues concerning number of dwellings, rather than a more general housing strategy, encompassing preferences and access to homes. The Association of Metropolitan Authorities initially welcomed HIPs, but found in practice that they did not allow as great a degree of local autonomy as was first thought (Association of Metropolitan Authorities, 1987). By 1981, the initial concept of a HIP as a housing department's equivalent to a development plan was further eroded when the timescale of the document was cut from four to two years.

Perhaps the major criticism of HIPs, concerned the way they developed into what are essentially expenditure control instruments. The tendency for such an evolution was recognised at an early stage. Watson et al. (1979) argued that HIPs were mainly introduced as a means of deflecting concern regarding public expenditure. By 1975 local government expenditure constituted 18% of Gross National Product and the simplest means of controlling this area was found to be to focus on capital rather than revenue expenditure (Means, 1994). The then SoS saw HIPs as a tool for increasing;

> ...the freedom of authorities to do the job as they think best, *within parameters agreed by central government.* (Shore, P., 1976, quoted in Murie and Leather, 1977a (authors emphasis).)

Clearly, this shows that from conception, there existed within HIPs an expenditure control motive that became more pronounced as financial budgets became constrained. It was stressed in Circular 63/77, *Housing Strategies and Investment Programmes: Arrangements for 1978/79*, that the whole exercise would be evolutionary, adapting as local and central government became more familiar with the process. This evolution has occurred, but perhaps not in the direction initially envisaged. Instead of evolving into a strategy document created and used by the whole local authority, it has become a means of financial control for the housing department, and for the Government to control (through the DoE) capital expenditure.

In an attempt to achieve more control over public spending, cash limits were applied to government expenditure in 1976/77, the same year as HIPs were introduced. Crofton (1977) argued that HIPs were introduced because the Treasury was faced with fluctuating inflation, making it difficult to forecast public expenditure. As Murie and Leather (1977a; 1977b) suggested, the crucial issues revolve around the availability of resources and the criteria for allocation between local authorities. One could argue, that the dominant role of HIPs had become one of prioritising and distributing scarce resources and the view that HIPs are used simply a means of obtaining funding for local authority housing projects is still prevalent (Carter, Brown and Abbot, 1991b, p.15).

Cole and Goodchild (1993) have summarised housing strategy formulation into an evolutionary process that can be categorised by three distinct phases. These phases can be seen to have resulted in housing strategies developing from the document based upon direct provision by the local authority of social housing, to a strategy which is far more 'open-minded'. Briefly they see the three phases as follows;

Phase 1 Comprehensive Housing Strategy. This is the early period of housing strategy evolution, summarised as one which stimulated research into the subject, and although being primarily housing department led, stressed the need for inter-departmental and inter-organisational collaboration regarding strategy formulation.

Phase 2 The Alternative Housing Strategy. This phase can be seen as one that occurred as a result of Whitehall-local government conflicts in the 1980s. Expenditure controls and a general 'disablement' of local authorities (Malpass, 1992) created within certain, predominantly metropolitan, authorities a mood of policy innovation, one of which was to rejuvenate and publish housing strategies, which examined an area housing situation comprehensively. These strategies were seen by the authorities who prepared them, as a tool for strengthening local democracy and highlighting broad housing issues, rather than another technical document (which many HIPs and housing strategies had become). The main criticism of these types of strategies was that they were too ambitious and, in terms of the HIP timescale, had unrealistic goals.

Phase 3   Enabling Housing Strategy. The current incarnation of housing strategies, focusing upon the need to work with other agencies to achieve housing objectives. The degree to which this is possible depends upon four areas through which the local authority can 'influence' others to achieve its policy, namely finance, land, planning and local community (Bramley, 1994b).

To the four areas in which Bramley suggested a local authority can influence policy implementers (Bramley, 1994b) one would add a fifth factor for successful enablement, namely knowledge. If the local authority is to work with others it has to know the bodies and agencies it is dealing with (the links discussed in the final section). Perhaps more importantly, it has to be aware of the factors that drive its new policy implementers, namely conditions in the housing market.

Since 1987, there has been renewed Government interest in the approach which local authorities adopt towards housing strategies. Coopers and Lybrand's Reports for the DoE examined methods by which the local planning department could monitor the housing market, in an attempt to make land release more responsive (Coopers and Lybrand Associates, 1987) (see Chapter Five). Work done at Leicester University in the early 1990s highlighted the way in which expenditure based plans (e.g., HIPs) related to physical development plans (Carter and Brown, 1990; Carter, Brown and Abbot, 1991a and 1991b). Perhaps the most important document in terms of how government viewed housing strategies was that prepared in 1992 by the Audit Commission (Audit Commission, 1992). The report produced a number of recommendations, many of which are in the process of being implemented. For instance, in 1993 a letter to all the local housing authority Chief Executives, from the DoE, stated:

> Ministers' view is that the HIP process should develop progressively in a flexible manner, which allows scope for the differing circumstances of authorities and the developing housing policies of both local and central Government. To facilitate this, the Department [of the Environment]

intends to invite all housing authorities to draw up annual housing strategy statements in which each authority describes the needs and resources for housing in their area, and the plans and programmes which the authority has for addressing them. Housing strategies should be developed in consultation with the Housing Corporation, housing associations, the private housing sector (both rental and owner occupied), housebuilders, the voluntary sector, tenants groups and other interested parties. They should encompass all relevant functions and resources of the authority in a corporate approach. (DoE, 1993d, para. 4)

This letter broadly implemented, albeit at a consultation stage, the findings of the Audit Commission report. Simply publishing such a letter could be seen as an illustration that local authorities, in the face of past DoE and government indifference, had neglected the housing strategy role of the HIP. Yet will the DoE and more recently the DETR look more positively at a fully surveyed, analysed and costed strategy than they had been the case in the past? It would appear that the government and DoE/DETR continued throughout the 1990s to be preoccupied with annual submissions, a belief which will have a negative affect on the development of truly strategic documents, which would require a longer term view. Perhaps most crucial for these 'new' housing strategies success is the way local housing authorities are in a position to enable housing development, through close contacts with other agencies, and not just those concerned with social housing, a view others have of the 'new' housing strategy (Cole and Goodchild, 1993).

In September 1994, the DoE requested Capita Management Consultancy to review the HIP process, reporting back in April 1995 (DoE, 1995b). The main thrust of the project was to examine the efficiency and effectiveness of the HIP process and recommend ways that it could be improved. The main focus was upon ways that the DoE could improve its part of the process, i.e. the publication of guidance notes, the means by which the bids are evaluated, etc. To enable the study to be representative of all participants in the HIP process, an extensive survey was carried out, with officials at the DoE (both national offices and regional offices), the Housing Corporation and Local Authorities, being interviewed. The study presents some interesting findings regarding HIPs and a useful graphical representation of the HIP process (DoE, 1995b, Annex 4). For instance, one question examined the perceptions which Local Authorities had regarding the DoE HIP objectives. The vast majority of respondents (83%) saw the DoE using this as a means of allocating or rationing resources.

Perhaps the manner in which housing strategies have evolved, becoming short term documents concerned with the technical process of financial resource distribution, is a reflection of local authorities becoming aware of what the DoE wish to see included in a HIP submission. Although HIPs still serve a distribution purpose for expenditure, it is questionable the degree to which they are useful, given that funding distribution is increasingly at the discretion of the DoE/DETR, rather than any published and recognised 'index' (Cole and Goodchild, 1993, p.9). A cynical view may be one that suggests local authorities, having seen ambitious, long term policy documents dismissed by the DoE (in favour of HIP bids that contain minimal discussion of policy and are dominated by easily achievable, short term policies), have altered the thrust of their strategy statements. The findings of Capita Management illustrate this quite clearly. What appears to have happened is that, far from the local housing authority being highly aware of the housing needs and demands in their particular area (although they may be), they have become highly adept at monitoring government policy. This can be seen in paragraph 3.19:

> All [local housing authorities] suggested that they 'tweak' their strategy statements to give the greatest emphasis to whatever has been highlighted in the strategy guidance even if their fundamental strategy has not changed. (DoE, 1995b, p. 14)

This 'tweaking' may illustrate the increasing sophistication of local authorities in producing strategies that appeal to the government. Similar competitive funding arrangements, such as City Challenge and Single Regeneration Budgets, have been introduced into other areas of local government. Local authority staff have become aware of what is required to win funds in such 'competitions' and one would suggest that the housing officers are no exception.

Nearly half of the authorities questioned in the survey would have produced a strategy that focused less on the Government initiatives (as highlighted in the pre-submission guidance notes) if they were preparing a document for their own use. Table 4.1, summarises the use local authorities make of the strategy document. This table illustrates that housing strategy documents are used infrequently as a means of Forward Planning by local authorities. This is perhaps to be expected, given the short term nature of the documents. Perhaps more encouraging is that 53% of the local authority respondents use the data required for HIP submissions to develop policy and to monitor performance.

**Table 4.1 Use of Housing Strategy Documents**

| Use of Strategy | % of Respondents (Respondents able to give more than one response) |
|---|---|
| Corporate/Strategic Management | 53 |
| Public Information | 50 |
| Internal Information | 33 |
| Consultation | 33 |
| Forward Planning | 28 |
| Policy Making | 23 |

**Source:** DoE, 1995b, Table 4

Working from this report, the DoE produced its publication, *Preparation of Housing Strategies*, which appears to be attempting to restructure the focus of housing strategies (DoE, 1995c) in light of the early 1990s discussion. This document highlights the areas that a local authority should examine when preparing a housing strategy, ranging from an assessment of the housing stock to energy efficiency. It stresses the need to assess the housing market and lists various sources of information that local authorities could employ to monitor the housing situation (see Chapter Five). Perhaps the most useful part of the document is that it exists at all, rather than anyone particular theme. In publishing it, central government has shown that it is aware that, in a practical sense, housing strategies have never fully materialised.

In 1996 the issue of local housing plans has developed further. The Environment Select Committee (HoC, 1996) expressed concern regarding effective formulation of housing need assessments. The Committee suggested that the DoE issue guidance to assist, planners in particular, draw up more effective regional and local housing plans. The government's reply to this request was that such calculations have tended to be the role of the housing department (DoE, 1996). However the government went on to state that there may be merit in research to investigate local housing needs assessments, as they put it:

> ...to avoid unnecessary disputes between developers and local authorities when the calculations are fed into the plan-making process. (DoE, 1996, p. 16)

To effectively achieve such a goal, it will be necessary for the local authority to develop a corporate structure allowing the housing and planning departments to work in a more corporate manner, and perhaps more importantly links with the agencies responsible for housing provision, in particular, housebuilders.

The DETR published a report in 2000 that presented a good practice guide for the preparation of local housing needs assessments (Bramley, Pawson and Parker, 2000). Although still focusing firmly on the role of the housing department, this document does highlight the need to work corporately across the authority and the need to involve, what they call stakeholders. One issue with this is that private housebuilders are seen as one of the stakeholders (along with tenants organisations, ethnic minority groups, etc.). One could argue that this results in housing strategies which are not of the type that are the focus of this work. Clearly the work of Bramley, Pawson and Parker is focusing upon housing needs and, as a result, will, by the definitions in earlier chapters, focus on social housing. This is an assertion that appears to have little to contradict it based on the evidence presented in the report.

Within the local authority, one department already has significant experience in dealing with the housebuilding industry, namely the planning department. It is the creation, or strengthening, of links between the planners and the housing officers (something that the Bramley, Pawson and Parker report do call for, if only weakly) that forms the next section of this chapter.

## The Link Between Housing and Planning Departments

The preceding section has examined the relationship, in terms of housing strategies, between local housing and planning departments and Whitehall as represented by the DoE and more recently the DETR. In terms of Figure 4.1, this chapter has so far concentrated most directly upon zone 1. This

## 88 The Formulation of Local Housing Strategies

section will concentrate more directly on the theme of co-ordination *within* the local authority, the horizontal links illustrated in zone 2 of Figure 4.1. As was shown from the preceding discussion such corporate links are increasingly being called for. In terms of the research questions in Chapter One, this will go some way to identifying the degree to which local authorities operate in a fashion that allows policies to be integrated and co-ordinated.

Throughout the 1960s and 1970s, there had been a tendency amongst local government managers and academics working in the area of public management to try to develop corporate management techniques. In the 1960s three reports highlighted problems of traditional management (Buchanan, 1963; Plowden, 1967; Seebohm, 1968). All these reports, which focused on specific areas such as traffic and social services, generally called for better integration between departments to improve local government policy implementation. Stewart (1971) reflected upon the climate that developed from the studies, eventually developing into local government reform (Redcliffe Maud Commission), which highlighted the idea of general management. In 1969, McKinsey and Co. examined ways of developing the management structure of Liverpool City Council, to ensure responsive and effective service provision. Other councils, such as Birmingham City Council and Cheshire County Council, were establishing central intelligence units to monitor and assess the demands placed upon the whole authority both at present and in the future (Greenwood and Stewart, 1974). Stewart (1971), stresses the danger in viewing policy planning as a set of procedures, arguing that it should be viewed as an ongoing process responsive to the needs of a management situation, stressing the corporate approach required to successfully achieve these aims. During the 1980s and 1990s moves to privatise service provision within the local authority framework, developed and evolved into 'best value' reviews. Although not necessarily conflicting with integration, it could be argued that focussing upon these areas for certain departments, as opposed to the council as a whole may have resulted in a feeling of exclusion for certain departments or services. At the very least it would have altered the appraisal of management policy, with time being devoted to highlighting the cost effectiveness of roles, rather than improving the communications between roles.

If the 1960s focus had continued throughout the 1970s and 1980s one would have expected HIPs and housing strategies to be fully reflective of the whole local authority. In theory, the increased use of such comprehensive, rational policy planning systems should be seen as a means of overcoming disjointed incrementalism (defined by Faludi as a piecemeal approach to decision determination (Faludi, 1973, p.150)) and the first step towards introducing a housing strategy in the fullest sense of the word. Yet is this the case? Circular 38/78, *Housing Strategies and Investment Programmes for Local Authorities in England: Arrangements for 1979/80*, stressed the need for housing departments to consult planning colleagues in the formulation of HIPs (DoE, 1978a). If a circular, published one year after the introduction of HIPs, has to stress that such communication should take place, it suggests that HIPs initially failed to carry out such integration. Morris (1980) suggested that, in the North of England, local authorities had increased the corporatism and integration between departments, but he found that this occurred predominantly in response to housing need. If the situation in this one area accurately reflects other areas of England and Wales, then, even after a relatively short period of time, HIPs were seen as a means of identifying and prioritising needs, rather than a means of forming a broad housing strategy, which identified demand for all types of housing.

Planners involved with the collection of statistical data and forecasts relating to future levels of housing provision are often those employed in the strategic planning process, based at County Council level (Unitary authorities are discussed below). These professionals tend to be the most knowledgeable in respect to forecasting techniques and household formation methods. Yet because they are employed by the County, they are not directly involved in the preparation of HIPs, a process that occurs at the District level. However they may well be involved indirectly, either through the publications they produce (ranging from structure plans to employment and household bulletins) or even directly through discussions with the officers in the districts. County/district relationships can differ, with some areas enjoying strong, efficient, informal links whilst other areas may well have rather more hierarchical structures, only consulting one another when required. Some counties may well have poorly developed information sections, with the result that strategic guidance and data are not available for the districts (beyond that contained in the structure plan). If this is the case, officers in the district may have to expand their role to assure that data and information, upon which a strategy can be based, is available. This county involvement adds a further element into the planner/housing officer relationship, and if Figure 4.3 was to be used as an illustration, one would suggest that this occurs within zone 2.

Metropolitan and unitary authorities have an advantage over the more traditional shire districts because, in Part 1 of unitary development plans, they have a strategic instrument. In these authorities, housing officers, planners concerned with local planning matters, and planners responsible for strategic policy are all employed by the same authority. This, in theory, should ensure co-ordination and involvement of all the local authority professionals, as the purely practical problem of being employed by different tiers of the local government has been circumvented, existing as it does within the one authority.

Why did the HIP process and the preparation of housing strategies fall to housing officers? Primarily this may have been the result of the way the HIP submission included a financial statement detailing the local authority's construction and rehabilitation agenda. This is clearly within the remit of the housing department, yet circular 38/78 stated:

> Local housing authorities should ensure that their policies and assumptions are consistent with regional strategies, structure and local plans and, where appropriate, inner area programmes; and should consult their planning colleagues at both the district and county level to achieve that result. (DoE, 1978a, para. 28)

This illustrates that corporate working was envisaged in the development of housing strategies.

Watson et al. (1979) believed that planners were not trained in the fields required to successfully implement HIPs (i.e., financial aspects of developments) and this, as much as the way in which they evolved, perhaps explains why housing officers became the central professionals in HIP implementation. Merret highlights that the Labour Government of the 1970s, faced with a fall in private housing production early in their term of office, then the need to cut housing expenditure by £150 million pounds in 1977/78, increased the role of public provision only to introduce increasing controls later in the term (Merret, 1979). Clearly the planning department may have found itself involved minimally in HIP and strategy preparation because, even from the outset, the view of the DoE was that the HIP submission would have more in common with a financial bid than a housing 'development' plan.

With hindsight, it would appear that an opportunity has been wasted and HIPs may not have realised their full potential in the late

1970s, due both to a lack of enthusiasm on the part of planners to become more central to the system, and to central government in seeing HIPs as being primarily a tool for expenditure control. Once local authority officers (in all departments) became familiar with HIPs as a housing department programme, the process has become departmentalised, and increasingly difficult to re-introduce as one that concerns planning *and* housing.

It has been suggested that to succeed in preparing integrated expenditure and development plans, similar to housing strategies, there is a need to combine the policies physically in one housing strategy document, treating land and capital in the same 'plan' (Carter, Brown and Abbot, 1991a and 1991b). If such a course of action were to occur, it would force co-ordination and inter department working. However, it may be problematic in the short term to prepare such a document in isolation, for instance a housing strategy, rather than the current development plan-HIP system that exists. What may be practical would be to prepare the development plan (as the document with the longest timescale of the two) and build the housing strategy around these policies. If there were to be a combination of HIP proposals and planning policies in one document, it might prove popular with the bodies who are increasingly relied upon to implement housing strategies;

> ...a consensus is emerging between 'planners' and 'developers' on the importance of policy planning but also of the need for *one* set of policies for housing, i.e. one plan document. (Carter, Brown and Abbot, 1991a, p. 3)

Generally, if the corporate ethos had been introduced earlier, then, by the time HIPs were introduced, a stronger cross-department consciousness may have developed. If departments had successfully embraced corporatism, as discussed earlier in this section, there may have been more success in allowing HIPs to fully embrace the wider objectives of all the council departments concerned with housing. Perhaps a problem of timing was therefore as much to blame, with the eventual erosion of HIPs into housing budget statements, as a result of an increase in financial constraints. It was apparent therefore that HIPs had arrived at a situation where they were being implemented primarily by one lead department, and rather quickly the ambitious objectives of developing an integrated housing strategy were sacrificed.

Moves towards corporatism have been less positive during the 1980s, because local government, finding itself 'attacked' by Whitehall, has had other priorities (Hambleton, 1988; Malpass, 1992). It should be pointed out that some authorities employed innovative management structures as a means of circumventing government control, and this has included interdepartmental working, albeit at a decentralised level (Lowndes and Stoker, 1992; Cole and Goodchild, 1993). However, as highlighted in the preceding section, since the end of the 1980s there has been a renewed interest in HIPs, and corporate approaches to policy formulation. The Audit Commission's 1992 study calls for an increase in corporatism, to ensure that the planning department and housing department are not pursuing conflicting policies. Carter, Brown and Abbot (1991a and 1991b) have suggested that there has been a renewal of interest in policy planning systems and the corporate ethos linking the producers of expenditure based plans (HIPs) and development plans. This, they presume, may be partly due to the Planning and Compensation Act 1991, which has increased the importance of policy documents. Another reason may be the view that local authorities are essentially enablers, facilitating development and, as Bramley states:

...enabling puts a premium on corporate working. (Bramley, 1994b, p. 146)

This move towards enablement can be seen in a wide range of both central government guidance (DoE, 1987a) and academic research (Goodlad, 1994; Jackson, Morrison and Royce, 1994).

Capita Management, in their report to the DoE (DoE, 1995b), suggested that the complimentary nature of housing strategies leads to the development of corporate liaison groups. Along with the housing department a number of other departments are frequently involved in housing strategy preparation (environmental health; finance; social services; planning; architects; legal). A study of Welsh local authorities (Littler et al., 1994) found that most authorities exhibited informal inter-departmental working structures. This was most noticeable in the smaller authorities, where officers were more likely to know each other personally, enabling the officers to know 'who to contact'.

The questionnaire survey carried out as part of this research (see Chapter Six below), highlighted the degree to which integrated housing strategy statements were prepared. Figure 4.4, illustrates that the vast

*Local Authority Housing Strategies and Joint Housing Studies* 93

majority of local authority departments (in the sample areas) do work together to prepare housing strategies.

The same questionnaire asked the authorities which department played the dominant role in the strategies' preparation. In the case of the metropolitan authorities from the 20 authorities who answered this question, 19 had a housing strategy prepared under the guidance of the housing department, whilst the remaining authority's housing strategy was prepared jointly by planning and housing. This is similar in the case of East Midland authorities, where 8 of the 15 respondents who answered this question had a housing department dominated housing strategy, two were planning department led whilst the remaining five had both departments playing an equal role. It is hardly surprising that the housing department takes the lead role as it is to the chief officer of this department that the request for a housing strategy is usually addressed. What is surprising is that the planning departments take the lead role in *any* of the strategies that are prepared.

**Figure 4.4 Are Combined Housing Strategy Statements Prepared?**

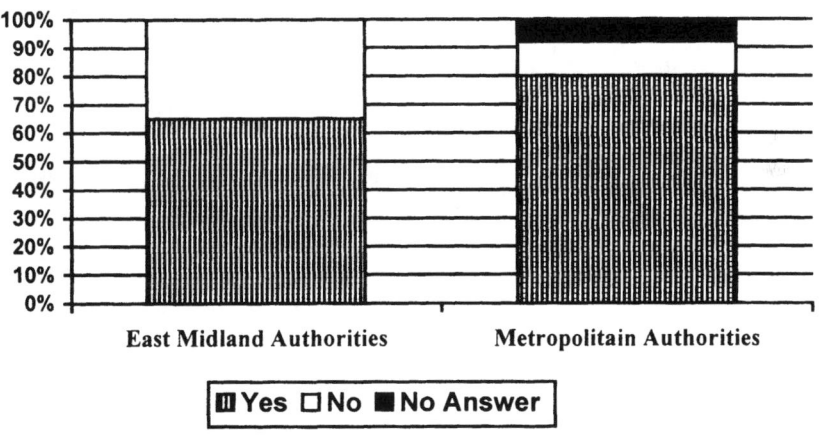

The two case study areas present an interesting comparison in this respect. As highlighted in Chapter One the case study councils of Mansfield and North West Leicestershire were chosen based upon economic factors. In terms of housing strategies both authorities prepared such a document, but in the case of Mansfield it was prepared by the Planning Department whilst in North West Leicestershire it was the responsibility of the Housing

Department. This, although not a selection criteria, is a fortunate difference in the two authorities as it allowed the research to contrast the styles of housing strategy formulation in an authority where such a document was prepared by a planning department with one prepared by a housing department.

The results of the empirical survey work give an illustration of the situation as it stood in 1994, however it gives no indication of the actual *degree* of interdepartmental working. For instance, the planning department may simply be asked for comments after the strategy has been prepared, and there may be little policy conception that involves both the housing and planning departments. Since 1994 there doesn't appear to have been much progress in determining the degree of interdepartmental working, with the closest being a study published in 1998 (Goss and Blackaby, 1998) which had a 40% response rate and found that the 'strongest' links were between the housing department and the social work department responsible for community care. There is obviously scope for further work in this area, in an attempt to determine the degree to which corporate management is utilised in the development of local authority housing policy, in the broadest sense. As Bramley states:

> Interdepartmental teamwork is not a new requirement in housing programmes; what is new is the emphasis on partnership with outside agencies, financial/commercial awareness, flexibility and entrepreunership. (Bramley, 1994b, p. 146)

Corporatism should not simply be seen as an internal management structure that the local authority alone should pursue. There is a necessity for corporate thinking to extend beyond town halls to include the other bodies and agencies who are involved in the housing market. The next section of this chapter will examine this area, with particular reference to the housebuilding industry.

## The Housebuilding Industry and Local Authorities

To prepare a strategy that reflects the housing market, information will have to become disseminated amongst the participants in zone 3. Not only will this allow all the participants to be aware of what is occurring in each other's 'specialist area', it will also engender a degree of trust. It could be suggested that these links may already occur in respect of housing associations and local authorities, due to the increased role of the former in providing social housing and, in the case of rural authorities, the use of exceptions policies (DoE, 1991e). Research discussed in *Evaluating the Low Cost Rural Housing Initiative* illustrates that, in an attempt to achieve low cost homes, relationships have developed between housing developers and local authorities (DoE, 1991e). This degree of inter-agency co-operation is encouraging, yet these instances tend to be focused on particular developments, not on perceptions and views of the local housing market. Chapters Five and Six illustrate the type of market information that may prove useful to develop the knowledge that the local authority has regarding their particular housing market and the degree to which the local authority officers communicate with other agencies.

As the local authority is now primarily seen as an agency of enablement, it is left to third parties to implement housing policy. To effectively carry out these policies, bodies such as housebuilders will therefore have to be consulted in the process of housing strategy formulation. DoE circular 63/77 *Housing Strategies and Investment Programmes: Arrangements for 1978/79* explicitly established the trend, by which housing provision was no longer to be a major local authority role. Instead, the HIP authority should concentrate on;

> ...relating their own proposals more explicitly to the housing contribution likely to be made by the private sector and other agencies. (DoE, 1977b, para. 5, part d)

Throughout the 1980s and 1990s the movement towards local authorities distancing themselves from direct housing provision has accelerated, leaving a system that relies on public policy to be privately implemented (Malpass, 1992). This section will examine the contacts that exist between the local authority and the housebuilding industry (mainly private housebuilding companies but also housing associations).

A questionnaire, examining the ways in which HIPs and housing strategy statements have attempted to reflect private housebuilding trends and perceptions indicated that 28% of those authorities who responded had attempted to gauge housebuilder opinion (Morris, 1980). Given that this survey was carried out whilst authorities were preparing proposals for only

96  *The Formulation of Local Housing Strategies*

the second round of HIPs, it is perhaps disappointing that such a low level of private involvement was apparent. This contrasts strongly with the view expressed in circulars (DoE, 1977b) that the HIP should be related to the private sector. Morris found that only 7 of the 23 housing policy statements examined actually discussed the role of the private house builder. However, such a poor reflection of housebuilder interest may be due to the housebuilding industry itself.

> It also seems often to be the case that the other agencies are not interested in housing strategies. A number of authorities who had consulted such organisations either discovered that they were not interested or that they provided little, if any, worthwhile information. (Morris, 1980, p. 52)

It should be borne in mind that Morris' survey took place in the late 1970s, when local authorities were still constructing between 75,000 and 100,000 dwellings per annum. It could be suggested that there was not the same necessity to develop links with the housebuilding industry, because the construction programme of the local authority itself could implement their housing strategy. A more recent survey reiterated that private housebuilders were only interested in HIPs if they were involved in contracting (Carter, Brown and Abbot, 1991a and 1991b), illustrating the view housebuilders have of HIPs and the strategy statement as essentially a social housing document. They suggest that developers see expenditure based plans as being largely irrelevant, since expenditure based plans in their present form do not contain any information that is of use to most developers. It may be the case that the housing department is, in its present form, not best placed to interact with developers, a role that could be filled by the planning department.

Throughout the 1970s, 1980s and 1990s there has been an increase in the links between developers and the local authority, primarily as represented by the planning department. Take, for example, the question of land availability. Debates and discussions between developers and planners can be seen to have been encouraged in circulars such as 10/70, (DoE, 1970) which stressed the benefits of regular consultations with representatives of the housebuilding industry and the need to ensure that land was available for at least five years future development (Cuddy and Holingsworth, 1985; Rydin, 1988). This discussion of land availability continued throughout the 1970s (see for example, DoE, 1972; 1973; 1975;

1978b) yet Rydin (1986) suggested that for much of the decade, the debate was distorted by the Community Land Act.

By the time the new Conservative administration adopted the Local Government, Planning and Land Act in 1980 (legislation which allowed the DoE to effectively *compel* local authorities to make an assessment of land availability), there had already been a significant move towards joint working with private housebuilders. For instance circular 44/78 *Private Sector Land: Requirements and Supply*, stated:

> Local authorities are asked to see that regular meetings are held as often as builders need them. (DoE, 1978b, para. 3)

These meetings were to be undertaken to allow the local authority to better understand demand patterns and the local land supply situation. The methodology for undertaking such an assessment was based upon a study of housebuilding land in Greater Manchester, undertaken in 1979. This Manchester study represented the first joint approach, involving both housebuilders and local authorities (Hooper, 1985). Yet the study has been criticised (Hooper, 1980; 1985; Hooper, Pinch and Rogers, 1988) mainly for the methodology employed to determine land availability. Yet it is not the way the study examines the number of housing units that is of specific concern for this thesis, rather the fact that it formalised the links between the planning authority and housebuilders (DoE, 1979), so that in the years that followed this pilot study, a number of updates were published (Findley and Bourke, 1988), each based on local authority-housebuilder dialogue. As the original study concluded:

> The indications are that the detailed discussions begun by this study between local authorities and builders will continue. Both parties agree that they have learnt a great deal from each other and this alone has made the study worthwhile. (DoE, 1979, para. 60)

Rydin (1988) saw joint housing studies as primarily being technical exercises with little political (councillor) involvement. She demonstrated that underlying conflicts between the participants in the process meant that the planners and the housebuilders did not trust one another. If this level of suspicion remains, and it pervades the whole council, not just the planning department, the implications for the development of housing strategies may well be serious. Conflicts between the local authority and the housebuilders can largely be seen to be a reaction to debates regarding future household numbers, i.e. how much land is actually available. Discussions concerning wider issues, not purely the details of land availability and housing allocations, may have greater success. Joint land studies had variable levels of success (Doak et al., 1987) and Rydin (1988) suggests that a lack of resources was a basic concern as was the availability of data (an issue that will be examined in the following chapters).

These 1980s 'housing studies' could be seen as fulfilling an ulterior motive. It has been argued (Rydin, 1986) that land availability studies were not so much a means of achieving better development, more a technique for shifting power towards developers and away from local authorities. She suggested that as part of a wider view to rationalise power, liberalising planning was the only way of achieving policy promises of more homes and increased home ownership. In this respect, a housing policy was achieved at the expense of a broad, accountable socially acceptable strategy, in favour of individual housebuilders' and developers' internal strategies. This supports the argument that, far from the Conservative government of the 1980s having a *housing* policy, they effectively pursued a *tenure* policy (Donnison and Maclennan, 1985). However, even if the motives behind the introduction of land availability studies in the 1980s were as politically motivated as Rydin suggests, such studies have been useful in that they so far as they bring housebuilders and local authorities together. This point cannot be stressed too strongly, as it is the discussion within land availability studies that will provide a useful foundation from which the working and co-operation between different bodies, required by housing strategies, can be developed.

Between 1980-1985 34 joint land studies had been undertaken. In the latter part of the decade (1986-1991) a further 26 were completed (Bramley et al., 1995). It has been suggested that housing forums and liaison groups may involve housebuilders to a lesser degree in areas where there is controversy regarding housing land (Bramley et al., 1995), and in such circumstances housebuilders may find greater benefits from involvement in EIPs, local plan inquiries, submitting planning applications and testing sites on appeal. Clearly this is a factor which may prove problematic in attempts to develop forums and discussion groups which involve the enablers of the housing market (the local authority) and the implementers of housing policy (the housebuilders).

## Figure 4.5 Current Existence of Housing Liaison Groups

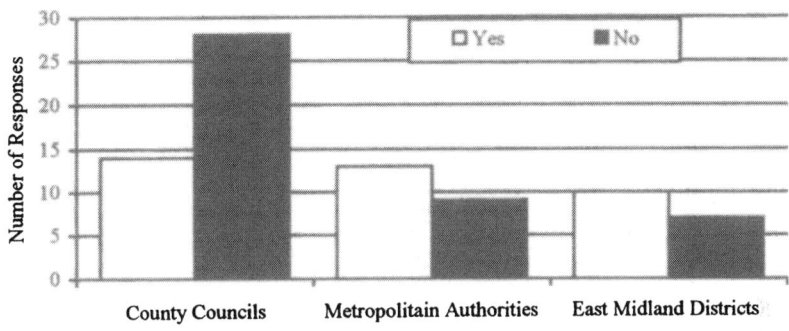

## Figure 4.6 Membership of Housing Liaison Groups

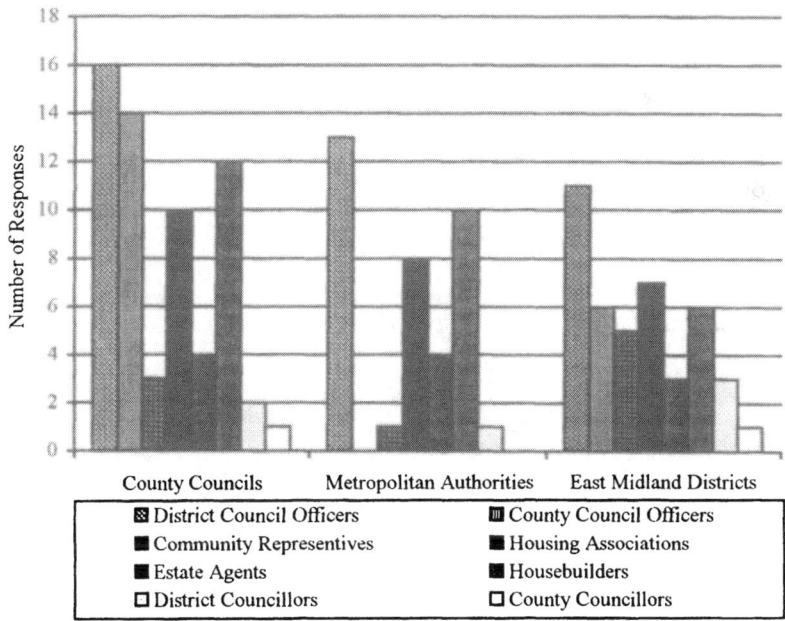

## 100  *The Formulation of Local Housing Strategies*

The questionnaire survey, discussed earlier and forming the foundation for Chapter Six, sought to ascertain the links between local government (at county, district, and metropolitan authority level) and other agencies, as indicated by the existence of some form of multi-body 'housing group'. Figure 4.5, highlights the results of the survey and indicate that the county councils have fewer groups of this type than the metropolitan authorities or East Midlands districts.

When the survey question was widened to include authorities where housing liaison groups had existed in the past, but currently no longer meet, a further 7 county councils and one East Midland district were found to have experience of this type of discussion group. Combining all the authorities which had, at one time or another, been involved in this type of group, it can be seen (Figure 4.6) that a wide variety of agencies have been involved. Housebuilders are seen to be involved extensively in these groups at all levels of local government, as are housing associations. If the enabling authority is to succeed then the involvement of such bodies will have to be developed.

Discussion in the mid-1990s highlighted that there is an expectation for local authorities to involve local housing associations and the Housing Corporation in the preparation of a strategy (DoE, 1995c, p33). This research tended to focus upon the way the local authority could provide land, for low cost housing development, focusing upon the manner in which one local authority worked with housebuilders to achieve this goal. Although this is important, it is only part of what a complete housing strategy should focus upon. This would suggest that there still exists (for the reasons outlined above) a view that the housing strategy is a housing department document. This is significant, as other work has shown that;

> ...there were few signs of any significant change in the involvement of the private sector, in spite of the fact that almost 40% of local authorities thought that the private sector would find HIPs useful: presumably the authorities did not think that they would find the private sector useful. (Carter, Brown and Abbot, 1991b, p. 15)

It is necessary to overcome this, and to fully integrate housebuilders in the development of housing strategies. This would be most likely to succeed if housing strategies were to be presented as a document which involves both the housing and planning departments.

## Local Authority Housing Strategies and Joint Housing Studies 101

Housing strategies would only benefit from greater involvement of the planning department, as the planners would bring to this 'marriage' the connections they have with the local housebuilding industry, built up through informal relations or more formalised land availability studies. This suggests that it is an internal, corporate approach that is required.

**Conclusion**

This chapter has focused upon housing strategies, highlighting their development and formalisation as part of the HIP process, illustrating that in the 1990s housing strategy statements became seen as a strategic document in their own right, separate from the HIP process. The links between departments within the local authority, and the history and current level of corporate working were discussed, and it was suggested that this is the foundation upon which a successful strategy will have to be based. The final part of this chapter investigated the links between the local authority and housing policy 'implementers', illustrating that the planning department is possibly the most useful at approaching bodies such as housebuilders.

The manner in which housing strategies have been examined in this chapter, not in chronological terms, but in terms of networks or connections, focusing upon how the agencies involved in preparing housing strategies (the local housing officers) work with others to design and implement policy, was felt to be most supportive for this research. Planning departments have a history of public consultation both through the policy formulation process and the consideration of planning applications. They have been seen to be the 'best suited' department to publicise and consult on housing strategy formulation (Jackson, Morrison and Royce, 1994). In addition it can be seen from the previous discussion that the planning department has had the strongest relationship with the housebuilding industry. Yet HIPs and housing strategy formulation have tended to be the consideration of the housing department. If the links between the housebuilding industry and the local authority are to be developed the planning department will be required to play an important role that will further increase the need to integrate the planning and housing departments in so far as they work upon housing strategies within a local authority structure. It has illustrated that there is a need for the planning department to be more closely involved in the preparation of strategies, which would allow planners to employ their experience of consultation exercises, in general, and links with the housebuilders, in particular.

To draw this chapter to a close it is useful to return to two of the research questions, namely the degree of policy integration between departments and the involvement of policy implementers. This chapter has shown through review of the literature that these areas have been priorities for a number of years. However the primary survey work also presented in this chapter has indicated that despite such long established calls for integration and co-ordination there is still work to be done to ensure local authorities both work corporately and co-ordinate externally. Where integrated housing strategies are produced the empirical surveys have demonstrated that they are largely led by the housing department.

# 5 Indicators of Housing Demand

**Introduction**

The discussion in Chapter Four highlighted that establishing relationships between local authorities and housebuilding companies should be seen as a prime objective of enabling authority's housing strategies, yet this is only part of the process. To ensure that the local authority has an adequate understanding of the housing market, it will have to make use of available information sources, monitoring data and using this data to make evaluations of the housing market. This chapter will discuss the work that has attempted to examine data sets that may be employed by local authorities, which will lead into Chapter Six, an examination of the data that local authorities actually monitored in the mid-1990s.

This chapter will therefore expand upon, and reassess, earlier work that has examined data sets, such as house prices and housing starts. Although primarily a review and analysis chapter, information gained from empirical research will also be contained in the discussion, essentially to illustrate points. Each individual data set will be analysed in terms of three 'themes'. Firstly each set will be examined in terms of availability. That is to say 'Is the data readily available to a local authority and can it be disaggregated to a level which may reflect specific housing markets?' Secondly, each possible set of data is then assessed with regard to the degree to which it may indicate demand. The final assessment concerns the degree to which data, if it were used to monitor housing markets, may be open to manipulation.

To try and ensure the assessment of each data set can be compared, each is scored in terms 'a' to 'e' with respect to these three assessment criteria. In terms of data availability the grading 'a' is seen to represent very available data, whilst the grading 'e' is seen to indicate data that is difficult to obtain. With regard to data reliability, grade 'a' demonstrates an ability to estimate demand, whilst grade 'e' indicates a poor likelihood of representing demand. In terms of the final categorisation, namely manipulation, grade 'a' indicates a believe that the data is difficult to manipulate, whilst grade 'e' suggests the opposite. The results of this assessment are presented in a summary table (Table 5.7) in the conclusion. It should be borne in mind that these assessments are based upon personal judgements on the face of the evidence presented in the discussion. Where this technique may be weakest is as a means of assessing the reliability of data sets as demand indicators. This may be better achieved through more statistically-based analysis, an area where future research could be conducted.

**Context**

Of all the work carried out, the most extensive, although not necessarily the most robust, series of studies were those commissioned by the Department of Environment, in the mid-to-late 1980s. The DoE commissioned Coopers and Lybrand to examine the housing market and the different techniques employed by local authorities in monitoring it. As they stated in 1985, the aim of the report was to;

> ...assess and report on the varying assessments and assumptions about new housing made by the planning authorities and housebuilders and to assess the extent to which both the provision in plans and land which is made available for housing takes account of the requirements of the market for new private sector housing. (Coopers and Lybrand Associates, 1985, p.1)

This report should be placed in the context of the period in which it was commissioned, a time when development pressures were extensive (see Figures 5.1 and 5.2) and in Whitehall there existed a view that the planning process was responsible for delays and hindrances in development (Thornley, 1991).

Clearly since Coopers and Lybrand carried out this study, the housing market has changed considerably (see Chapter One). As a result this chapter will update the work of Coopers and Lybrand through an

*Indicators of Housing Demand* 105

**Figure 5.1 Total Private Sector Housing Completions: Great Britain (1980-1998)**

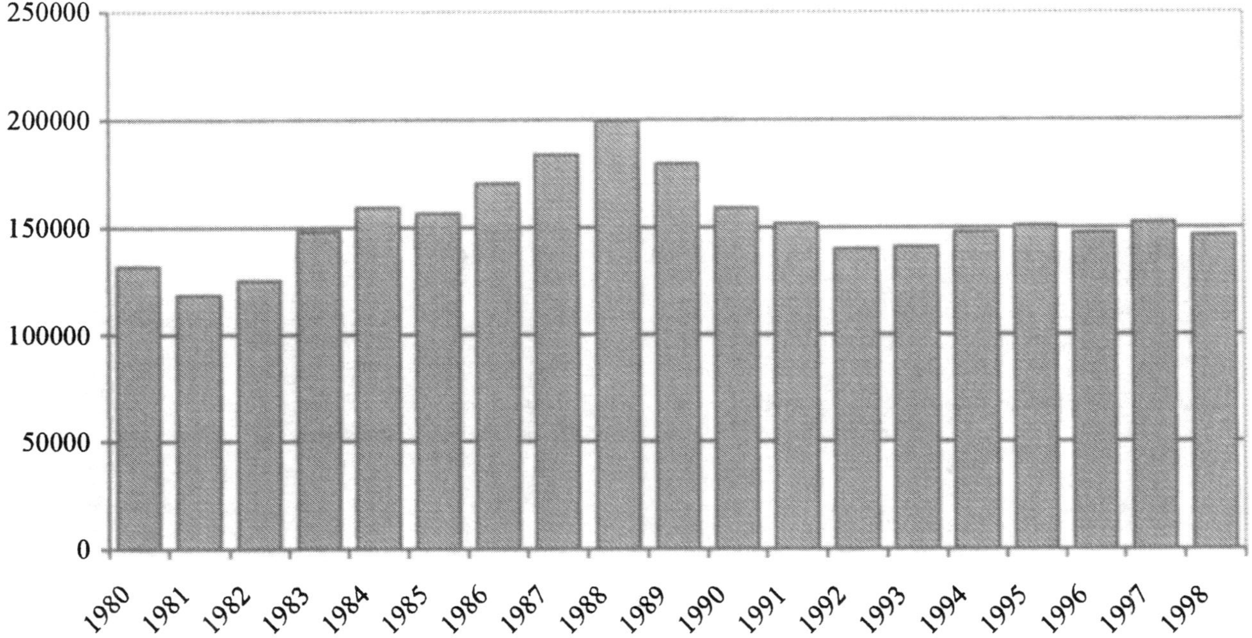

**Source:** Housing Statistics and Data Division of the DoE and DoE 1993a: Wilcox, 2000, Table 19h

106  *The Formulation of Local Housing Strategies*

examination of the situation in the 1990s, a decade that has so far seen the development of a stronger planning system, a weaker housing market, and greater access to information (i.e. access to the Land Registry information).

In addition to these changes in the housing market, the recent advice on housing strategies and calls for greater information on which to base housing provision forecasts (see previous chapters) suggests that there is a need to re-examine the area of data reliability. This chapter will discuss these areas and, where applicable, illustrate the discussion with data from the case study areas (the districts or, where data availability allows, the two more specific housing markets ie. Ashby and Mansfield).

Figure 5.1, gives some indication of this development pressure, by highlighting the growth in private residential development completions throughout the decade. It can be seen from Figure 5.2 that applications for planning permission also increased in the late 1980s, which could be seen as being illustrative of an increase in development pressure. Yet is this data reliable as an indicator of development pressure? Are other data sets such as planning appeals, estate agent sales rates or viewing figures for new homes more reliable? More importantly, is the data available at a level localised enough to be useful for local housing strategy formulation? These are the questions that this chapter will seek to answer.

One of the most important findings of the Coopers and Lybrand reports is the proposition that debate should be about how the development process can be adapted and enhanced to become more responsive to demand signals. This is an important development. Debates between planners and developers have centred around the allocation process, the quantitative argument regarding the number of units that will be required for the plan period and where these units will be situated (Hooper et al., 1985; Rydin, 1985; Short, Fleming and Witt, 1986; Bramley et al., 1995). As was shown in the last section of Chapter Four, even the forum for debate between housing developers and the local authority has tended to focus upon the number of housing units required rather than a general discussion of housing trends, changing conditions in the market, etc.

Within a plan-led process, as currently exists through Section 54(a) of the Planning and Compensation Act 1991, it is vital to overcome these traditional areas of confrontation and enter into a consensus regarding housing projections, switching the arena for debate to location, tenure and type/style of dwelling. However, as Chapter Three highlighted, there is still significant uncertainty regarding household projections, and it is perhaps beneficial, if housing strategy formulation concentrates on 'proportions'

Indicators of Housing Demand 107

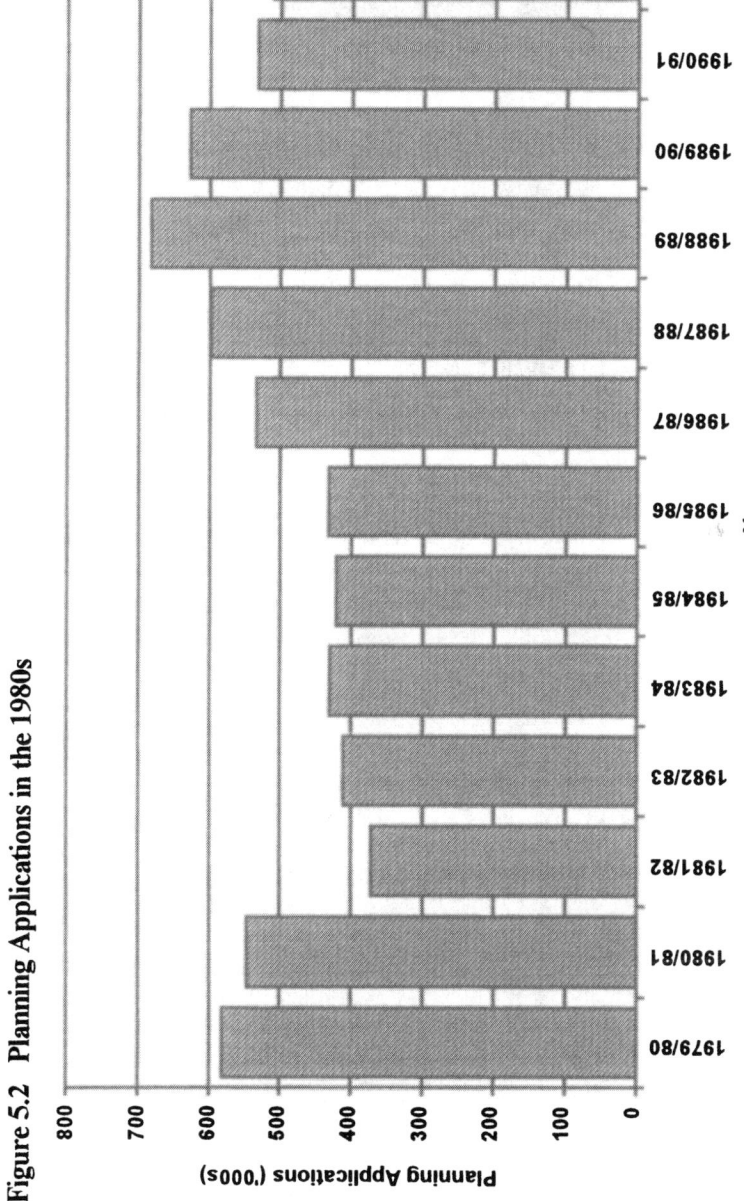

Figure 5.2 Planning Applications in the 1980s

**Source:** Table 1.1, *Development Control Statistics: England 1991/92*, DoE, 1993
**NB** From 1986/87 onwards the types of development suitable for inclusion in this table increased.

rather than projections. What this 'proportional debate' might focus upon is the degree to which the different housing tenures and housing providers would meet overall housing need, highlighting areas where the housing market is not meeting these requirements. To effectively achieve such an objective, there is a need for reliable data. For instance, recent work (Bramley et al., 1995) has highlighted that, increasingly, an ability to understand house price changes and differentials is necessary if housing needs are to be effectively met.

The indicators that Coopers and Lybrand suggested as useful for the monitoring of the housing market were quite wide-ranging, yet they basically fell within three categories: policy and economic predictors; housing market statistics; professional judgements. The following discussion will initially examine policy and economic predictors before examining the combined subject of housing market statistics and professional judgements.

**Policy and Economic Predictors**

These are essentially an analysis of what effect policy initiatives, both at local and national level, will have on an area's housing markets. One would expect, housing markets to be strongly related to economic growth predictions and economic evaluation of an area, and it is therefore to be expected that econometric forecasters may be able to provide this type of analysis. Cambridge Econometrics, whilst preparing long-term regional projections, have presented changes in GDP; consumers expenditure; employment and population, as being reliable long-term macro-economic indicators (Cambridge Econometrics, 1995; 1996). Although this report focused upon the regions, other macro-economic forecasting agencies have examined similar indicators whilst preparing growth prospects for districts (Henley Centre, 1994). Although useful, these forecasts do have limitations, especially cost. As an expense, this may not be one which local authorities feel they can justify. In addition, the forecasts may not be any more robust than those generated by local authority officers themselves, based on their own perceptions of the economic prospects for the area. One would envisage that this 'in-house' forecasting can be supplemented through the monitoring of a number of data sets, an area that the rest of this chapter will focus upon.

The Coopers and Lybrand report is decidedly lacking in discussion of localised economic indicators that may reflect housing market demand. This is perhaps one of its greatest omissions, given that effective demand is strongly underpinned by macro-economic forces. Some estimate of the income,

*Indicators of Housing Demand* 109

or possible economic well-being of households will allow a housing strategy to estimate the need for social housing vis-à-vis housing for owner occupation. The two practical indicators identified by Coopers and Lybrand were;
1. Employment change
2. Infrastructure and Economic Development Projects

To a degree, infrastructure and economic development are not pure indicators of market demand, more accurately they could be seen as a reflection of the way future political will shapes a housing market. However, it must be appreciated that both public projects and private sector investment decisions will have an effect on housing markets.

Coopers and Lybrand suggested that this type of data should be viewed as '...background' (Coopers and Lybrand, 1987, para 1.6). The use of these indicators as purely background does not appear to be in harmony with the aims of the reports, (see page 1 of the 1985 publication), as it has been argued that builders view the current and future employment base of some areas as '...a key indicator' (Coopers and Lybrand, 1987, Para 2.43). It would be anticipated that the local authority might consider that there is a strong relationship between policy and development, or else why would policies be pursued? To create growth in an area, the local authority may develop a portfolio of policies ranging from those concerned with housing to others focusing upon employment, one complementing the other.

**Table 5.1 Unemployment in the Case Study Areas, March 1996 (%)**

|  | Leicestershire | Burton on Trent TTWA | Nottinghamshire | Mansfield TTWA |
|---|---|---|---|---|
| Unemployment | 6.0 | 7.2 | 9.3 | 13.0 |

**Source:** Leicestershire and Nottinghamshire County Councils Unemployment Bulletins

Statistical data concerning employment levels can be a useful indicator of economic change, with the employment rate and its movements giving some indication of general job security. This data is presented in a number of official documents, but it is published more regularly in the CSO publication 'Labour Market Trends' (formerly, pre-1996, 'Employment Gazette'). This publication highlights employment statistics (one of the major factors affecting housebuilders perceptions of an area) in terms of parliamentary constituencies. In urban areas, this will mean that the designated area could well be at a level below that of the district, and therefore more likely to reflect housing market areas. Alternatively, if the area is rural in character, it could encompass a large number of housing market areas. In addition, the statistics produced in the journal are current, being usually only two months out of date.

At the local level employment data is relatively straightforward to obtain. In terms of the case study areas both County Councils compile regular employment bulletins, which provide detailed information on the unemployment rates for males and females in the counties travel to work areas. Table 5.1 indicates the unemployment rates in Nottinghamshire and Leicestershire and compares these with the rates for the travel-to-work area within which Ashby and Mansfield are situated. Using these definitions is the closest to defining unemployment in a housing market. As was discussed in Chapters Two and Three the geographical definition of a housing market can be rather complex and open to a large degree of uncertainty.

Employment data, although published regularly, is not without critics. It has been noted by many that, throughout the 1980s, levels of unemployment have been 'hidden' behind a number of different definitions. For instance youth training programmes to remove the youth unemployment from the official employment rate, or legislation which has limited the extent to which certain groups can register for unemployment benefit and therefore be reflected in the official figures. The evidence for this cynicism ranges from academic work (Fothergill and Beatty, 1996) to journalistic analysis. For instance, Hutton (1996) indicates that there have been more than thirty changes to the definition of 'unemployment'. Clearly such inconsistency in definitions is not supportive of data set monitoring. Despite the fact that there are limitations with the data, it is still employed. For instance Bramley and Watkins (1996) use data on unemployment rates from the claimant count, divided by an estimate of the number of economically active persons in the district.

The close relationship between effective demand for housing and the economy is not difficult to trace. Obtaining a mortgage is a long-term commitment, both on the part of the mortgagor and the mortgagee. Both parties have to be of the opinion that the house is affordable and job and income security is at a high enough level to ensure regular repayments are maintained. Unemployment data may therefore give an indication of the likely need for affordable social housing vis-à-vis other travel-to-work areas. The temporal data is perhaps more useful than simple 'snap-shot' statistics, as time series illustrate whether or not unemployment is rising or falling. Indicating whether or not a housing market has the potential to support owner occupation or requires affordable housing.

One of the most useful published sources for income data is 'Regional Trends', published by the Central Statistical Office, in which housing data is disaggregated in terms of districts, and which also contains information on economic activity levels. The problem with this data is that there appears to be a time lag between data collection, compilation and publication. For instance, disposable income statistics are produced at a county level with a three year time lag (Table 14.4 in the 1993 edition), whilst gross weekly full time earnings are produced with only a one year lag, in the same table. District statistics include employment (three year lag), economically active persons (three year lag), and owner-occupation levels (three year lag) presented in Tables 15.1 - 15.2.

The New Earnings Survey presents average weekly earnings at a county level, illustrated in Table 5.2. In terms of the case study counties, employment in Leicestershire is the most well paid, higher than the average for the East Midlands as a whole, whilst Nottinghamshire is just below the regional average. Using this average income data it is possible to develop an estimate of an 'affordable' house price, both for a single male income and a single female income (single person households are forecast to be the fastest growing household type (see Chapter Three and Holmans, 1995)). The methodology for such an estimation is based upon the assumption that the householder has accepted a 90% mortgage and the lending institution is prepared to lend 2.5 times the annual income (currently, 2001, many lenders are prepared to lend 3.25 times a single income which may, if the same calculation was done now, increase the 'affordability' level).

When this estimation is compared to actual house prices that are being realised in the areas concerned, it is clear that some areas are more 'affordable' than others. Using the Halifax data for the last quarter in 1994 illustrates that, in all five East Midland Counties, the average house price was less than what the average single male income could afford. For single females, the situation is totally reversed and almost across the region homes are more than £10,000 too expensive for a single income female. This is purely illustrative and is based on simple calculations. If a more complex income estimate were to be used, such as that produced from Bramley's housing and planning model (Bramley and Watkins, 1996) then the situation may produce different levels of 'affordable' housing. What is clear, however, is the fact that dual incomes are often necessary to be able to enter owner occupation and if household incomes were taken into account homes would appear far more 'affordable'. Such average income and

Table 5.2 Average Gross Earnings in the East Midlands 1994 (£s per week)

| | Single Male | | Single Female | | Average Semi-Detached House Prices (Halifax 1994 Q4) |
|---|---|---|---|---|---|
| | Male Average Earnings | House Price Affordable From this Income | Female Average Earnings | House Price Affordable From this Income | |
| Derbyshire | 325.90 | £47,000 | 227.20 | £32,800 | £42,963 |
| Leicestershire | 327.80 | £47,350 | 232.50 | £33,600 | £48,278 |
| Lincolnshire | 307.50 | £44,500 | 221.90 | £32,000 | £41,939 |
| Northamptonshire | 339.20 | £49,000 | 235.60 | £34,000 | £44,052 |
| Nottinghamshire | 322.00 | £46,500 | 231.50 | £33,400 | £43,305 |
| E. Midlands | 325.00 | £46,950 | 230.50 | £33,300 | £44,171 |

**Source:** Government Statistical Survey, 1995, Table e110.2 and e113.2; Halifax

## Indicators of Housing Demand 113

average house price conceal areas where income (or house prices) are either above or below these figures, further indicating the need for a 'local' focus.

Affordability indicators are examined in a number of publications. The Housebuilders Federation produces a monthly publication entitled 'Housing Market Report', a publication which can be used to indicate the state of the housing market, particularly the market for new homes. It contains a section on the economy, reproducing a number of indicators of national and regional economic health. Whilst the majority of this information can be obtained elsewhere, for example the Department of Employment for the unemployment statistics, it does provide a readily accessible data source for this information, as well as housebuilder perceptions (see below). The publication also contains statistics and indicators of confidence and affordability. The confidence statistics are not regionally disaggregated and are simply based upon national polls carried out by organisations such as MORI and Gallup. Perhaps the feature of the 'Housing Market Report' which is most useful is its affordability index. Although this only gives a broad indication of trends, it is classified regionally. This index is created by compiling a number of different statistics. Initially, the average weekly earnings from the 'New Earnings Survey', for both males and females, is established to obtain the average income for both a dual-income couple and a single male income. The average property price, as highlighted by the DoE/DETR 5% sample, is then determined for each region. Assuming that the average mortgage is for 80% of the homes value, the percentage of income required to service the loan is determined. This then gives a time series which can be used to see if affordability in each region is improving or deteriorating. Whilst it gives an indication of the ability to buy market homes, the approach is open to challenge, as it understates the cost of house purchase. This is because account is only taken of interest repayments, the additional cost of insurance and repayments being ignored. Such hidden costs may be around 25% of the total outgoing involved in buying a home. Perhaps more significant is the fact that the index may be demographically limited, in-so-far as it concentrates on dual-income households and single income males. Take, for example, the fact that demographers suggest that there will be an increase in lone parent households (Murphy and Berrington, 1993; Tilling, 1995), a household group dominated by female household heads. Clearly affordability for this group has been ignored.

The DETR publication 'Housing and Construction Statistics' contains data which is of use when ascertaining the economic strength of an areas population. In one table there is a regional breakdown of house purchase which not only highlights the average dwelling price, it also contains the average recorded income of borrowers. This can only be used as an indication of a region's ability to maintain housing costs of different magnitudes. As this data is derived from the DoE 5% survey, it could be assumed that there would be the same capability of disaggregation to a county level that can occur with house prices (Nicol, 1994).

A general knowledge of this type of information will allow housing strategists to be aware of economic characteristics, both economic characteristics in general, and (where data exists) of more disaggregated areas (districts, travel-to-work areas, etc.) which would be closer to housing market areas. It might be suggested this is already being done by many County Councils' (or Metropolitan Authorities') Research and Information groups, usually a team within the planning department, collecting and collating this centrally produced data. Therefore the local authorities charged with preparing housing strategies should be able to obtain information regarding the economic situation of the households within their district. This would provide a degree of guidance as to what type of home may be required in the housing market, a general view that may be supported by the use of other indicators and demand monitors (which will be discussed below).

**Statistics and Judgements**

The second type of demand indicator is collected and collated by the various agencies with an interest in the working of the housing market, often augmented by value judgements. Perhaps the examination of this type of information provides the best and most robust method of market monitoring, as it can be analysed to show movements or trends. This is in direct contrast to the monitoring of policy options, affordability indices and income statistics. These have many uncertainties regarding future projections, even before they are interpreted in terms of demand. A first-hand examination and analysis of reliable statistics is more robust than those which are based on the successful outcomes of various policies, or a third party's interpretation of trends. It was from statistical indicators such as these that Coopers and Lybrand recommended the five indicators for practical use. The indicators that they supported were:

1. An indicator of house price movements.
2. Some form of 'planning indicator'.
3. An 'estate agent indicator'.

4. A 'builders indicator'.
5. An indicator of migration.

As these are arguably the most reliable indicators, it is clear that a detailed investigation of them is called for.

One major limitation which many of the statistics appear to suffer from is the determination of a base level of demand. To be able to use statistics to indicate fluctuations in demand, there is a need to determine and establish a relative base level. If the trend is viewed from a base level occurring in a buoyant (or alternatively depressed) economy or housing market, the analysis of future movements may not present a realistic picture of demand. For example, inquiries at an estate agent may increase, but it may have previously been low and is simply returning to an equilibrium level. Alternatively, the sales rates of new houses on a large site in the South East of England may prove to be over ambitious for a small site elsewhere. Therefore it is vitally important to ensure that market monitoring is continued from year-to-year; quarter-to-quarter; month-to-month, in an effort to ensure that an effective time series is developed. An effective time series will allow changes to be placed in a context.

In addition to the problem of developing a 'base' level from which changes in demand can be measured effectively, there is an additional problem. It is almost impossible to examine the housing market, its supply and demand, in a state of 'quarantine', and land and housebuilding can never be seen as isolated factors and activities. A major problem with many of the suggested indicators is that they appear to assume that trends which are being highlighted are isolated and detached from other effects. Clearly this is not the case. Both economically and spatially housing market areas are inextricably linked. For instance, assume that one housing market experiences demand at a similar level to a neighbouring housing market, but supply is constrained in one more than it is in the other. The surplus demand from one area will be transferred to the second best alternative (Bramley, 1993; 1995). This will then reflect on the indicators of that area, suggesting higher demand here than would be the case. A fine line exists between classifying this as unsuccessful effective demand and latent demand (see Chapter Three above). One argument is that the would-be householders do not have the economic strength for their first choice housing market, therefore they cannot support effective demand. Yet they are forced to utilise a sub-optimum solution and effectively demonstrate greater demand in an area where it is met more freely than areas where it is not. This is the fundamental problem with most of the indicators, as they are not robust or sophisticated enough to overcome in-built supply constraints.

116 *The Formulation of Local Housing Strategies*

It is clear, therefore, that if the indicators are reliable in other respects they will have to be placed into the context of wider economic trends and past movements of indicators. If this is not done there is a significant danger that the indicators will be misinterpreted.

*Local Authority Data*

As this research examines housing strategies prepared by local authorities it is appropriate to commence this discussion with an examination of the data that may already exist internally, due to the fact that the local authority is responsible for the collection and collation of a number of different data sets. The housing department, planning department and building control section are all associated with housing and to varying degrees produce data that may indicate market demand. These data sets can be seen as gauging demand or need at different parts of the housing pipelines discussed in earlier chapters.

*Housing Department* Housing departments usually have a list of households and persons who not only require housing, but meet various criteria, both established nationally and by the local housing authority concerned. Can this truly be classed as a demand indicator? It may give some indication of need (and even this assertion is questionable (Dyer, 1993)), but it cannot be said to indicate market demand. This is due to the fact that, almost by definition, those who are accepted onto housing lists are not the type of households able to easily afford market housing. For instance, local authority tenants are more likely to be on low incomes and reliant on benefits (Table 23, Maclennan, Gibb and More, 1990), and would therefore not appear to be the sort of economic group that housebuilders would ordinarily cater for. The residualisation of the tenure (Morris and Winn, 1990; Forest et al., 1990; Malpass, 1990), removing many of the more economically active households through 'Right-to-Buy' (RTB) and leaving a far from attractive housing stock, highlights why housebuilders may not see waiting lists as a reliable indicator. Even as an indicator of housing need the reliability of waiting lists is open to question.

Local authority housing is offered at below market rents (although the gap has decreased over recent years) and therefore demand exceeds supply, with the result that some form of rationing is required (Maclennan, 1991). As households tend to add themselves to housing waiting lists only if there is a perception that a positive outcome will occur, a list which suggests a five year wait will discourage certain households. This is especially the case for those households which are not in a high category of need as established by the points system, favoured by 62% of local authority housing departments, (Institute of Housing, 1990). In addition, the local authority housing stock may be managed in terms of subsections of the district. Through the RTB this may create a situation where certain local authority housing market areas have no housing stock. If an area has no local authority houses then it would appear that there is no demand for housing in that area if waiting lists were simply used on their own. The waiting list will not reflect the housing need of that area, as there can not be a choice in an area where no housing stock exists. This situation is worse in rural areas, where the local authority stock may be so small, that a number of settlements have no local authority homes at all, with the result that they can not be specified as a location for housing. In addition there may be a significantly lower turn over of homes in rural areas, resulting in waiting lists being longer and households perceiving no chance to obtain a home, thereby electing not to register.

**Table 5.3 Housing Waiting Lists (1995)**

|  | Waiting List | LA Housing Stock | HA Housing Stock | Total 'Public Sector' |
|---|---|---|---|---|
| Mansfield | 1,605 | 9,004 | 1,268 | 10,332 |
| NW Leicestershire | 1,840 | 5,478 | 1,187 | 6,687 |

**Source:** Interviews and Section A: Dwelling Stock of NW Leicestershire and Mansfield from 'Needs Appraisal', HIP1 for the DoE, April 1995

Although there are limitations with this data, it is useful to focus upon the situation in the case study districts. As can be seen in Table 5.3, the local authority housing stock in the two case study districts differs significantly. If this data is compared with the housing departments waiting list figures, it transpires that NW Leicestershire has a more significant problem of housing need than Mansfield as it can be seen from the table that there are far fewer local authority homes, relative to the waiting list, in NW Leicestershire than in Mansfield. The table also indicates the degree to which this local authority stock is supplemented by housing association units, producing a figure for total public housing stock. Even with this additional figure taken into account there is still a greater level of need in NW Leicestershire. This may indicate house prices are lower in Mansfield, allowing marginal owner occupiers to access this tenure rather than public

118  *The Formulation of Local Housing Strategies*

housing. In relation to the population, in NW Leicestershire 2.28% of the population are on the housing waiting list, compared to 1.59% in Mansfield.

Coopers and Lybrand appeared to accept the significant limitations endemic within waiting lists, and did not suggest their utilisation as an indicator of housing demand.

*Dwelling Vacancy and Occupancy Rates* Another possible indicator identified by Coopers and Lybrand is the level of dwelling vacancies, the assertion being that a high level of vacancy suggests low demand. High demand would, all things being equal, encourage the re-use of empty dwellings. Figure 5.3, illustrates the manner in which the percentage of empty dwellings changed between 1971 and 1990. It can be seen that the highest rates of vacancy were between 1979 and 1983 (a period of recession in the housing market) whilst the lowest figures were in the early 1970s (a period when the housing market was buoyant). Yet the vacancy rates do not appear to illustrate all the housing market changes one would expect. For instance between 1987 and 1989 the housing market was booming, to such a degree that one would suggest vacancy rates should realistically be lower, possibly as low as the 1970s figures. Yet it is only in the peak year of 1989 that the rate falls below 2.5%.

Although Dorling's work focuses on the national situation, the vacancy rate data which is available from the Census is capable of disaggregation to a level which may reflect housing market areas (enumeration districts). However, Census data is too infrequent to be employed as a market indicator, and is also lacking in the detail needed. For example in the 1991 Census the data concerned with vacancies simply separated all vacant accommodation into: new and never occupied; under improvement; and others (OPCS, 1992a; 1992b).

This final 'catch all' category tends to include the majority of the stock (75% in the case of Nottinghamshire) (OPCS, 1992a, Table 54). It could be argued that to provide a worthwhile indication of vacancy rates this category should be disaggregated further, but as the Census stands there is no means of determining *why* these properties are vacant. However positive signs developed in the 1991 Census through the inclusion of data which disaggregates the vacant stock in terms of house type (Table 62). Yet an overall assessment is that, in their present form, vacancy rates are not particularly useful as a data source for the development of housing strategies.

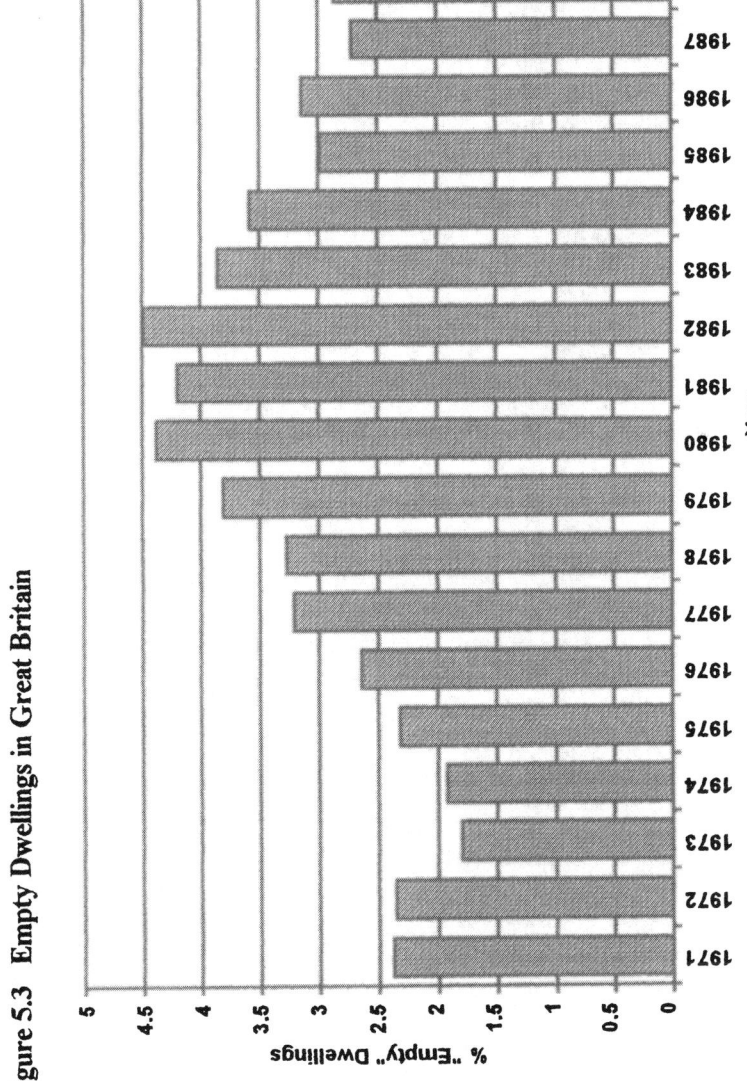

Figure 5.3 Empty Dwellings in Great Britain

Source: Dorling, 1991, Table 4

120 *The Formulation of Local Housing Strategies*

For instance a recent Audit Commission publication (Audit Commission Update, 1998) does highlight that target setting for re-lets in the social housing sector may create problems with this indicator, as any change may be a result of the local authority focusing on reducing how long a property remains vacant.

Vacancy rates are compiled annually as part of the HIP submission process. As can be seen in Table 5.4, the housing departments of Mansfield and NW Leicestershire have estimated the vacancy rates in both the public and private sector. The methodology for the compilation of this data is contained in the notes provided with the form. These state that the number of vacant dwellings can be estimated from council tax records or a local survey, not the census, recognising the static and problematic nature of this data set.

**Table 5.4 Vacancy Rates in the Case Study Districts (%)**

|  | Local Authority | Housing Association | Private Sector | All Dwellings |
|---|---|---|---|---|
| NW Leicestershire | 1.4 | 3.2 | 5.5 | 4.7 |
| Mansfield | 6.1 | 2.4 | 5.9 | 5.8 |

**Source:** Section A: Dwelling Stock of NW Leicestershire and Mansfield from 'Needs Appraisals', HIP 1 for the DoE, April 1995

It would appear from this table that the vacancy rates of the private sector in both districts are very similar. However, there is a significant difference in the local authority sector. It can be seen that Mansfield has a vacancy rate four times higher than NW Leicestershire. This may suggest less need for social housing in Mansfield than in NW Leicestershire due to the fact that higher housing need may force greater utilisation of the housing stock. Yet there is a doubt regarding what vacancy rates actually indicate. High vacancy rates, as well as emphasising a low demand, could also demonstrate an extremely active and fluid market, with strong demand where dwelling turnover is high. Clearly, the important factor is the length of time the property is vacant. This would allow vacancy rates to become an indicator of 'property turnover'. As King stressed in 1987, there is a tendency for structure planning authorities to treat vacancy rates, even when used in important population forecasts, as remaining constant between census years at between 4-5% (King, 1987b).

Occupancy rates, although similar to vacancy rates can be seen as a separate indicator. Again this is data which is available in the Census and therefore suffers from the problems mentioned above, although it can, in its most direct form, give some indication as regards the prevalence of concealed households. Take, for example Mansfield District. Table 24 of the Census (OPCS, 1992) suggests that 3.6% of households in that district have four or more persons over eighteen years of age. This would ordinarily mean that a number of these persons would be hoping to set up their own home and, if this number is unduly large compared to other areas, it might indicate some level of demand. If this number were to be examined in conjunction with the areas affordability and income rates, the demand could be segmented in terms of the supply 'housing pipelines' (see Chapter Two).

*Planning Department* The debate regarding the relevancy of planning indicators was extensively covered in the Coopers and Lybrand studies, not altogether surprising given that it was the planning system which the reports aimed to influence. The planning process generates considerable data related to market demand, for instance, planning applications and planning appeals, both included in the Coopers and Lybrand studies. These involve two forms of data:

1. Data that the planning department collates and monitors.
2. Data that is available to the planning department, but which might require some form of processing.

Included within these data types are: number of actual planning enquiries; the level of applications concerning small sites; the degree to which planning consents are amended; and the densities of developments in applications. Other suggested data sets involve the statistics that are compiled by the building control department, as part of their role in monitoring construction standards (starts and completions). There is also a fourth type of indicator which is an amalgamation of building control and planning statistics. Two of these (time to take up planning permission and depletion rates) were discussed by Coopers and Lybrand.

In 1982 Brotherton examined the use of development control data as a means of determining zones of development pressure (Brotherton, 1982). In 1984 Healey and McNamara critically examined how far Brotherton's findings could be relied upon elsewhere (McNamara and Healey, 1984). Although a number of their observations concerned Brotherton's detailed findings regarding areas under pressure, they also suggested that there were significant dangers in using development control records in an unrefined manner. They argued that simply using planning applications would include applications which are not for residential development. This is obviously the

## 122  The Formulation of Local Housing Strategies

case, and as with all of these 'planning based indicators' there is a need to filter applications which are for developments other than residential. McNamara and Healey agreed with Brotherton that the potential for monitoring land and property development from development control data was significant. This data was further examined by the DoE in 1993, where a study sought to determine the usefulness of one part of this data source (PS3 returns) to gain information on land availability (DoE, 1993b). The study stated that although, in general PS3, returns contained useful information, they were not without errors, ranging from transcription problems to uncertainties over which sites should and should not be included. In terms of this thesis PS3 returns are not particularly useful, as their prime focus is to inform a third party. They are useful for the district themselves only in so far as they summarise the data that the local authority would already possess.

*Planning Applications* The assertion that, if demand is high, there will be a higher number of applications, appears to be sound. Nevertheless, using planning applications is not without limitations. The drawback that is possibly the most important currently, is that arising from Section 54(a) of the Planning and Compensation Act 1991, the presumption in favour of the development plan. Arguably, planning applications will fall away once a conservation minded development plan is in operation, due to developers perceiving little chance of gaining permission due to Section 54(a). As a result subsequent housing strategies, if number of applications are used as an indicator, may be produced with the assumption that there is little demand. Yet is this the case? It may be that a self perpetuating spiral has been created, as housebuilders simply submit fewer applications as a result of the planning regime in operation. Another factor is that the number of applications may fall away due to the economic situation that exists in the housing market at any point in time. As can be seen in Figure 5.2 the number of applications fell annually from 1988/89, when the housing market entered its period of decline. It is noted that this figure is based on all planning applications, not just those for residential development. Yet a disaggregation to isolate residential planning applications could be achieved by the local authority itself, from its own databases. One would suggest that an examination of residential applications alone would indicate a steeper decline in applications over the same period. For instance between 1990/91 and 1991/92 applications for major residential developments fell by 12% (year on year) whilst all planning applications only fell by around 8% (authors analysis of DoE, 1992e; DoE, 1993e).

Indicators of Housing Demand 123

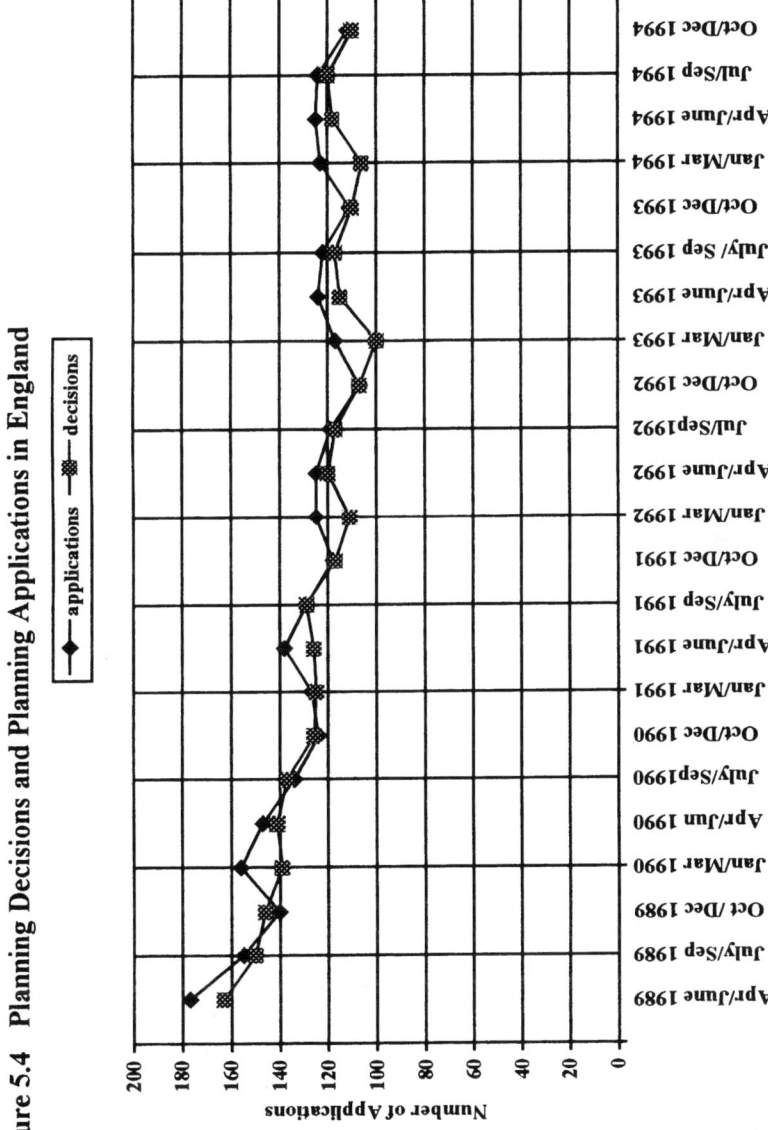

Figure 5.4 Planning Decisions and Planning Applications in England

Source: DoE Development Information Bulletin, Table 1

124  *The Formulation of Local Housing Strategies*

The DETR publish tables of planning applications and decisions on a quarterly basis, but the data is only disaggregated to a district level to highlight decisions and the speed with which they are made. Figure 5.4 plots decisions against applications to ascertain whether or not the data could be employed interchangeably. It can be seen that decisions tend to lag applications by one quarter, which supports the eight week decision time for planning applications. If this is borne in mind decisions may be a reasonable proxy for applications. However this should only be problematic for those using the DETR published data, one would argue that as the local authorities record planning applications themselves they will be able to monitor this data with greater certainty and disaggregation than an outside observer or an academic.

This data concerns all planning applications, not just those for new residential development. Examining the DoE information bulletin further it is clear that applications for new dwellings have been relatively constant at between 13% and 16% of all planning applications for much of the 1990s. One would not expect such difficulties to be apparent within the local authority. It is only those of us examining the DoE data, which aggregates the statistics, that encounter problems in definitions.

Using this data to examine the situation in the case study districts highlights that, whilst both districts have encountered a gradual decrease in the number of planning decisions since the early 1990s, the decrease in NW Leicestershire does not appear to have been as dramatic as Mansfield. If the assumptions regarding decisions following applications are correct and new build residential planning applications have remained at a constant percentage in these two districts, this suggests that the market in NW Leicestershire has not suffered as significant a slump as Mansfield. Figure 5.5 highlights this in a graphical format.

Early in the 1980s there emerged a pro-development political climate (Thornley, 1981; Montgomery and Thornley, 1990). This coupled with the presumption in favour of development (Circular 22/80) placed the developer lobby in a strong position (Rydin, 1983). The issues that Coopers and Lybrand examined were therefore the result of a different type of development process, reflecting the situation that occurs when the developer-planner balance is weighted towards the developer. One of the limitations identified was that there were no means of separating demand-inspired planning applications from those which are made for land bank creation or speculative purposes. In addition, difficulties were identified regarding multiple applications, which in

*Indicators of Housing Demand* 125

**Figure 5.5 Planning Decisions in the Case Study Districts**

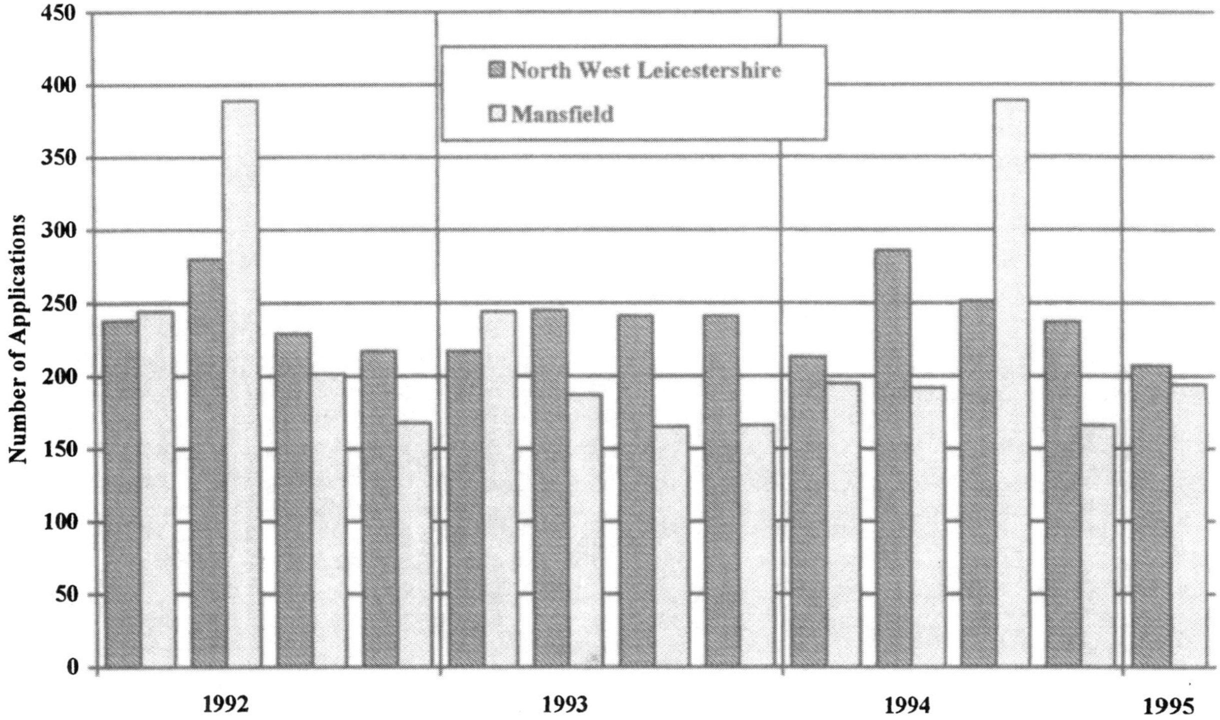

**Source:** DoE Development Information Bulletin, Statistics of Planning Applications

126  *The Formulation of Local Housing Strategies*

itself could be seen as a demand indicator. If a number of applications are submitted for the one site, there would have to be a means of adjusting the data to ensure that over-counting did not occur.

One of the problems Coopers and Lybrand identified was the possibility that if applications were accepted as an indicator of demand, this could be prone to distortion by builders who manipulate the statistics through submitting applications that they have no intention of developing. This is a problem, but it is arguable to what extent builders would do this, especially as charges for application are now considerable. The cost of a planning applications is significant, both in fees and in the amount of time that the applicant has to spend on case presentation and background research. It might be suggested that small building companies, in particular, may not have the resources or the long term view required to 'manipulate' planning applications.

*Number of Planning Appeals*  The number of appeals lodged against negative planning decisions may be one indication of demand. If high market demand exists, the applicant may feel that the cost (both financially and in terms of time) would be outweighed by the rewards of a successful appeal, creating a situation where appeals are more likely. The alternative view to this is that if demand were uncertain there would be limited subsequent effort once an initial application has been refused. However, it could be argued that what is perhaps most important to developers is not so much the demand, but the possibility of getting the right 'result'. Appeals are related to both the national policy, local policy and the consistency of local decisions, in fact the confidence that the applicants have in obtaining planning approval. Figure 5.6 highlights how appeals rose in the 1980s before falling from 1988/89 onwards. The assertion that this fall is due to a fall in demand would probably be a reasonable one. An argument exists that it may have continued into the 1990s, not necessarily because of demand, but because developers cannot see a successful outcome from their efforts, through the plan-led system. It would make an interesting study to see if this was the case as more plans became adopted.

The data used in this figure concerns all appeals, not just those lodged against refusals for residential development. However, as it is the local authority which defends the appeal, it should be in a far better position to monitor the exact number of residential appeals. Again the data available to the researcher is aggregated by the DoE and now the DETR, making it difficult for a study such as this to examine this area in as much detail as the local authority officer can.

Indicators of Housing Demand 127

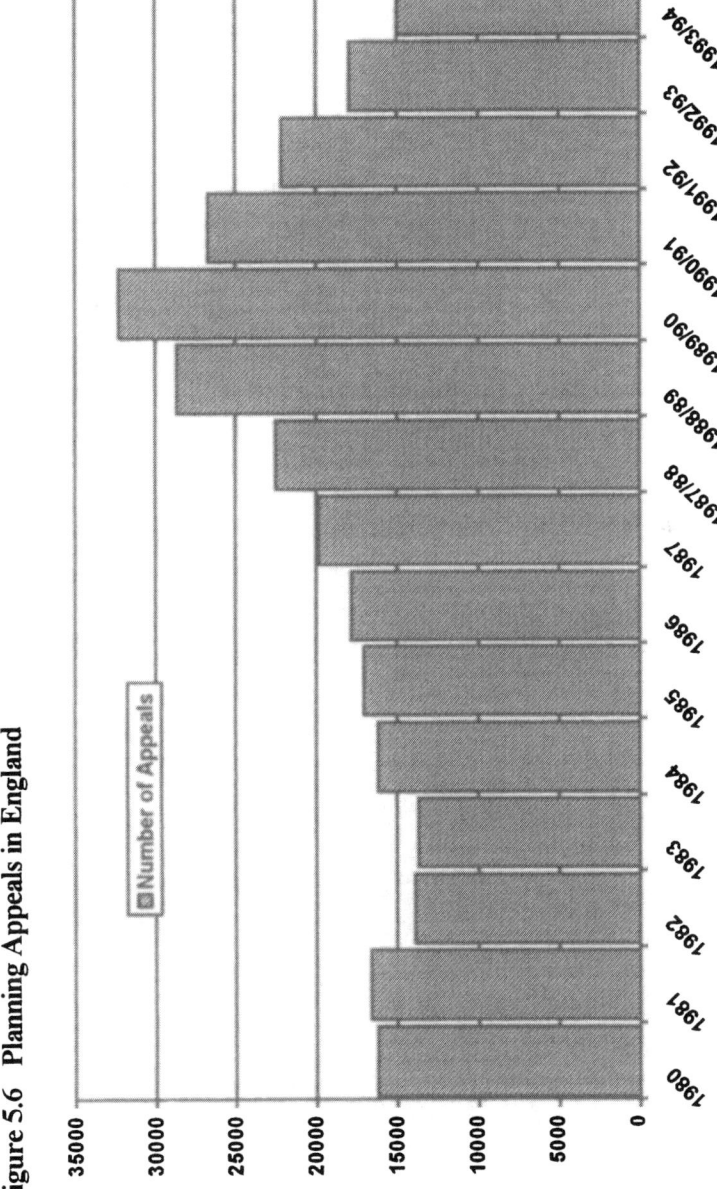

Figure 5.6 Planning Appeals in England

Source: DoE, 1993e, Table 7.1; DoE, 1995d, Table 6.4

Not withstanding the general criticisms, if a local authority were to employ either appeals or planning applications as a means of monitoring changes in demand, the degree of disaggregation and detail may be considerable. For instance, planning applications could be compiled in terms of specific housing markets, then in terms of the type of home that the developer is wishing to build. If there were changes over time this may suggest changes in the demand patterns, as interpreted by housebuilders.

*Enquiry Levels* This is an indicator which would be relatively easy to compile and monitor, but it is very problematic in so far as it is easy to manipulate. Housebuilders enquiring about sites have very little commitment to make, and if it were to become known that such a measure was being used as an indicator, housebuilders could enquire about several sites in order to present an inflated picture of demand. The only justification for the use of such an indicator would be if it were to remain informal. However, even if enquiry monitoring were to remain secret, there is still no way of ensuring that the enquiries are for genuine development or simply speculation. If the enquiry is genuine, problems remain regarding the degree to which the enquirer envisages the site as a long-term investment, a land bank for future demand, or a means of meeting short-term demand. The degree to which enquiries can both be knowingly manipulated or become biased by speculative investigations means that it is perhaps one of the least attractive indicators.

Although discussed by Coopers and Lybrand, they did not recommend this form of data as a viable indication of market demands.

*Development of Small Sites* If there is high demand in an area, sites which may not have been the first choice for developers would become more attractive. It could therefore be suggested that an increase in the development of small sites would therefore indicate an increase in housing demand. Yet, what could be defined as a small site? A far more useful data set to monitor would be the increase/decrease in the percent of planning applications on windfall sites (i.e. sites on land not identified for housing in policy documents or land availability studies). An allocation for windfall sites is common practice in the land allocation process at the local level. For instance, in NW Leicestershire it has been estimated that 400 dwellings will be provided on this type of site, so it is feasible that estimates of future supply from this source can be compared with what has actually occurred.

Yet, even if the definition was expanded to reflect windfall sites, there are still problems with this type of data. The importance of small windfall sites depends to a great extent on the degree to which planning policy constrains larger site developments. In a rural area, for instance, planning policy may only allow infill sites. If small sites were to be used as an indicator the figures would clearly show high levels of demand. If builders who normally develop sites with in excess of fifty units, for instance, start to look at sites where fewer than ten units can be accommodated, it could show that demand is high enough to alter strategies. Yet, even here, it must be placed into the context of the planning policies operating in the area at the time.

*Amendment of Planning Applications* Although this data cannot truly be classed as a 'stand alone' demand indicator, it may give an indication of changes in market structure. For instance, if a re-submission changes the site from detached to terraced housing it may indicate that housebuilders realise that the market structure in a certain area has changed. This would be a relatively robust and easily collated method of differentiating market demand. However, it is not totally free of limitations. Re-submission may be for internal reasons within housebuilding companies, as the original application may no longer fulfil the company's corporate strategy. For instance, a national company may find a house type sells well in one particular area but badly throughout the country as a whole. Removing this size and design of dwelling from the housebuilder's portfolio would, therefore, be due to national criteria, and would not reflect local market preference.

*Starts and Completions* Starts and completion data is published by two agencies, the Department of Environment Transport and the Regions (DETR) formerly the DoE, compiling building control statistics, and the National House Building Council (NHBC) through their role in housing standard control. As the NHBC class starts as 'registration of a start', which has to be made at least twenty one days in advance of construction commencing, starts which do not actually materialise, may therefore be included. In the study period the NHBC estimate that 97% of actual recorded starts will result in construction (NHBC, 1993). The DETR define a construction to have started when the foundations are laid (DoE, 1993a). There are similar differences in the definition of when dwellings are completed. The NHBC define a completion as having occurred when the house is complete in respect of the NHBC's own

## Table 5.5 Starts and Completions in the Case Study Districts

|  | North West Leicestershire | | Mansfield | |
|---|---|---|---|---|
|  | Starts | Completions | Starts | Completions |
| 1986 | 60 | 46 | 37 | 53 |
|  | 59 | 59 | 48 | 29 |
|  | 67 | 74 | 60 | 23 |
|  | 54 | 67 | 31 | 8 |
| 1987 | 31 | 38 | 87 | 42 |
|  | 97 | 82 | 98 | 115 |
|  | 71 | 60 | 36 | 40 |
|  | 139 | 107 | 37 | 64 |
| 1988 | 78 | 24 | 36 | 83 |
|  | 90 | 72 | 84 | 55 |
|  | 103 | 125 | 88 | 99 |
|  | 98 | 95 | 79 | 52 |
| 1989 | 66 | 93 | 98 | 79 |
|  | 123 | 49 | 75 | 138 |
|  | 74 | 79 | 77 | 87 |
|  | 79 | 85 | 86 | 63 |
| 1990 | 88 | 77 | 63 | 89 |
|  | 58 | 127 | 44 | 79 |
|  | 105 | 49 | 106 | 39 |
|  | 42 | 50 | 57 | 39 |
| 1991 | 100 | 95 | 33 | 61 |
|  | 111 | 104 | 39 | 69 |
|  | 88 | 88 | 36 | 16 |
|  | 83 | 60 | 47 | 31 |
| 1992 | 83 | 69 | 106 | 62 |
|  | 145 | 81 | 78 | 35 |
|  | 64 | 106 | 81 | 89 |
|  | 87 | 112 | 28 | 48 |
| 1993 | 95 | 108 | 46 | 70 |
|  | 142 | 97 | 122 | 72 |
|  | 96 | 90 | 138 | 83 |
|  | 101 | 116 | 73 | 75 |
| 1994 | 166 | 79 | 45 | 91 |
|  | 87 | 120 | 48 | 78 |
|  | 99 | 102 | 108 | 128 |
|  | 90 | 105 | 37 | 82 |
| 1995 | 74 | 129 | 86 | 36 |
|  | 80 | 83 | 115 | 17 |
|  | 91 | 150 | 130 | 126 |
|  | 55 | 74 | 48 | 95 |

**Source:** DoE, Housing Data and Statistics Division

technical requirements. This is prior to occupation, but is seen by the NHBC as generally signifying that the house is ready to be occupied (NHBC, 1993). The DoE/DETR regard a house as having been completed when it becomes ready for occupation, whether it is in fact occupied or not (DoE, 1993a). There is, therefore, a wider difference in the definition of a start than a completion, yet it is in the compilations of completions that significant problems arise (Gillen, 1994b).

With a few exceptions (Ball, 1983; Gillen, 1994b; Gillen et al., 1995) little academic work has examined the problems and incompatibilities with these data sets. Even the work that has examined this area has tended to avoid recommending one data series. In terms of housing strategies it would appear that local authorities would be best placed to employ the DETR building control based data. Building control data is collated 'in house' by the local authority themselves and it includes building inspections that have been carried out by the NHBCs building inspectors. It would appear that the data can, therefore, be tailored to the exact requirements of the individuals analysing the data, for instance the building control officers could be requested to record starts in terms of housing types or market areas.

The primary limitation with this data is the fact that in its published form (in the Housing and Construction Statistics) there can be a time lag. This is due to some authorities submitting the figures on time whilst others delay. The DETR require virtually complete responses from each authority before it can compile and prepare the statistics to be published. Yet this would not be a problem at the local level. If the data were to be employed by the local authority, before it was sent to the DoE for collation, the onus would be on the local authority officers to produce monthly/quarterly data on time.

According to Ball (1983), the cost to the housebuilder of holding completed dwellings is prohibitive, with the result that housebuilding companies build for a quick sale. This should ensure that housing output closely follows the level of demand. As a result, starts and completions, if taken as a representation of housebuilder activity, may be used as an overall indication of market demand e.g. the higher the level of starts the greater the level of housebuilder confidence in a buoyant housing market. Yet there are other factors which can affect the statistics, for example, the weather, or delays in the production of materials. This could present a fall in the starts or completions data which would be the result of factors outside the realm of the housing market and housing demand.

There is an argument, however, that starts and completions could be indicators of past demand being met, and may only indicate future markets if

132  *The Formulation of Local Housing Strategies*

past trends continue. This may be the case with regard to completions as the construction process results in present completions being a reflection of decisions and opinions on the market which were taken, on average, a year to eighteen months previously (dependent upon the time taken to gain planning permission and construct). This assertion may mean that as a long term indicator they are less reliable. If they are examined in terms of changes in the number of starts (or completions) of house types, they will, in part, reflect where the housebuilders see the greatest potential market. However they may also reflect the areas of greatest potential profit.

Ball (1983) suggested that a combination of starts and completion data, to form 'net starts' may be the best measure of output. He saw net starts as being the addition to the number of homes being constructed, in effect total starts minus total completions, in any one time period. He stated that this would act

> ...as an indicator of new commitments of capital to housebuilding. (Ball, 1983, p. 106)

Figure 5.7, highlights net starts in the two case study districts. If Ball's assertion is correct, then it suggests that since 1994 both districts have experienced limited new capital commitments to housebuilding. This is in contrast to the situation earlier in the decade when greater capital investment occurred, suggesting that the housing markets of these two districts have declined since 1990.

It could be argued that housebuilders would only add additional new capital to housebuilding if they foresee a market for the completed product, therefore this indicator may be of use. However, it will still meet the problems that have been indicated to exist in the collection of starts and completions.

One adaptation of start and completion data is to examine the time between start and completion, essentially the time to build. The assertion is that the shorter the time period, the higher the demand. However the speed of development may reflect more than market demand. The weather can often affect build times, as can the builder's own strategy, or the cost of the finance. Perhaps the greatest problem with such an indicator is that of comparability. It would be almost impossible to highlight an individual development rate as an 'average' which would provide a benchmark to allow future completion

*Indicators of Housing Demand* 133

**Figure 5.7 Net Starts in the Case Study Districts**

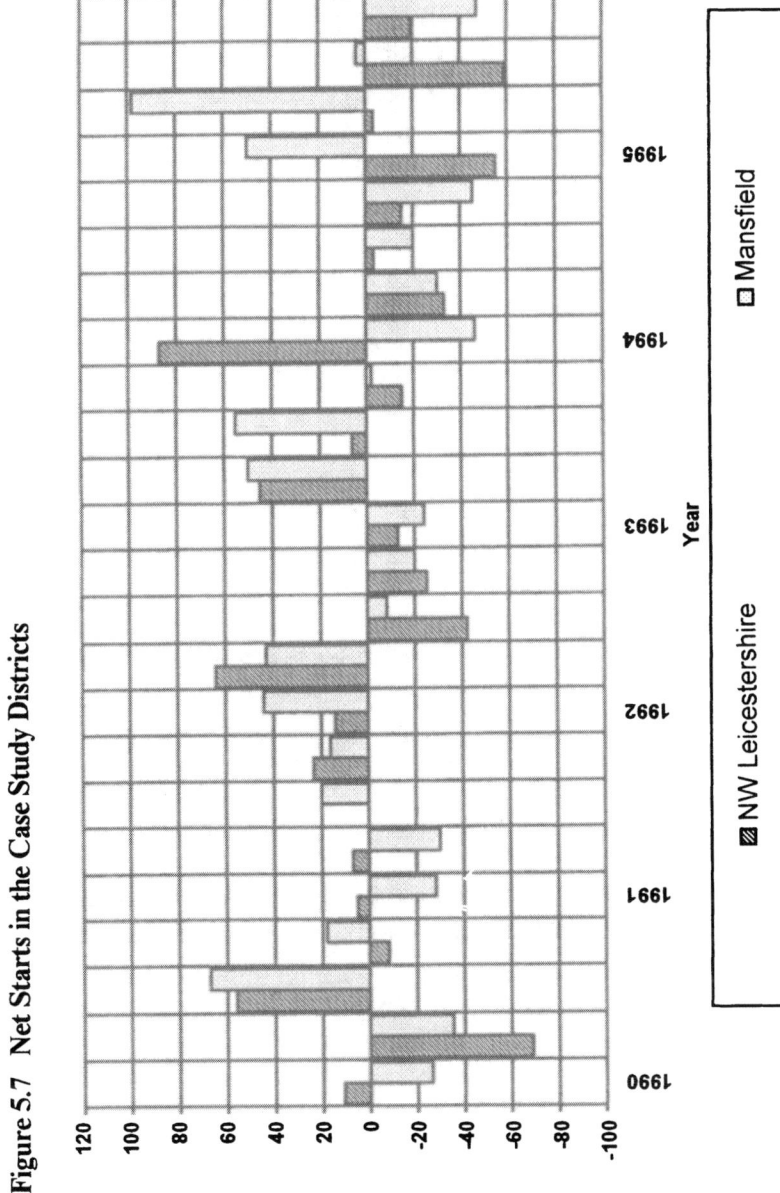

Source: DoE, Housing Data and Statistics Division

## 134 *The Formulation of Local Housing Strategies*

speeds to be evaluated. To be effective this indicator requires good time series from a representative number of sites. Again such data could be developed from that which is already collected and held within local authorities. If this is not possible the NHBC compile data which highlights time taken to build homes, and this may be employed.

Start data can be developed to provide a useful indicator through recording the identity of the builder. If one builder, prior to completing a site in a housing market area, starts a second development (a strategy which would result in the building company effectively competing with itself) it would most probably be due to high levels of demand at the initial development. This information could be easily monitored through recording developers who are active in an area.

*Depletion Rates of Allocated Sites and Time to 'Take Up' Planning Permissions* If sites which are allocated for housing are developed early in the life of a policy document, then there is an argument that demand is high. Coopers and Lybrand suggest that depletion rates are a one sided indicator, which may reflect high demand, through high rates of depletion, but may not necessarily imply low demand if allocated sites remain undeveloped. This assertion is valid given the fact that the housebuilder's or landowner's own strategy may be paramount, (as in the time to 'take up' planning permissions) effectively curtailing development even when demand is high (Rydin, 1985). In addition, further limitations may be a result of the planning process itself. For instance, phased developments may force developers to postpone a development, whilst the demand exists in the housing market to justify full completion of the site.

Time to 'take up' planning permissions would combine the planning departments' approval date, with the start date recorded by building control officers, essentially a measurement of the duration of planning permissions. The supposition is that if the time between the approval and commencement of construction is short, demand is high, whilst a longer timescale is evidence of a lack of demand. Again, there is the problem that a bench mark needs to be set as the 'average' length between approval and commencement. If this is established by looking at past trends, then the period examined would have to be accepted as a period of average demand. In addition the general economic and political conditions will have to have been similar, in the benchmark period, to those currently in existence.

As with many of these indicators, there are a number of reasons, apart from changes in demand, which may cause take up times to vary. The strategy of the housebuilder, or motive of the planning applicant, are obviously the most important and are also the most difficult to examine. Bibby and Shepard, in an examination of the usefulness of PS3 returns as a means of monitoring housing land availability, focused directly upon the major limitation of this type of data (DoE, 1993b). In their examination they studied the duration of planning permissions in English districts, between 1988 and 1991. Their findings illustrated that, in 1988, the duration of planning permissions in the South East (the region generally accepted to have the greatest housing demand) was 26 months. This relatively short period was not matched by any other region, except the North (DoE, 1993b). Although the study suggested that planning officers generally accepted that the shorter the duration of the planning permission the greater the market demand, it did illustrate that there could be practical reasons, other than demand, for planning permissions being utilised quickly. The overall conclusion that Coopers and Lybrand reached with regard to Building Control/Planning Department data was that:

> ...with the exception of the proportion of permissions implemented within each year to expiry, there would be little value in attempting to use planning indicators of demand. (Coopers and Lybrand Associates, 1987, para. 2.25)

It would appear that they decided to use time to 'take up' planning permission as the base for this form of indicator.

Guillou (1990, pp. 137-140) suggests that planning indicators are accepted primarily because there is little alternative. He argues that an indicator is proposed with very little analysis as to what it actually indicates nor how it could be developed to indicate demand. The internal strategies of the builders and problems encountered during a construction process could have as much of an effect on the proportion of starts as changes in demand. One of Guillou's arguments is that this indicator tends to abstract the dynamic nature of planning permissions into a static entity. He suggests that permissions are continually added to the 'pool', which would therefore undermine any contention (suggested by figures built upon a base year's permissions) that demand is constrained by supply. This contention is valid to a degree, yet the expectation is that an increase in the proportion of dwellings completed in any one year would reflect the conditions prevailing within the current or contemporary permission 'take up'. This would result in higher depletion rates being placed in context by higher numbers of applications. If both indicate the same trend it would reflect demand more accurately, as it observes the situation at different 'ends' of the development process.

Yet even if the indicator were to be widened to look at both ends of the development process, the individual problems, discussed above, would remain. Guillou argues, convincingly, that the existence of outline and reserved matter consents, as well as detailed applications, results in an obscure acceptance of what actually constitutes a permission. Clearly, it would be inappropriate to compare reserved matters with detailed permissions due to the differences in available time. For instance, in the case of reserved matters applications, there is an expectation that 100% would be implemented within two years. Similarly, outline permissions may not contain enough detail with regard to the type and number of houses that will actually be built. Guillou argues that only applications which are in the full detailed state should be included and permissions which are complicated by planning agreements should be excluded.

Research has shown that areas with different planning policies tend to attract different categories of developer (Rydin, 1985). In areas with planning constraint and high demand, land is treated as an investment by speculators who would view outline planning permission as a tool towards value enhancement. Paradoxically, it would appear that low construction rates are the result of higher demand for housing, because companies orientated towards speculation are more active than those which generate the majority of their profits through actual construction. One would have to concur with these criticisms, yet the major benefit of this sort of data is the fact that it is readily accessible to the planning officers themselves. With increased use of computers in local authority offices, this should allow for greater flexibility in the use of such data and given time and a reliable data base, this sort of data has a contribution to make to housing market monitoring.

*House Builder Data*

One would anticipate the most reliable information regarding housing markets will be from the housebuilders themselves. As housebuilders are profit making companies they will have to be acutely aware of market demand, the type of property which is being demanded, and the number of houses this demand will be able to sustain before it is fully met. Housebuilders would therefore appear to be a very useful source of housing market data. Market researchers in housebuilding companies are charged with the responsibility of determining demand in an area. The methods employed can range from sophisticated geo-demographic analysis, employing

## Indicators of Housing Demand  137

population projections, to highly localised market knowledge and the reliance on personal contacts. Coopers and Lybrand suggested that builders identify sites through a general investigation of an area's economic prosperity, employment prospects, infrastructure plans and other major investments in the area. This may be the mainstay of many housebuilding companies, yet it is clearly not the only factor which housebuilders are concerned with.

Although the expectation is that all housebuilders undertake some sort of survey, it is still arguable whether or not the data can be used practically by local authorities to monitor housing markets. Firstly there is the question of actually obtaining the data from the housebuilding industry in a form that can be utilised. Housebuilding is highly competitive and information that may prove useful to a competitor is closely guarded. In addition there may be a problem of integrity of data. If the housebuilders perceive statistics would present a case which would be beneficial to their own strategy they may prove enthusiastic and helpful. Yet if the data demonstrated low demand then this information could well be withheld.

Housebuilders, market researchers and land buyers appear to have no long-term objectives, taking one site at a time and being primarily concerned with sales on a particular site (Orchard, 1992, p.11). There is a possibility that they will therefore tailor market research towards the requirements of each individual site, on an ad-hoc basis. Guillou (1990) suggests that, within market areas builders assess development potential on a site specific basis. This may appear to be a wasteful exercise which involves frequent reiteration of efforts. However, it could be suggested that builders strategies will result in a 'chain' of development in a given area. Therefore, almost by default, a large builder may have a number of sites, or potential sites, at any one time, resulting in an ongoing appraisal of demand and an understanding of a local housing market. Ball suggests that most large housebuilding firms carry out highly detailed market research of local housing markets, to identify gaps in current supply (Ball, 1983), whilst examining the market to identify areas where profits will be highest and competition will be low. What becomes clear from both this and other discussions is that it is no simple matter to classify 'housebuilders' (Ball, 1983; Gillen, 1994). In terms of using housebuilders as a data source, it is therefore important for the local authority to be aware of the type of company from which they are gathering information.

Site identification does not necessarily result in development. Effective demand might not be strong enough, nor of the right 'type' to interest a particular developer. Yet the majority of developers remain committed to broad site identification (i.e. area rather than specific sites), followed by demand appraisal before committing themselves to more specific site identification. Some of the major builders do take a more strategic view and have commissioned academics working in the demographic field to highlight areas that have demographic potential. This may be an indication of housebuilder concern regarding the extent of future markets. One could argue that during the early 1980s, demography, general economic circumstances, availability of housing finance and planning controls created a situation where the housing market boomed and housebuilders could build almost anywhere and make a profit from the product. With many of these factors either disappearing or becoming weaker in the 1990s, a more considered appraisal and identification of sites on the part of housebuilders would have been be required. In the first decade of the $21^{st}$ century the situation has become more complicated with some of the factors of the 1980s operating alongside some of the 1990s.

One significant difference between housebuilder indicators and those mentioned previously is that housebuilders not only record and monitor data, they actually change policies and strategies, in the short term, in the light of what this data shows. For instance, if sales rates are low for eight weeks, the developer will re-appraise the marketing strategy and promote the site more aggressively. As a result the subsequent sales figures may increase significantly. If sales rate were to be used as an indicator this change could be interpreted as an increase in demand. Alternatively, if sales are proceeding beyond expectations, the housebuilder may re-appraise the situation and decide the properties are being offered at too low a price. If prices are raised the final units on this site might take longer to sell and may suggest demand has slackened, whereas in effect it has remained the same and the market conditions have changed. This monitoring and altering of the sales conditions highlights the major drawback with all the housebuilder-based indicators, which have essentially been developed to examine the ongoing success of any development, or group of developments.

In discussion with housebuilders, it transpires that there exists a sales expectation which reflects the seasons. The general expectation is that twice as many homes would be sold during the summer months than in the autumn and winter. On the face of it, this would seem to be legitimate, given the fact that during the spring and summer the day light hours are longer and there is more opportunity for would-be home buyers to view properties, whilst during the Christmas and New Year period households tend to be otherwise engaged. Whilst this may be the case in the new housing market, an examination of all property transactions presents a different perspective.

*Indicators of Housing Demand* 139

Figure 5.8 Quarter on Quarter Percent Change in Property Transactions

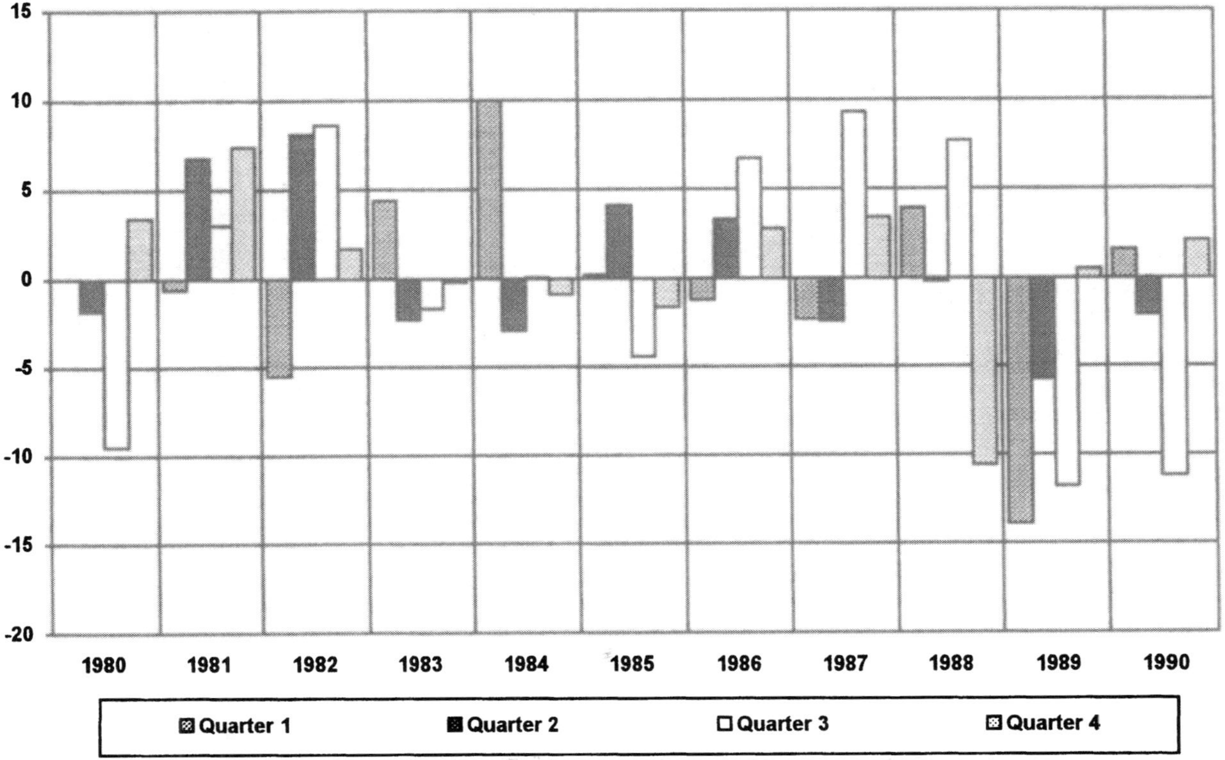

Source: CML/BSA, Housing Finance, 1995, Table 19

Figure 5.8 presents the quarter-on-quarter change in property transactions for the 1980s. If the views of housebuilders are to be supported, one would expect more positive changes in property transaction in the summer months than the winter. However it would appear from this figure that quarters two and three experienced more falls in the number of property transactions than quarters one and four. In essence the winter quarters have more buoyant housing markets than those of the summer.

The data that underlines property transactions is based upon the 'particulars delivered' processed by the Valuation Office and the Land Registry, and it has been argued that a time lag of between one and two months exists from actual transaction completion to the data being processed (CML/BSA, 1996). However, the 'particulars delivered' upon which transaction data is based, may in fact lag behind the housing market to a far greater degree than anticipated. If it were to lag the market by 2-3 months, then the quarterly changes would fit with the expectations of housing professionals.

As can be seen from the preceding discussion there is a case for monitoring the housebuilding industry. One would suggest that this could be gained from building links with private housebuilding companies, the kind of links that could be seen to develop from the co-ordination of policy and implementation that has been discussed in earlier chapters. Apart from this general approach to greater co-ordination between the local authority and housebuilders, there is a need to examine the type of market monitoring information that may be provided by housebuilding companies.

The subsequent discussion will examine the data that may be expected to be collated by housebuilding companies for their own marketing information and may therefore already exist in a form useful for housing strategy formulators.

*Sales to Reservation Ratio* This indicator utilises the number of reservations which proceed to completion, as opposed to those which are simply reservations and fail to materialise in the form of firm sales. The expectation is that a fairly low ratio could be construed as reflecting high demand, whilst a high ratio would suggest that demand is weak. Clearly the different 'tactics' of the housebuilders will have a profound affect upon the series. If the builder has a strong commitment to reducing cancellations (Bateman, 1993) through tackling the after-sales 'remorse' period, then the expectation is that they will have a smaller cancellation rate and a stronger sales-to-reservation ratio. Arguably, a low ratio would be expected as reservations require a down-payment. This could ordinarily mean that a high percentage of reservations actually develop into fully completed transactions. Yet discussion with housebuilders and an examination of sales literature indicates that some reservation deposits were as low as £20. Relative to the price of a house, £20 is not a major penalty to incur if the housebuyer decides to cancel.

*Sales Times and Sales Rates* The time for units to sell, or the number of units sold in a given period, are two suggested indicators. Sales times, although not extensively used by the housebuilding industry, could be employed in a number of ways. Two possibilities are the length of time between the commencement of marketing the site and sale, or the time between approval and sale. Discussions with housebuilders have shown that sales rates are widely used, both for monitoring their own developments and for determining which house type should be placed on particular sites. There are essentially two ways that sales rates are calculated and both techniques have a similarity, in that the figure is presented as a weekly average. The overall sales rate is the weekly average rate since selling commenced, whilst the alternative establishes an eight week rolling average sales rate. If the length of time taken to sell a unit is comparatively short, and there is a high sales rate, then the implication is that there is a high demand. Similarly, if the development is proving to be unattractive, then sales times would increase and sales rates would fall. These indicators would suffer from the same problems of fluctuating housebuilder strategies, accounting for higher (or lower) than expected sales rates. As a result, there is a degree of uncertainty regarding how much of the improved sales time is due to demand changes and how much is due to marketing.

*Visitor Based Statistics* New home developments are usually laid out in a way that allows the on-site sales team to keep a track of all the visitors that call at the site. Therefore the sales staff have an indication of the number of visits, whilst additional data is gathered from individuals who visit show homes or ask questions of the sales team. There are a number of ways the data can be analysed. For instance, the number of visitors that it takes to generate a sale is one that can be used. Similarly the proportion of visits that result in a reservation. These will give an indication of the attractiveness of the product on sale and will be used by the housebuilder in conjunction with other indicators to alter marketing policy. Perhaps the least attractive method of estimating demand is to simply investigate the visitor numbers, which would probably be more useful as a measure of the success of advertising in the area. Whilst it appears to be plausible that a low ratio of visits to sales or reservations illustrates a high demand all the qualifications that have already been raised in this discussion of housebuilders will have to be borne in mind.

*The Proportion of Houses Sold Prior to Completion* If demand in a given area is high, the expectation is that houses would sell prior to their completion. Clearly, this is a modified form of sale time indicator and at best this indicator will only present a reflection of higher demand. Coopers and Lybrand were of the opinion that this was the indicator which was the most independent of housebuilder's strategy and marketing (Coopers and Lybrand, 1987, para. 2.31). They also highlighted, as with all the indicators, a problem with definition. As already stressed (see above) the definition of when a property is complete is liable to significant interpretation (Ball, 1983; Gillen, 1994b). Arguably this is not insurmountable, and the possible adoption, for monitoring purposes, of a 'standard time' when a dwelling is recognised as complete (for instance, when it becomes liable to council tax) may overcome this problem.

Perhaps the most significant problem with such a definition is that it may indicate very little. The NHBC in their publication *Private Housebuilding Statistics* produce a table that sets out the time to build. This indicates that the median time for construction appears to be around eight months (for both traditional and timber frame construction methods). Yet it is possible to build a house in under eight weeks, and if the NHBC figures are the median, some housebuilders must be constructing homes in short periods of time. Two to three months is similar to the time it takes to complete the legal formalities associated with house purchase, which may allow a situation where a house can be 'built to order'.

A move towards 'just-in-time' construction has been highlighted as a feature of past building strategies (Ball, 1983, p.105). It might be suggested that short build times may result in almost all homes being sold prior to completion, allowing housebuilders to build to demand. If this is purely due to current economic circumstances, then the indicator may become useful in the future. However short construction times and a move towards increased sales prior to completion may be an indication of future trends within the structure of the housebuilding industry. This would place housebuilding in the same role as an office furniture or motorcycle dealership, where customers order the product and have to wait a number of weeks for the factory to deliver.

'Superhomes', a concept that was introduced by Laing in the mid-1980s, took 'just-in-time' construction to its extreme. Containerising all the

## Indicators of Housing Demand 143

materials necessary for one house ready for shipment to the site, allowed output in excess of 3,000 units per annum. However, it was discontinued in 1989, suggesting that the company may have over-purchased materials and found that the holding costs were prohibitive, during a down turn in the housing market. Some of those involved in the 'superhomes' concept have suggested that one of the reasons for its failure was a lack of technology to support accurate stock control, distribution and ordering (Hooper and Nicol, 2000).

Of all the possible housebuilder indicators Coopers and Lybrand suggested sales prior to completion as a robust indicator (Coopers and Lybrand, 1987, para. 2.32). The problem with builders' strategies skewing indicators has been discussed above. Guillou (1990) highlighted the manner in which this indicator remained prone to mis-interpretation due to alterations in strategy. For instance, if the number of completed dwellings declines due to housebuilders strategy, a 'ripple effect' may be created. The overall demand may remain the same, yet would-be house buyers perceive that the supply has been constrained, therefore competition results in a higher proportion of sales prior to the dwelling being completed.

> In such a situation the proportion of advance sales could rise even if demand remained unchanged. Indeed, the proportion could still rise if demand were to fall, provided that the fall was more gradual than had originally been envisaged. (Guillou, 1990, p. 146)

Guillou contends that some housebuilders could pursue an aggressive pre-completion marketing strategy. If this type of company were to increase its market share, it may result in the figures regarding pre-completion sales increasing. If other things were to remain equal, this could well result in the indicator suggesting a higher demand than may actually exist. This line of argument would not appear to be very convincing, as aggressive marketing is common throughout the housebuilding industry. Site publicity runs virtually in tandem with development on all sites, reaching its zenith once the first show home is complete. Publicity and marketing will remain at this level although the majority of the development may not be complete.

In practice, there appears to have been little done to try and develop these potential indicators as individual data sets. Perhaps this is due to the secretive nature of the housebuilding companies who may perceive such information as commercially sensitive (see Chapter Seven). Steps have been taken by Hampshire to compile all of these indicators into an aggregate format (Hampshire County Council Planning Department, 1988 and 1990). In this case a questionnaire sent to 54 different firms asked their opinion on the strength of current demand in terms of property types and in terms of housing market areas. The housebuilders were also asked for their perceptions of future housing demand, again by house type and area, and their impression on land supply in an effort to form a complete picture of housebuilders' perceptions.

Housebuilder data would not appear to be reliable for use in market monitoring. This is not to say that housebuilders should not be involved in the process in some way (see below), but the data they monitor would not appear to be particularly useful for the local authority. This appears to be the view expressed by the local authorities themselves (see Chapter Six).

*House Prices and Land Prices*

Economic theory suggests that if demand is high and supply is constrained, the good which is being demanded will rise in price. The monitoring of house and land prices would therefore seem to provide a useful indication of demand. These indicators received strong support from Coopers and Lybrand, who recommended house price data as being particularly useful in this regard. Initially, one would have to stress that there are a number of different sources that can be utilised to gain information on house and land prices. If this is added to the problems that are endemic within each source of data, it becomes clear that there exists greater uncertainty in this data than the Coopers and Lybrand studies appear to suggest.

As discussed in earlier chapters, housing markets are difficult to identify, due partly to their fluidity and partly to substitution effects of neighbouring housing markets, different housing types and different housing tenures. However differences in house prices are related to geography, as a result, if similar properties in different areas are achieving different prices then this can be used as an indication of possible market areas. House prices would not only allow an indication of the spatial delineation of house type markets, through the differences in house prices between similar house type areas, an estimation of the buoyancy of different areas could be made. It would appear that house prices could support market identification as well as monitoring changes in demand.

*House Prices* There are essentially two methods by which house price data can be collected. The first and perhaps the easiest method is to utilise the data sets prepared by either the Halifax or Nationwide Building Society or to examine the house price statistics compiled by the DoE/DETR. These sources are based on transactions, which have been funded by the lending institution concerned (in the case of the Halifax and Nationwide) or the sample financial institutions for the DoE/DETR surveys (Pannell and Champion, 1992). The second alternative is to carry out a perception-based study. This can range from the regular Inland Revenue publications (Valuation Office Agency, 1992) through the monitoring of property professionals' opinions, to investigations of property papers themselves (Foulkes and Woodhead, 1986).

Houses are perhaps one of the most unusual goods currently purchased in the UK, placed in such a position by their uniqueness and cost. Looking at the cost implications first, Nicol (1994) demonstrates that the vast majority of would-be homeowners have to obtain funding from lending institutions to be able to afford property. However the number of transactions that have proceeded without any formal funding is significant and as a result a number of property prices will not be recorded in any mortgage based house price dataset. If these concealed transactions are similar across all housing types, than there may not be a significant area of concern. However, it would be more realistic to expect that the houses which are not reflected are of certain types e.g. retirement type properties bought without a mortgage by households selling large properties, in later life, to replace them with smaller, cheaper properties; or very expensive and large properties purchased by wealthy individuals. Alternatively there may be an under-representation of inner-city properties, through 'red-lining' policies or the non-borrower ethos endemic in some cultures. If this is the case, then it is questionable the degree to which house price data-sets based on actual transactions can accurately reflect all housing markets.

The group of householders who commit themselves to a mortgage to be able to afford to buy a home find themselves connected to world-wide economic trends. In the 1990s the macro-economic policies of the government resulted in a distinct interaction between macro-economic policy and the micro-economics of individual housing markets, through the manipulation of interest rates. This changed slightly when the Bank of England became responsible for setting rates, there is an argument that the connection still exists though less formerly than in the past. Such connections have created a situation where house price movements may have as much to do with changes in the supply of housing finance as changes in local demand.

The second idiosyncratic feature of housing is that no house is exactly the same as any other. Even new-build houses are essentially unique,

146 *The Formulation of Local Housing Strategies*

occupying different geographical locations and finished to different specifications. As time progresses, this uniqueness becomes more distinct, as different owners customise houses, through decoration and modification. The result of this is that it is extremely difficult to determine an all-encompassing 'average house price'. The chances of any housing mix traded in one period being the same as that traded in subsequent periods is small. A simple time series is not comparing 'like-with-like', and this has only been attempted on one occasion (Evans, 1978). Even in 'like-with-like' comparisons a problem of comparability remains. Improvements may have been undertaken in the property in question between the two sample periods. As a result some of the properties' price increases may be due to improvements in the structure or decor of the building, rather than house price inflation.

**Table 5.6 Comparison of House Price Series Characteristics**

| Data characteristics | DoE 5% Sample | Halifax Series | Nationwide Series |
|---|---|---|---|
| Mortgage approval or completion stage data used? | Completion | Approval | Approval |
| Coverage National UK | Yes | Yes | Yes |
| Regional | Yes | Yes | Yes |
| Quarterly transactions (approx. 1993) | 6,000-7,000 | 30,000-36,000 | 10,000-12,000 |
| Lowest workable disaggregation level | County or metropolitan district | Postcode | Postcode |
| **House Price Categorisation?** | | | |
| Type of house | Yes | Yes | Yes |
| Age of house | Yes | Yes | Yes |
| Purchaser type | Yes | Yes | Yes |
| **Data Publication Frequency?** | | | |
| monthly | No | Yes | Yes |
| quarterly | Yes | Yes | Yes |

The Halifax, Nationwide and DETR series all produce indices of house prices. The use of indexing techniques is an attempt to introduce a degree of consistency in the mix of houses traded in any one period. As can be seen in Table 5.6, the Halifax has the largest data set of the three and has a reasonably robust index. The DETR only presents a 5% sample, but this reflects both bank and building society lending. However, the index is not equipped with the statistical techniques necessary to fully overcome differences in the housing mix. Although the Nationwide has a smaller dataset than the Halifax it has the most sophisticated and robust techniques for reducing sample variations (Nicol, 1994; 1996). The indices prepared by the lenders and the DETR tend to be presented in an aggregated format, and detailed breakdown of house types, as exists in the 'raw data', is limited. Within a given region, the indices are presented in terms of property age (new or second hand) and type of buyer (existing owner occupier or first-time buyer). This technique is useful for monitoring house price trends for specific categories, for instance new properties, first time buyer properties or properties which have been formerly owner occupied. The Nationwide index is believed to reflect 85-90% of characteristics which influence house prices (Fleming and Nellis, 1993). Therefore a comparison of the indices almost certainly reflects changes in house price and not house mix, between the various groups. If house price changes are to be taken as an indicator of demand, the index will be the best means of determining within which group that demand lies.

The Nationwide is often accused of being a building society orientated towards one area of the country, and due to its smaller transaction base not truly reflecting the properties traded in anyone period. It is almost impossible to gain a detailed insight into the geographical distribution of mortgages as the society view this data as confidential, yet an estimate can be made. Figure 5.9 compares the Nationwide and Halifax regional branch base with that of the population in general. As mortgages could be provided by the estate agencies of the lenders (Nationwide Estate Agents and Halifax Property Services) or by independent brokers, Figure 5.9 may only give an indication of possible mortgage distribution and therefore transaction base of the two societies. If the branch distribution illustrated in Figure 5.9 is an accurate reflection of the institutions lending patterns, then the following can be surmised. Clearly, the Nationwide data is limited in regions within which it does not have a strong presence, yet it is better represented in other areas of the country, e.g. London, the South East, East Midlands and East Anglia.

As can be seen in Table 5.6 the Halifax and Nationwide data-sets can be disaggregated to a post-code level. As a result, if this data is used it

148 *The Formulation of Local Housing Strategies*

**Figure 5.9 Branch Distribution of the Nationwide and Halifax Compared to the Regional Distribution of the Population**

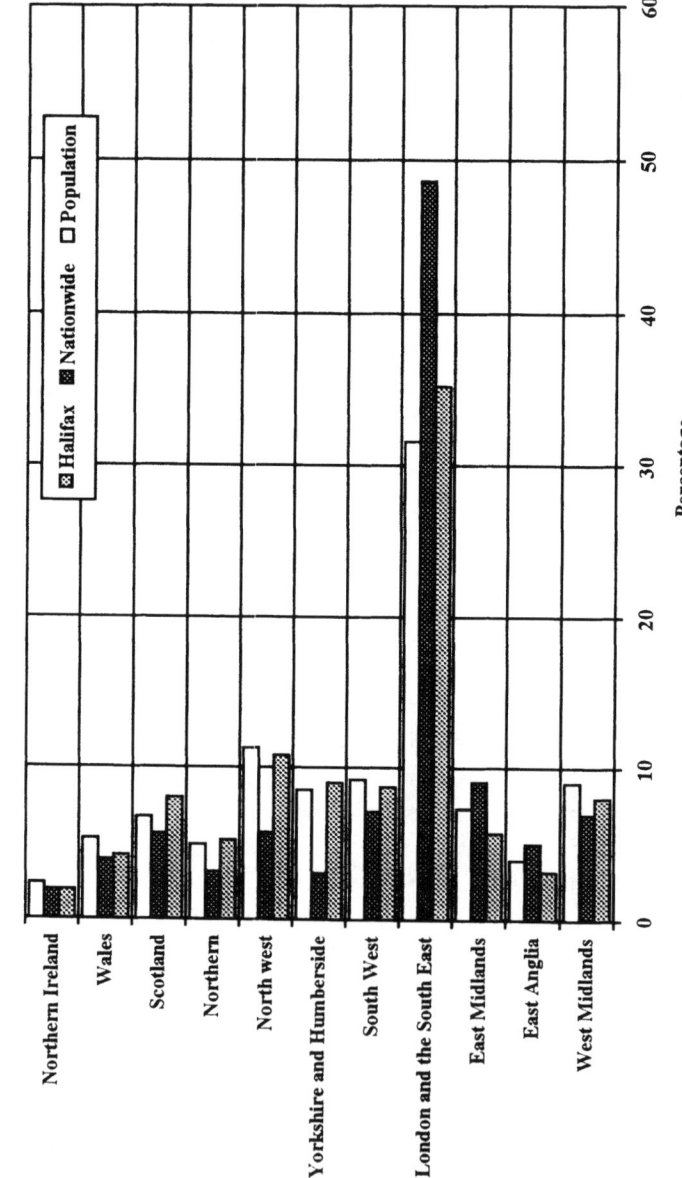

**Source:** Population, Church, 1993; Branch networks, authors analysis

could be constructed so as to accurately indicate housing market areas. However, one major problem with this source of data is that the sample size for any particular housing market area may be too small to allow accurate trends to be monitored. The DETR data should also be capable of disaggregation to a similar level. However, a number of the transactions recorded do not include enough data to allow the government compilers to record them in terms of housing market areas. As the DETR sample is much smaller than that of the two lenders, if it were to be disaggregated further than a county level the sample size would become unreliable. For instance the data for Nottinghamshire in the last quarter of 1994, was based upon a sample of 119 transactions.

One problem with transaction data is that to be recorded, the housebuyer has to purchase a home with a mortgage, as highlighted above this may create a situation where certain types or location of homes are under represented. Perception-based data is not limited by actual transactions, and can be adapted to reflect housing markets with greater ease. As well as being able to accurately reflect market areas, it can be developed in such a way as to uncover future market expectations. However its major limitation is that it is extremely reliant on both the professional expertise and the goodwill of the individuals who are providing the information. For this type of data there is a significant overlap with surveys of estate agents which have been carried out by a number of planning authorities (Wiltshire, 1981) and is investigated below. Examination of newspaper advertisements as a means of monitoring house prices has been undertaken by some councils (Hertfordshire County Council, 1988). Dorset County Council (Foulkes and Woodhead, 1986) monitored newspaper advertisements for a number of years, supplementing this data with both estate agent surveys and the regional data from the Nationwide Building Society. Overall, Dorset C.C. found that there was a degree of comparability between the data sets statistics, suggesting that they reflect actual house prices accurately and sale prices can indicate what the market is willing to pay. However one would suggest that this may not be the case in a depressed housing market, when would-be homeowners would expect to pay less than the asking price. It would appear that a 'portfolio' of the different sources of house price data creates the most robust, yet flexible, house price monitor.

Coopers and Lybrand examined house prices in conjunction with estate agent indicators, reaching the conclusion that data on house prices, from the large chains of estate agents in particular, would be forthcoming. The large estate agency chains have in the past, often been tied to lending

150  *The Formulation of Local Housing Strategies*

institutions, for instance Black Horse Agencies (Lloyds Bank), Cornerstone Estate Agents (Abbey National), Halifax Property Services and Nationwide Estate Agents. Although Cornerstones is no longer part of the Abbey National, most of the other connections still exist. Clearly, collecting information from the local branch of the Halifax estate agency business would supplement the nationally produced series and, along with informal house price monitoring (of property papers), can form a clear indication of house price trends in any housing market area.

However there is more to the utilisation of an indicator than simply obtaining a data source. It is crucial to identify what the data is showing and how it can be analysed to benefit the wider objectives. Guillou has examined the adoption of traditional economic theory to house price movements, and the effect on house prices as a result of changes in supply and demand. The conclusion reached was that;

> ...a rise in price may be associated with an increase in demand, without a rise in the number of transactions, or with no change in demand and a fall in the number of transactions. (Guillou, 1990, p. 119)

The supply of homes is therefore crucial and, as the housing market is dominated by second hand homes, it is the aspirations and intentions of existing homeowners which can affect house price movements as much as new supply. The monitoring of house prices could therefore have ambiguous interpretations. The elasticity of the various ratios further complicates the situation. Elasticity is determined by a number of factors ranging from the availability of substitutes to the possibility of new purchasers entering the market. Elasticity of demand is the rate at which demand expands against the rate at which price falls. Using price changes as an indicator of demand, it is necessary to understand what the elasticity of housing demand will be prior to contemplating its implication. The commonly held perception of the housing market is that it is characterised by an inelastic supply, which limits the amount of land available, as well as the time taken for it to become available (Lavender, 1990). If this is the case, then house price changes will be a reflection of a constrained supply, relative to actual demand. Even this assertion does not explain all the possible causes for house price changes;

> High house prices could either indicate that there are large numbers of relatively well paid households seeking housing and able to pay the high prices, or that the local housing market is relatively constrained and that

*Indicators of Housing Demand* 151

**Figure 5.10 Comparison of House Prices in the Case Study Areas**

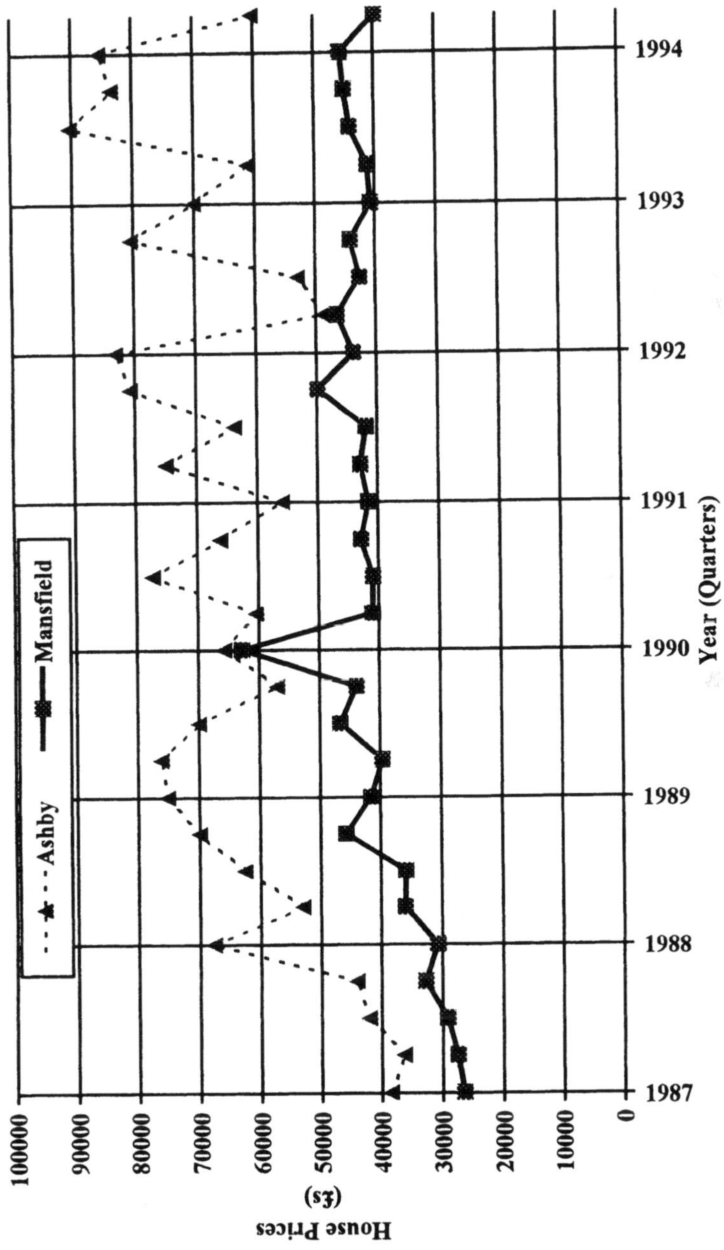

Source: Halifax Data

> there is something of an under-supply of housing, which could arise from a lack of available land for new development. Alternatively, there could be changes in the market for which developers are building, or from some combination of all these factors. (Barlow, 1990, p. 19)

As can be seen in Figure 5.10, Ashby has higher house prices than Mansfield, suggesting, if the indicator is accurate, that the market is constrained and demand outstrips supply. However, the Ashby series also indicates the problem with house price data as an indicator, at the local level. Clearly the time series is erratic, increasing one quarter only to fall dramatically the next. This inconsistency is not so apparent in Mansfield, where a far more consistent trend can be seen. This may indicate differences in the sample upon which these series are based. For instance, a small sample can be unduly affected by either a very expensive or very inexpensive property being included in the sample. The number of transactions funded by the Halifax is commercially sensitive and the company would not wish this to be made public. However, from the data supplied to the author by the company it is clear that Mansfield can have around five times as many Halifax-funded transactions as Ashby.

Coopers and Lybrand concluded that the rate of house price change would be the best way of utilising house price data.

> A higher than average rate of increase in prices is thus usually a direct indicator of unsatisfied effective demand. (Coopers and Lybrand, 1987, para. 2.12)

To develop this successfully, a time series would be required, because simply comparing the house prices in one area with those of another would only illustrate the fragmented and geographical nature of the housing market. To demonstrate changes in demand in one area, it is necessary to create a time series illustrating price changes. From this an allowance will have to be made to remove any price changes that may be due to either simple inflation or a change in national housing policy, for instance lending criteria.

To construct such an indicator, house price series for similar types of property in similar market areas will have to be compared. The choice of comparative areas is therefore extremely important. If the market areas being compared are similar in every respect, apart from demand, then the expectation is that house prices will increase faster in the higher demand area. However a number of policy options by both local authorities and builders could result in house prices retaining parity between the areas therefore concealing demand.

Similarly, if the areas adjoin each other and one area has a generally higher-priced housing stock than the other, then demand which culminates in transactions may be found to transfer to the cheaper area. If supply remained the same in this area, then house prices could rise faster in this area than in the more expensive area. Clearly this would be seen to indicate a higher effective demand, which is in effect latent demand.

*Land Prices* Land prices could also be employed as an indicator of housing demand. Coopers and Lybrand suggested three possible ways in which land price data could be developed. Two are open to questions as to their usefulness, whilst the third would appear to be more practical.

They suggest land price level; land costs as a percentage of final house selling price; and rate of increase of land prices as useful indicators. Arguably, land price level is a purely static measure which would prove to be of no use when indicating demand. Similarly, land value as a percentage of house price would at best only show that certain areas have high land prices relative to house prices, and make no attempt to explain the situation in terms of both planning controls, desirability of one certain site, or strategy of the builder. The final indicator suggested, is the rate of land value increase. Clearly this can be presented as a time series and on first glance would appear to be useful. The Coopers and Lybrand study believed that this would be the best indicator, but they themselves recognised severe limitations with this type of data.

The major doubt surrounds the collection and comparability of land price data. Land can be purchased in a number of ways by developers, ranging from outright to option purchase. These different purchase methods may mean that land prices are not comparable. Further incompatibility is a result of the fact that land is a heterogeneous commodity, where it is almost impossible to compare the raw price data of land traded in one period with that traded in another.

Coopers and Lybrand believed that actually obtaining data, ignoring the incompatibility problems for a moment, would be almost impossible. Land price data is information that most housebuilders would feel unwilling to divulge. The result would be that any sample of land prices would only be a reflection of land bought at auction. They suggested that this would result in a sample that is both too small and perhaps unrepresentative of all land traded. The conclusion they reached was that land prices would be extremely

154  *The Formulation of Local Housing Strategies*

difficult to both monitor and compare. In addition, they suggested that this work might also reciprocate indicators suggested by house prices, especially new house prices. This is because residual valuation methods means that builders land bids are constructed around new house prices. Keogh (1989) highlights that land price data is extremely limited, and all officially published data is based upon Inland Revenue 'particulars delivered'.

It would appear that land prices are problematic and they were not suggested as an indicator by Coopers and Lybrand. Keogh (1989) suggested that on the basis of information published at that time it would be difficult to construct a clear interpretation of land market activity. Whilst recognising these limitations, there would appear to be a place for the use of land prices, whilst in the longer term compiling an improved index. Land prices movements would be expected to be a lead indicator of estimates of demand. Land price rises would therefore indicate a builders expectation of changes in demand. To be able to use this information as a pre-indicator of demand, a robust data set is needed. To achieve this, examination would have to change from actual transactions to perceptions. Arguably, the Valuation Office Agency (VOA) data is the best for this as it marries perceptions with actual land transactions obtained from 'particulars' delivered. In addition, the officers employed by the VOA present new data in a format which makes some allowances for incompatibility in the data (VOA, 1995).

*Estate Agent Data* The discussion regarding house prices highlighted the use of estate agents perceptions of the market, as a way of supplementing formal transaction based house price series. Coopers and Lybrand proposed to develop estate agent monitoring beyond this, to reflect estate agent 'business'. Estate agency is the means of collating disparate and geographically separated goods into one convenient location, that is then accessed by would-be home buyers. In addition, some estate agents are also property managers for residential lettings. Clearly, estate agents may therefore be able to give an indication of the demand for owner occupied and privately rented housing.

Would-be homebuyers investigate certain properties, after setting themselves both economic and geographical parameters (Maclennan, Munro and Wood, 1987). It is when this moves from informal 'window shopping' and collection of property particulars to something more substantial that estate agent data will become tangible. Would-be homeowners who actually confirm with the estate agents what properties they are looking for and record interest in certain properties may create a data base of applicants that can be used as a market indicator. It has been suggested that:

> ...in principle this represents a powerful indicator, relating directly to the intentions of prospective house buyers. (Guillou, 1990, p. 140)

Again, this indicator would be prone to seasonal fluctuations, and it is perhaps its role in comparing the demand for housing markets that is important, rather than its use as a time series.

The first indicator suggested by Coopers and Lybrand concerned the ratio of applicants to instructions to sell the higher the ratio, the greater the demand. The second suggested indicator concerned the ratio of applicants to the number of sales.

The major dilemma with these indicators is the trustworthiness of the appropriate data. It was accepted, when the indicators were proposed, that there may be some difficulties with 'double-counting' applicants who express an interest in homes in more than one area and of more than one type. Although it was envisaged that:

> ...the numbers would not represent the level of demand, but the relative numbers for different house types and locations would suggest relative demand pressure. (Coopers and Lybrand, 1987, para. 2.35)

Applicants who either cannot buy the house, or are not genuinely interested in purchasing, also distort the picture of demand presented by the estate agents.

The third indicator suggested by Coopers and Lybrand is based on appointments to view per sale. This appears to be a development of the other two indicators, yet it will still be prone to some inflation through double counting and the inclusion of non-genuine viewings. This indicator would largely be affected by the property mix on an estate agent's books. For instance, if the estate agent has an unusual property, it may attract, as Guillou calls them, 'sporting' viewers, who have no intention of purchasing the property. This will boost the appointment to view figures, beyond a level that is founded on simple demand.

Once again, there is the problem of issues affecting the demand indicators which are not directly associated with demand. Guillou (1990, p.141) highlights the problem of a positive increase in the indicator caused by a reduction in supply rather than an increase in demand. In the housing market, which is so reliant on housing chains, the estate agency indicators may therefore represent excess demand in certain links of the chain. The housing supply may be there, yet due to facts such as the economy or negative equity, households may not be willing to move to free the chain. The demand will then be met as far as possible by new builders who view estate agents as:

> ...the prime source of information about the second hand housing market. (Orchard, 1992, p. 20)

The net effect may be that the housing market will encounter 'blockages' which will be overcome through tangential 'pipes'. When these blockages clear, there will be a situation of 'tandem' housing supply in certain locations. Although the new housing market is unlikely to have a major effect on 'flooding' the market nationally, it may result in a localised oversupply. The result of this is that latent demand from neighbouring areas could become redirected.

Even with these reservations, estate agents have a role to play in developing housing market indicators, both in terms of improving house price series and estimating consumer demand. Coopers and Lybrand's suggestion of an indicator which highlights the relative levels of demand has been developed by Guillou (1990, p.141), highlighting a cross-sectional spatial approach, rather than a time series. Evidently, this comparison of areas, rather than one area over time, is appropriate for the determination of market areas. Taking this further, Guillou believes markets could be compared, forming a snapshot of demand, and this could be developed as a spatial ratio. He suggests that this could be employed to allow household allocations to be distributed in line with house type and location preferences. Evidently, the would-be householders' interest, as reflected by estate agents, would therefore partly determine the district housing allocations. For an integrated strategy, this may have, as he points out, limitations, in that it only reflects owner occupiers preferences. Arguably this is not a major problem, as housing allocations in plans, are largely utilised by development for owner occupation at the present time.

Coopers and Lybrand perceive that monitoring estate agent data may be a means of determining migration. The migration indicator they proposed would appear to be a rather grand title for what is essentially a measure of interest in certain types of house. As an indication of where demand is coming from, either the market area concerned, the district, the region or elsewhere, this will only be reliable as far as applicant numbers reflect actual demand. Applicants from outside the housing market area may be more reliable than those from within, because they will have had to travel to view properties. This effect may differentiate them from 'sporting' applicants. The data compiled by estate agents, although problematic in one respect and appears to have been embodied with greater attributes by Coopers and Lybrand than actually exists, is still useful and should be collated.

The crucial question is: how co-operative will estate agents be? The large chains, such as Halifax, Nationwide and Black Horse may see their involvement as adding prestige, similar to the compilers of house price statistics (Nicol, 1994). Coopers and Lybrand perceived co-operation from a number of the national chains (para. 2.40). They believed that, as many of them are now public companies, there may be little problem of confidentiality. This is a questionable argument, as the expectation is that transaction and applicant data would not be in the public realm, simply through being a public company. Wiltshire, the county with one of the longest histories of monitoring housing market demand, has had significantly differing results from their surveys of estate agents. Questionnaire surveys have been sent to local estate agents annually since 1981, although 1987 was only a limited house price survey. The response rate was high in 1981 (73%) but has fallen back so that the 1992 survey received only a 36% response rate. This may in part be due to the fact that the sample size has increased, by almost 300% since 1981. The result of this is that the estate agents who are willing to help were the only ones asked in 1981, whereas the wider survey may include estate agents who were excluded initially because they were not in a position to be supportive to the survey. The responses have been used to develop increasingly sophisticated indicators of markets, in terms of supply/demand, land and house prices, and in terms of geography. This spatial element has been developed into a breakdown of the county's housing market areas. In addition, it has been adapted to graphically show which regions and towns exert migrant pressure into the delineated market areas (Wiltshire County Council, 1993, Figure 24).

Similar work has been carried out and utilised by other counties (Hampshire County Council, 1990). It is apparent that estate agents are, to an extent, willing to help formulate policies concerning housing demand. Informal discussions with eight estate agents in Mansfield did indicate that there would be a positive response to a request by the local authority for estate agents to contribute to housing market monitoring.

The use of this source is not one that can be discounted and it is, despite its limitations, a useful means of determining the type of housing

158  *The Formulation of Local Housing Strategies*

demanded and the spatial orientation of those demanding it. It is also one of the few means of evaluating the private rented sectors demand and supply.

**Conclusion**

This chapter has attempted to examine a number of different *possible* housing market indicators that could be employed within the development of integrated housing strategies. Although it has examined the positive aspects, as well as the limitations of each data set, this discussion has not conducted any statistical analysis with regard to the reliability of the data sets. This is an important area and is perhaps one that future research could examine. It also focused on the situation in the mid 1990s, when the field work for the study was carried out.

Table 5.7 summarises some of the main findings of this discussion. It examines each indicator individually, giving a rating from a to e in terms of three categories; availability of the data; degree to which it may indicate factors other than housing demand; degree to which it can be manipulated. The ratings have been given purely as a result of this chapter's discussion and do not reflect any of the views of districts either in the East Midlands or elsewhere that have employed such data (an area discussed in the next chapter).

This table is simply a means of summarising the discussion in this chapter, and it is not intended to be viewed as a 'stand-alone' justification for any data set. Clearly the local authority's own data scores highly mainly due to the fact that it can be compiled by the officers concerned and can reflect particular market areas. The data that would have to be provided by outside agencies is not so highly ranked due in part to the availability (i.e. relies on the goodwill of housebuilders or estate agents) and secondly it could be seen to be easily manipulated. One would suggest that the weakest column is perhaps that which concerns the degree to which the indicators reflect demand. This is the area that requires more robust possibly statistically based analysis.

Data availability scores highly if it is easily available to a local authority and can be disaggregated to a district or housing market level. Low scores are obtained if the data is only available at the assistance of a third party. Degree to which the data indicates housing demand is based upon the discussion that has highlighted that some data sets may be just as likely to illustrate operations other than housing market demand. If this is the case then the data will be given a low score. The degree to which the data can be manipulated is based upon a premise that certain sets of data may (for one reason or another) be prone to corruption. If the

Table 5.7 Summary of Indicators Discussed in this Chapter (a=best e=worst)

| Indicator | Availability | Indicates Demand | Manipulation |
|---|---|---|---|
| Employment change | b | c | a |
| Income | c | b | a |
| Affordability | c | d | c |
| Housing Department Waiting List | a | e | c |
| Vacancy Rates | c | d | b |
| Planning Applications | a | b | c |
| Planning Appeals | a | c | c |
| Enquiry Levels | a | d | e |
| Small Sites | a | d | c |
| Density of Developments | a | d | c |
| Amendment of Planning Applications | a | d | c |
| Starts and Completions | a | b | c |
| Sales to Reservation | c | d | d |
| Sales Rates | d | e | d |
| Visitor Based Statistics | d | e | e |
| Prior to Completion Sales | d | c | d |
| House Prices | c | c | c |
| Land Prices | d | d | d |
| Estate Agent Data | d | c | d |

data can be easily manipulated to show something other than actual demand it will be given a low score.

The indicators discussed in this chapter are by no means exhaustive, and there is no reason why local authorities should not employ other techniques when forming and monitoring the effectiveness of housing strategies. What this chapter has achieved is to highlight the fact that each of the indicators has limitations, but if these are understood and, in some instances overcome, a number of these data sets may be useful for a local authority as tools for housing market monitoring. What must be stressed is that to be successful in developing a housing strategy, the local authority must monitor as many data sets as possible. A widespread 'portfolio' of housing market information should be seen as the best means of monitoring changes in the housing market.

It should be noted at this point, however, that different actors and agencies may be concerned with different time horizons in relation to their objectives and strategies. For instance housebuilding companies may be described as viewing the housing market in the short term and seen to examine marketing based indicators which illustrate short term changes. Alternatively land release policies are based on long term policies developed as a result of large scale forecasting methods. Again this different emphasis indicates the need to develop a portfolio of monitoring methods. In this case such a portfolio is necessary to ensure small scale frequent fluctuations in housing preference can be seen whilst larger scale changes that will take longer to develop are not ignored.

Although this chapter has been broadly based on practical work carried out by Coopers and Lybrand, the question still remains, what methods of monitoring are practically used by the local authorities. This question is the central theme of the next chapter which will highlight the use of these data sets by county councils; metropolitan authorities and district councils.

# 6 The Use of Data by Local Authorities in England and Wales

## Introduction

The previous chapter examined both the positive and negative attributes that many of the possible indicators possess. This review did not, however, consider the extent to which local authorities monitored housing markets, and the extent to which they found certain types of data both useful and easily accessible. This chapter will focus upon this area by considering the results of a major empirical survey, undertaken in order to identify which monitoring methods local authorities use.

Prior to presenting the result of this research it is necessary to examine the methodology behind the survey and indicate which authorities received a questionnaire. In devising the questionnaire, it was appropriate to assess the manner in which each tier of local government monitored the housing market. Therefore, questionnaires were sent to all counties, all metropolitan authorities outside London and all the district/borough councils in the case study region (the East Midlands).

The work undertaken prior to conducting the survey (see earlier chapters), suggested that although the links between policy makers (local authorities) and policy implementers (housebuilding companies) are vitally important, there may have been a perception by public authorities that housebuilding companies may be unhelpful. In terms of specific housing market data, there was a doubt regarding the degree to which the housebuilding companies may provide the type of information discussed in the previous chapter. It was necessary, therefore, to briefly ascertain the degree to which housebuilding companies would provide the type of

162  *The Formulation of Local Housing Strategies*

information that may prove useful, and this was achieved through another questionnaire survey. This short, purely supplementary, questionnaire is also examined in this chapter. As with Chapter Five, a table will be presented in the conclusion, summarising the majority of the questionnaire results.

**Questionnaire Methodology**

For the purposes of comparability, the questionnaires were almost identical. The specific data sets that were the focus of questions in the survey were largely based on Coopers and Lybrands work. It was perceived that these may be the data sets that have been monitored, due to the fact that this work called for such monitoring in the 1980s. The questions on data sets were supplemented by a number of other questions, many of which have already been discussed in this research. Other questions were asked that have not been used for this research, but have been used elsewhere (for instance questions on housing figures and statutory plan periods). Although the questionnaires were essentially identical the response rates differed, as did the time-table and scale of the surveys. There follows an examination of the methodology of each questionnaire in turn.

*County Council Questionnaires*

County planning officers have a pivotal role in determining strategic future housing allocations, through the structure plan, with which all districts have to comply. Although not a housing authority, it was felt that county councils may be responsible for significant research as they determine the level of future housing provision, and it may therefore be appropriate to determine the manner by which housing markets are monitored. This was undertaken through a questionnaire survey of all 47 County Councils in England and Wales, in the summer of 1994, with the initial questionnaire being sent out in May and a reminder being sent to those that had not responded, in July. This 'two-wave' method resulted in a very good response rate. By December 1995, 43 counties had returned the questionnaire (a response rate of 91%).

*Metropolitan Authority Questionnaires*

An examination of the situation in metropolitan authorities is worthwhile, as this type of governmental structure is in a unique position, combining both the strategic aims underlying structure plans with the detailed site specific features of a local plan. The view the authorities take may be of use, as the Local Government Commission's recommendations have, since the survey was carried out, resulted in an increase in the number of new unitary authorities. In addition, it was envisaged that, as metropolitan authorities are also housing authorities, it may provide useful details as to the way local authority departments can integrate the relevant activities of housing and planning departments to provide a housing strategy.

This survey was sent to all the metropolitan authorities outside Greater London, 36 authorities in total. The first questionnaire was again sent out in May 1994, with a reminder sent out in July. The response rate was high, as 25 of the 36 sent were returned, but by comparison to the very high rate of returns of the county councils, this was disappointing, just below 70%.

*East Midlands District Councils*

The initial intention was to view this element of the survey as the most important, as it was intended to provide detailed information to be used in the determination of the case studies as well as details of the situation that exists at the district level. This may have meant that the case studies would have only examined the situation in proactive authorities, as they would have been likely to provide the most comprehensive responses. A more robust approach would be to use other methods of identification, such as different levels of economic growth, house price change, demographic movement, etc. As the districts are housing authorities, it was envisaged that there may well be an insight into the integration of housing and planning functions in the formulation of housing strategies, similar to the metropolitan authorities. The questionnaire was sent to all 39 local Councils in the East Midlands and the response rate was 51% (20 returned), the lowest of all the Council surveys. Although this may result in the analysis made from the returns being less robust than the others, it was felt that reminders and further questionnaires may only reciprocate work that would be carried out in the detailed examination of the more local case study areas. There was also a worry that

164  *The Formulation of Local Housing Strategies*

if the survey was too aggressively pursued, it might cause ill feeling amongst the officers interviewed latter in this study.

*Housebuilder Survey*

A short questionnaire was submitted to 100 housebuilders operating in Britain. The selection criteria was firmly biased towards housebuilders working in and around the East Midlands, with 51 being sent to either the East Midlands regional offices of national housebuilders or to housebuilding companies which only operate in this region. To allow some comparison with the industry at a national level, 49 questionnaires were sent to housebuilders operating in other regions. The questionnaire was sent to housebuilding companies of varying sizes, from volume housebuilders to small locally-based building companies. This provides a reflection of the industry and its attitude to providing data to planning authorities. As at December 1995, the response rate, at 53%, had been surprisingly good, considering the competitive (and therefore possibly secretive) nature of the industry.

**The Survey Results**

One section of the planning authority questionnaire attempted to identify the source of the most commonly used household estimates and projection data. What was surprising was the degree to which central government data was not entirely relied upon. In the case of the counties, there were 15 responses acknowledging the use of DoE household data, 9 the use of data provided by the OPCS (although it should be noted that the OPCS do not provide household projections) and 32 the use of other forecasts or data. Of course, the authorities stating that they utilised the DoE/OPCS data may use it for background data in their own forecasting methods, rather than simply taking the projections at face value. Concerning the 32 authorities using their own forecasts, the majority of these are prepared in-house using population models, which reflect local characteristics other than head-ship rates and migration assumptions. A significant number of counties reported using the model developed by Anglia Polytechnic University (The Chelmer Model). The Chelmer Model uses the Registrar Generals' population estimates as the starting point, then projects the population, deriving household and dwelling projections from the population projections.

A supplementary question asked if these counties use their own economic development policies as an indicator of possible market demand changes (see Table 6.43). In answer to this question, 49% stated that they did use their own policies, whilst 32% answered no (the remainder did not answer the question). It would appear, therefore, that a high number of County Councils were using sophisticated methods for household projections and population analysis, many of which take into account the economic performance of the area and future growth potential.

In the case of metropolitan authorities, there is a similar situation as regards the use of forecasting models. Of the 25 authorities responding, four used all three sources of data, seven used just two, whilst the remainder used one in isolation. In terms of popularity, the DoE data was utilised by 25%, the OPCS statistics by 42.5% and the remaining 32.5% used other data sources. One interesting finding is that many of the authorities co-operate and prepare forecasts as if the Metropolitan county still exists. For instance, the Tyne and Wear authorities have an overall research arm, the Tyne and Wear Research and Intelligence Unit. A similar situation exists in Greater Manchester, where the information unit of the old Greater Manchester Council, has been funded by the ten Metropolitan Districts, to carry out strategic research for the city as a whole. It would appear that some cities still retain some cohesion as regards their overall strategy, undermining, at least in this respect, the criticism that the introduction of unitary authorities has resulted in a breakdown of co-ordination.

**Table 6.1 Number of Counties Defining a Housing Market Area Based Upon**

| District Council Area | 13 |
|---|---|
| Housebuilder Survey | 2 |
| Estate Agent Survey | 4 |
| Own Perception | 14 |

As discussed in earlier chapters, difficulties arise in trying to define a market area. All 43 counties considered this question, and 58.1% did take account of market areas in determining the geography of their housing allocations. As can be seen in Table 6.1, relatively few counties

166  *The Formulation of Local Housing Strategies*

had taken into account any definition other than their own perception of a market area or the straightforward definition based on district council areas. However as argued in Chapter Three, housing markets are fluid and are rarely, if ever, delineated in terms of government administrative boundaries.

A number of Councils used a mixture of the above methods, whilst others felt that different methods proved more reliable, for instance travel-to-work areas (in the case of Somerset), or socio-economic links with the county town (in the case of North Yorkshire). Market areas were used infrequently by the metropolitan authorities, with only 32% distinguishing between the housing allocation in terms of housing markets. This may partly be due to the fact that metropolitan areas are usually smaller, have dense development patterns and perhaps more importantly, minimal choice for land release.

The differentiation of housing market areas by East Midlands districts was even weaker. Only 11% of those responding to the questionnaire differentiated and identified housing markets within the area. This is perhaps the most disappointing of the responses, as it clearly indicates that the districts, i.e. the authorities responsible for identifying sites, payed little attention to housing markets. On a positive note, it could be argued that the officers have a knowledge of their area which allows them to identify markets by 'hunch'. This informal market identification may result in a positive outcome, but it clearly is not a robust or transparent method of market identification.

**Table 6.2  Make Up of Housing Liaison Groups**

|  | Counties | Metro-Authorities | E. Midland Districts |
|---|---|---|---|
| District Council Officers | 16 | 13 | 11 |
| County Council Officers | 14 | - | 6 |
| Community Reps. | 3 | 1 | 5 |
| Housing Associations | 10 | 8 | 7 |
| Estate Agents | 4 | 4 | 3 |
| Housebuilders | 12 | 10 | 6 |
| District Councillors | 2 | 1 | 3 |
| County Councillors | 1 | - | 1 |

This leads on to the need to examine the extent to which authorities consult with other agencies in determining housing allocations, allowing other agencies concerned with housing to have an input into policy formulation. In the case of the county councils, only 32% currently have a Housing Liaison Group (HLG) whilst a further 16% have had such an organisation in the past. This relatively low positive response rate may be in part due to slightly problematic wording in the question, which may have defined the type of group too narrowly. This may have led to some counties considering that their multi-party housing forum was not applicable, as it was not called a 'Housing Liaison Group'. Table 6.2 highlights the make-up of HLGs that existed in the counties, metropolitan authorities and districts. Clearly, some counties consulted broadly, regarding the housing situation, and the number of views that are expressed can only be beneficial in obtaining a better understanding of the needs and demands of the area. On average, between 3-4 different agencies were consulted by those authorities active in housing discussion groups.

Metropolitan authorities have had a slightly more proactive role in developing links with agencies, with just over 50% of those responding indicating that they had liaison groups or similar bodies. As these are unitary authorities, there is no county tier which would have to be included. Perhaps most surprising is that there is not a stronger involvement with housing associations, given that the metropolitan authorities also have a housing function. This may seem to suggest the integration between housing and planning departments is not widespread, an assertion countered by Table 6.3.

**Table 6.3  Authorities with Integrated Housing Strategies**

|  | Yes | | No | | No Answer | |
| --- | --- | --- | --- | --- | --- | --- |
|  | % | Nos. | % | Nos. | % | Nos. |
| Metro Authorities | 80.0 | 20 | 12.0 | 3 | 8.0 | 2 |
| E.Midland Districts | 65.0 | 13 | 35.0 | 7 | - | 0 |

In the case of district councils in the East Midlands, only 10 respondents stated that a Housing Liaison Group currently existed, whilst one authority answered that such a group had existed in the past. Of the 11

168 *The Formulation of Local Housing Strategies*

that had experience with Housing Liaison Groups, the agencies listed in Table 6.2 had been involved. As with the metropolitan authorities, there is an expectation that the housing function will result in considerable housing association involvement. In this case, it is more widespread at 63%.

Two questions were asked towards the end of the questionnaires sent to the housing authorities. These questions examined the way departmentalism is tackled within the districts and the metropolitan authorities, and the degree to which housing strategies and policies are integrated. When asked if integrated housing strategies are prepared the following answers were given (actual numbers are presented as well as the percentage figures).

The level of integration and corporatism is encouraging, but there is still a significant proportion, particularly in the East Midlands, which adopt a separatist, disjointed approach. A supplementary question sought to determine which department takes the lead role in the preparation of this strategy. In the case of the metropolitan authorities, nineteen of the twenty which had answered the question indicated that it was the housing department, the remaining authority stated both departments played an equal role. In the case of the East Midlands, fifteen authorities answered, eight confirming that the housing department took the lead role, two the planning department and five indicating that both departments were sharing the lead role equally.

Examining the detailed use of market indicators, the questionnaires disaggregated indicators into five distinct categories, similar to those discussed in the earlier chapter, and determined primarily by the source of the information:

- Internally generated statistics and data collated by government departments.
- Estate agent statistics, including house and land prices.
- Housebuilder statistics.
- Survey use.
- Economic indicators.

*Internally-Generated Data*

There is an expectation that this data would be the most commonly used, as much of it is already in the possession of either the local authority or a body

**Table 6.4 Waiting Lists - Employment and Usefulness**

| | Used in the Past | | | | Used Presently | | | | Useful | | | |
|---|---|---|---|---|---|---|---|---|---|---|---|---|
| | Yes | | No | | Yes | | No | | Yes | | No | |
| | % | Nos. | % | Nos. | % | Nos. | % | Nos. | % | Nos. | % | Nos. |
| Counties | 48.8 | 21 | 39.5 | 17 | 30.2 | 13 | 58.1 | 25 | 25.6 | 11 | 44.2 | 19 |
| Metro-Authorities | 72.0 | 18 | 16.0 | 4 | 68.0 | 17 | 20.0 | 5 | 56.0 | 14 | 8.0 | 2 |
| E. Midland Districts | 65.0 | 13 | 25.0 | 5 | 65.0 | 13 | 25.0 | 5 | 45.0 | 9 | 15.0 | 3 |

**Table 6.5 Waiting Lists - Ease of Use (Absolute figure is given in brackets)**

| | Difficult % | Straightforward but Time-consuming % | Easy % |
|---|---|---|---|
| Counties | 2.3 (1) | 32.6 (14) | 41.9 (18) |
| Metro-Authorities | - | 40.0 (10) | 32.0 (8) |
| E. Midland Districts | 15.0 (3) | 30.0 (6) | 25.0 (5) |

170  *The Formulation of Local Housing Strategies*

**Table 6.6  Housing Association Waiting Lists - Employment and Usefulness**

|  | Used in the Past | | | | Used Presently | | | | Useful | | | |
| --- | --- | --- | --- | --- | --- | --- | --- | --- | --- | --- | --- | --- |
|  | Yes | | No | | Yes | | No | | Yes | | No | |
|  | % | Nos. | % | Nos. | % | Nos. | % | Nos. | % | Nos. | % | Nos. |
| Metro-Authorities | 40.0 | 10 | 44.0 | 11 | 40.0 | 10 | 48.0 | 12 | 52.0 | 13 | 8.0 | 2 |
| E. Midland Districts | 25.0 | 5 | 50.0 | 10 | 30.0 | 6 | 50.0 | 10 | 55.0 | 11 | 10.0 | 2 |

**Table 6.7  Housing Association Waiting Lists - Ease of Use (Absolute figure is given in brackets)**

|  | V. Difficult | Difficult | Straightforward but Time-consuming | Easy |
| --- | --- | --- | --- | --- |
| Metro-Authorities | 8.0 (2) | 20.0 (5) | 32.0 (8) | 8.0 (2) |
| E. Midland Districts | - | 30.0 (6) | 15.0 (3) | 15.0 (3) |

with strong links to the local authority. To be a useful monitoring tool, it must be possible to develop the data into a time-series as this will illustrate trends and, if the data is reliable, be interpreted to show changes in housing preference and market demand.

In the case of the question concerning the possible use of the Local Housing Authority waiting list as an indicator, Table 6.4 highlights the percentage (and absolute number) of county councils, metropolitan authorities and East Midlands districts which have used, or currently use, this data. It should be stressed that the questionnaires to the metropolitan and East Midland authorities specifically identified this question as an indicator of social housing need and, therefore, this question was far more specific than that directed at the county councils.

Metropolitan and district authorities may utilise housing waiting lists to a greater extent because these councils are also housing authorities. As a result, it is of more practical use for these authorities, as they have responsibility for the direct provision of housing. Perhaps the most significant reason is due to the fact that the data is readily available, from within the authority. The authorities that do use this data seem to find it a useful indicator. However, this argument does not seem to be totally supported by the evidence gathered from the questionnaires. Table 6.5 shows that it is county councils which seem to think the data is easy to collect, whilst districts in the East Midlands appear to believe it could be difficult.

Waiting lists may be useful and used widely, but, as an indicator of need, let alone demand, they are problematic. The problems with waiting lists have been discussed in earlier chapters and elsewhere (Clark, 1990). Notwithstanding these criticisms, waiting lists can still form part of a portfolio of housing *need* indicators. This may be why the housing authorities (metropolitan authorities and the East Midland districts) find this data more useful than county councils, as they are responsible for some forms of direct housing provision and therefore use the data in a practical way, when allocating the housing stock.

A further question concerned the use of housing association waiting lists. A problem with this data is that, as some housing associations expressly house only certain categories of people (the elderly, the disabled, etc.), they may only be useful as an indicator of housing need for certain groups. Table 6.6, highlights the use of housing association waiting lists. Clearly, there is a different attitude towards this data in the shire districts than in metropolitan authorities. The districts would appear to be of the

172 *The Formulation of Local Housing Strategies*

opinion that housing association waiting lists would provide a useful indicator, but only around one-third of districts who responded to this said they undertook collection of this data. The Metropolitan authorities used this data more frequently, but there were less positive replies to the indicators usefulness.

Table 6.7 shows the percentage of respondents who had opinions regarding the ease of use of housing association waiting list statistics. Again, it is the Metropolitan authorities, which seem to present a negative picture of this data, with only 8% considering it as an easy data source to monitor and collect whilst 8% suggested it was very difficult.

In keeping with an examination of social indicators, the metropolitan authority and district council questionnaires examined two additional areas. The first question concerned the prevalence and usefulness of housing needs surveys as a means of demonstrating housing needs. From Table 6.8 it is clear that only a relatively small percentage of authorities have used these in the past, and, in the case of the metropolitan authorities, a little under one third are actually currently embarking upon such a study.

As regards the proportion which found housing needs surveys a useful tool in determining the housing situation of the district, 76% of metropolitan authorities (19 actual respondents) believed they were useful, more than the 60% of East Midland districts (12 respondents) which found them to be useful. It is, perhaps, surprising that such a high proportion consider housing needs surveys to be useful, as relatively few authorities undertake such studies. This situation is particularly noticeable in the case of the metropolitan authorities, and could perhaps be partly due to the different circumstances in operation in these authorities. As a result of Annex A of Planning Policy Guidance Note 3, (DoE, 1992a), authorities with 'rural' areas have been able to implement 'exception' policies. This allows these authorities to release land in exceptional circumstances, when a specific local housing need has been demonstrated to exist, and one widely accepted way of doing this is through a housing needs survey. There is also a significant difference in the perceived difficulties involved in carrying out a survey, as can be seen in Table 6.9. Clearly, housing needs surveys are not easy to conduct, but, if the responses of the East Midlands authorities are any indication, they are not as difficult as some (the metropolitan authorities) perhaps believe.

**Table 6.8 Housing Needs Surveys - Employment**

| | Used in the Past | | | | Used Presently | | | |
|---|---|---|---|---|---|---|---|---|
| | Yes | | No | | Yes | | No | |
| | % | Nos. | % | Nos. | % | Nos. | % | Nos. |
| Metro-Authorities | 32.0 | 8 | 60.0 | 15 | 32.0 | 8 | 56.0 | 14 |
| E.Midland Districts | 30.0 | 6 | 55.0 | 11 | 45.0 | 9 | 45.0 | 9 |

**Table 6.9 Housing Needs Surveys - Ease of Use (Absolute figure is given in brackets)**

| | Very Difficult | Difficult | Straightforward but Time-consuming | Easy |
|---|---|---|---|---|
| Metro Authorities | 36.0 (9) | 28.0 (7) | 20.0 (5) | - |
| E.Midland Districts | 10.0 (2) | 30.0 (6) | 30.0 (6) | 5.0 (1) |

## 174  *The Formulation of Local Housing Strategies*

Since the survey was carried out housing need surveys have increased in popularity and status and improved in procedure and they are supported through planning guidance and circulars (DETR, 1998, 2000). Bramley, Pawson and Parker (2000) have prepared a guide to practically preparing housing needs policies, and although useful this does indicate that housing strategies continue to be departmentalised documents (this is an issue that will be returned to in the conclusion).

The next indicator that was examined in all three council questionnaires was the use of vacancy rates, commonly derived from census data, with the result that it is at its most reliable when the census is recent. The census breaks the data down into enumeration districts a definition that can contain as few as 200 households. As these are localised they may be combined (if necessary) to form housing markets. The data gives details on:

- Households with residents.
- Vacant accommodation.
- Accommodation not used as a main residence.

It also reflects the manner in which these figures are compiled in terms of house type, and other variables. Vacancy Rate use is highlighted in Table 6.10.

As can be seen in the table, East Midland districts and metropolitan authorities have used vacancy rates to a limited degree, whereas county councils appear to have used these statistics considerably. The authorities are of the opinion that this data is one of the least useful of the indicators, probably due to the fact that the census only gives a 'snapshot' of the housing situation at one time. The useful indicators are those which show changes over time, allowing the market monitoring process to demonstrate if the demand is increasing (in this case, represented by decreasing vacancy rates) or if demand is falling (increasing vacancy rates). Clearly a survey which is only decenial is problematic in this respect, despite the fact that the data can be 'tailored' to specific housing markets.

In the late 1990s there was an increased focus on urban capacity and efforts were made to achieve better use of the existing built stock (DETR, 2000). As a result vacancy focused studies have become more prevalent and one would argue that that in urban areas vacancy rates should have become more reliable as a result of greater empirical research.

Table 6.10  Vacancy Rates - Employment and Usefulness (%)

| | Used in the Past | | | | Present Use | | | | Useful | | | |
|---|---|---|---|---|---|---|---|---|---|---|---|---|
| | Yes | | No | | Yes | | No | | Yes | | No | |
| | % | Nos. | % | Nos. | % | Nos. | % | Nos. | % | Nos. | % | Nos. |
| Counties | 65.2 | 28 | 20.9 | 9 | 58.1 | 25 | 27.9 | 12 | 32.0 | 14 | 23.2 | 10 |
| Metro-Authorities | 36.0 | 9 | 52.0 | 14 | 36.0 | 9 | 56.0 | 14 | 24.0 | 6 | 44.0 | 11 |
| E. Midland Districts | 30.0 | 6 | 45.0 | 9 | 20.0 | 4 | 55.0 | 11 | 30.0 | 6 | 35.0 | 7 |

Table 6.11  Vacancy Rates - Ease of Use (Absolute figure is given in brackets)

| | Very Difficult | Difficult | Straight forward but Time-consuming | Easy |
|---|---|---|---|---|
| Counties | 6.9 (3) | 13.9 (6) | 18.6 (8) | 20.9 (9) |
| Metro-Authorities | 12.0 (3) | 32.0 (8) | 24.0 (6) | 12.0 (3) |
| E.Midland Districts | 20.0 (4) | 35.0 (7) | 20.0 (4) | - |

176  *The Formulation of Local Housing Strategies*

**Table 6.12  New Dwelling Starts - Employment and Usefulness (%)**

|  | Used in the Past | | | | Present Use | | | | Useful | | | |
|---|---|---|---|---|---|---|---|---|---|---|---|---|
|  | Yes | | No | | Yes | | No | | Yes | | No | |
|  | % | Nos. | % | Nos. | % | Nos. | % | Nos. | % | Nos. | % | Nos. |
| Counties | 67.4 | 29 | 27.9 | 12 | 62.8 | 27 | 34.8 | 15 | 48.8 | 21 | 11.6 | 5 |
| Metro-Authorities | 64.0 | 16 | 24.0 | 6 | 68.0 | 17 | 24.0 | 6 | 52.0 | 13 | 16.0 | 4 |
| E. Midland Districts | 70.0 | 14 | 20.0 | 4 | 70.0 | 14 | 20.0 | 4 | 50.0 | 10 | 5.0 | 1 |

**Table 6.13  New Dwelling Starts - Ease of Use (Absolute figure is given in brackets)**

|  | Very Difficult | Difficult | Straight forward but Time-consuming | Easy |
|---|---|---|---|---|
| Counties | 4.7 (2) | 4.7 (2) | 44.2 (19) | 23.3 (10) |
| Metro-Authorities |  |  | 20.0 (5) | 44.0 (11) |
| E. Midland Districts |  |  | 45.0 (9) | 25.0 (5) |

## The Use of Data by Local Authorities in England and Wales 177

Table 6.11 highlights that the perceptions regarding the ease with which vacancy rates can be collected, and broadly reflect the use of this indicator. Some of the authorities mentioned using similar, but alternative methods for monitoring household vacancies, such as household/dwelling ratios. If these associated indicators were included, this would result in the actual number of authorities who monitor this area being greater than shown in the table.

Another indicator, new dwelling starts, was seen to be one of the most popular of the indicators (Table 6.12) and a very high percentage of counties, metropolitan authorities and districts have used, and continue to use, new dwelling starts. It should be noted that a number of the respondents who answered negatively to using housing starts, did indicate that they used housing completions (Gillen et al., 1995). Completions would suggest the use of a similar type of indicator (see the previous chapter). As expected from such a popular indicator the percentage finding it useful is high and this degree of popularity may have something to do with the relative ease with which the data can be collected. Table 6.13 highlights the percentage of authorities that found the data very difficult; difficult; straightforward; or easy, to use.

Clearly, districts as represented by the East Midlands and metropolitan authorities, are strong advocates of housing start data, finding the data both useful and relatively straightforward to employ.

The most commonly-used indicator employed by planning authorities is the actual number of planning applications (Table 6.14). In theory, the greater the number of applications, the higher the level of demand. This data is already collected by the Department of Environment, Transport and the Regions on PS1/ PS2 forms (DoE, 1993e) and therefore the authorities already prepare the information.

The districts provide the counties with the information before it is passed on to the DETR and therefore the data is fed through all tiers of the planning system. What is perhaps surprising is the fact that, although the data is widely collected, it is not seen as being particularly useful (this is especially noticeable in the case of East Midland districts). Although one county stated:

> Analysis of planning permissions/allocations and completion rates is central to strategic housing work.

178    *The Formulation of Local Housing Strategies*

**Table 6.14  Planning Applications - Employment and Usefulness**

|  | Used in the Past | | | | Present Use | | | | Useful | | | |
| --- | --- | --- | --- | --- | --- | --- | --- | --- | --- | --- | --- | --- |
|  | Yes | | No | | Yes | | No | | Yes | | No | |
|  | % | Nos. | % | Nos. | % | Nos. | % | Nos. | % | Nos. | % | Nos. |
| Counties | 65.1 | 28 | 27.9 | 12 | 62.8 | 27 | 30.2 | 13 | 48.8 | 21 | 11.6 | 5 |
| Metro-Authorities | 64.0 | 16 | 24.0 | 6 | 60.0 | 15 | 36.0 | 9 | 52.0 | 13 | 20.0 | 5 |
| E. Midland Districts | 75.0 | 15 | 20.0 | 4 | 75.0 | 15 | 20.0 | 4 | 35.0 | 7 | 20.0 | 4 |

**Table 6.15  Planning Applications - Ease of Use (Absolute figure is given in brackets)**

|  | Difficult | Straightforward but Time-consuming | Easy |
| --- | --- | --- | --- |
| Counties | 4.7 (2) | 51.2 (22) | 20.9 (9) |
| Metro-Authorities | 4.0 (1) | 48.0 (12) | 32.0 (8) |
| E. Midland Districts | - | 40.0 (8) | 35.0 (7) |

The Use of Data by Local Authorities in England and Wales 179

Table 6.16 Planning Appeals - Employment and Usefulness

|  | Used in the Past | | | | Present Use | | | | Useful | | | |
|---|---|---|---|---|---|---|---|---|---|---|---|---|
|  | Yes | | No | | Yes | | No | | Yes | | No | |
|  | % | Nos. | % | Nos. | % | Nos. | % | Nos. | % | Nos. | % | Nos. |
| Counties | 44.2 | 19 | 44.2 | 19 | 34.9 | 15 | 53.5 | 23 | 27.9 | 12 | 41.9 | 18 |
| Metro-Authorities | 20.0 | 5 | 68.0 | 17 | 20.0 | 5 | 72.0 | 18 | 24.0 | 6 | 60.0 | 15 |
| E. Midland Districts | 30.0 | 6 | 45.0 | 9 | 30.0 | 6 | 45.0 | 9 | 10.0 | 2 | 45.0 | 9 |

Table 6.17 Planning Appeals - Ease of Use (Absolute figure is given in brackets)

|  | Difficult | Straightforward but Time-consuming | Easy |
|---|---|---|---|
| Counties | 6.9 (3) | 46.5 (20) | 20.9 (9) |
| Metro-Authorities | 12.0 (3) | 28.0 (7) | 40.0 (10) |
| E. Midland Districts | 5.0 (1) | 40.0 (8) | 20.0 (4) |

Planning applications would appear to be an example of how, once systems are in operation, the periodic task of examining and updating the data is not difficult, and Table 6.15 shows that the majority of respondents see it as a straightforward operation, and very few see it as a difficult series to collate.

If planning applications are monitored, then there is also the possibility of monitoring a number of other indicators, either for monitoring on there own, or for how the different data sets relate to planning applications. Planning appeals are one example of this kind of indicator. It is envisaged that planning appeals may provide an indication of changes in demand; the greater the percentage of refused planning applications resulting in appeals, the greater the demand (see Chapter Five). To use this indicator effectively, residential planning applications will have to be monitored along with the number of refusals. This data can then be combined with the number of appeals lodged. Table 6.16 highlights which authorities currently monitor, or have monitored, planning appeals. This table also highlights the usefulness of the indicator.

Clearly, with the exception of county councils, there is little utilisation of planning appeals as an indicator. This could in part be due to the fact that appeals may have as much to do with the appellants' perceptions of success as demand (see Chapter Five). Table 6.17 illustrates that it is not a perception of difficulty that precludes appeal data being used. Therefore the assumption must be that, as an indicator of housing demand, the number of appeals may be open to misinterpretation.

Another possible indicator developed from statistics that the local authority itself collects is the amendment of planning applications. The assumption is planning application amendments will highlight the way in which developers perceive the market is changing. For example, altering a site for ten family homes to eight bungalows may reflect a change in the market. As can be seen in Table 6.18, few authorities seem to use the data and there is a view that it would not be particularly useful. One or two authorities had ceased to collect this data because during the period in question applications were at a low ebb. This is short sighted, as to successfully employ such data as a market monitor, a complete time series would be necessary.

The planning application itself can contain even more data that may be of use, for instance the density of housing applications (Bramley et al., 1995). If this is to be successfully employed, it should show an increase in

The Use of Data by Local Authorities in England and Wales  181

Table 6.18  Amendment of Planning Applications - Employment and Usefulness

| | Used in the Past | | | | Present Use | | | | Useful | | | |
|---|---|---|---|---|---|---|---|---|---|---|---|---|
| | Yes | | No | | Yes | | No | | Yes | | No | |
| | % | Nos. | % | Nos. | % | Nos. | % | Nos. | % | Nos. | % | Nos. |
| Counties | 13.9 | 6 | 72.1 | 31 | 13.9 | 6 | 72.1 | 31 | 18.6 | 8 | 55.8 | 24 |
| Metro-Authorities | 16.0 | 4 | 76.0 | 19 | 16.0 | 4 | 80.0 | 20 | 28.0 | 7 | 52.0 | 13 |
| E. Midland Districts | 35.0 | 7 | 50.0 | 10 | 35.0 | 7 | 50.0 | 10 | 15.0 | 3 | 40.0 | 8 |

Table 6.19  Density of Applications - Employment and Usefulness

| | Used in the Past | | | | Used Presently | | | | Useful | | | |
|---|---|---|---|---|---|---|---|---|---|---|---|---|
| | Yes | | No | | Yes | | No | | Yes | | No | |
| | % | Nos. | % | Nos. | % | Nos. | % | Nos. | % | Nos. | % | Nos. |
| Counties | 20.9 | 9 | 69.8 | 30 | 9.3 | 4 | 81.4 | 35 | 18.6 | 8 | 55.8 | 24 |
| Metro-Authorities | 28.0 | 7 | 64.0 | 16 | 24.0 | 6 | 72.0 | 18 | 36.0 | 9 | 48.0 | 12 |
| E.Midland Districts | 25.0 | 5 | 55.0 | 11 | 20.0 | 4 | 60.0 | 12 | 35.0 | 7 | 40.0 | 8 |

Table 6.20  Density of Applications - Ease of Use (Absolute figure is given in brackets)

| | Very Difficult | Difficult | Straightforward but Time-consuming | Easy |
|---|---|---|---|---|
| Counties | 16.3 (7) | 25.6 (11) | 34.9 (15) | 4.7 (2) |
| Metro-Authorities | - | 16.0 (4) | 44.0 (11) | 24.0 (6) |
| E.Midland Districts | - | 25.0 (5) | 35.0 (7) | 10.0 (2) |

**Table 6.21 Depletion Rates for Allocated Sites - Employment and Usefulness**

|  | Used in the Past | | | | Used Presently | | | | Useful | | | |
| --- | --- | --- | --- | --- | --- | --- | --- | --- | --- | --- | --- | --- |
|  | Yes | | No | | Yes | | No | | Yes | | No | |
|  | % | Nos. | % | Nos. | % | Nos. | % | Nos. | % | Nos. | % | Nos. |
| Counties | 34.8 | 15 | 55.8 | 24 | 34.8 | 15 | 55.8 | 24 | 34.8 | 15 | 30.2 | 13 |
| Metro-Authorities | 28.0 | 7 | 56.0 | 14 | 32.0 | 8 | 56.0 | 14 | 48.0 | 12 | 24.0 | 6 |
| E. Midland Districts | 25.0 | 5 | 45.0 | 9 | 25.0 | 5 | 45.0 | 9 | 30.0 | 6 | 35.0 | 7 |

**Table 6.22 Depletion Rates for Allocated Sites - Ease of Use** (Absolute figure is given in brackets)

|  | Very Difficult | Difficult | Straightforward but Time-consuming | Easy |
| --- | --- | --- | --- | --- |
| Counties | 4.7 (2) | 16.3 (7) | 46.5 (20) | 11.6 (5) |
| Metro-Authorities | - | 8.0 (2) | 44.0 (11) | 24.0 (6) |
| E. Midland Districts | - | 15.0 (3) | 35.0 (7) | 15.0 (3) |

## The Use of Data by Local Authorities in England and Wales 183

housing densities as demand increases, yet there may be significant problems with this data. For example, as all sites are different, the topography may affect the density, or the fact that the house types will rarely be comparable within the one housing market. With this in mind it is perhaps surprising that although low, there is a positive response to the use of the indicator (Table 6.19).

One reason for this level of usage may be the fact that it is not a particularly difficult data source to monitor. This may, in part, be due to increased use of computer-based application filing systems, although this is speculation, as no question was asked concerning the filing systems used. One authority did indicate that a computerised monitoring system was being set up and it would improve accuracy and efficiency, although it did highlight the fact that significant staff resources are required to 'feed the system' (response on one of the questionnaires).

Table 6.20 indicates that the authorities which use this indicator most and find it most useful also find it the most straightforward. However, the counties with a low level of use appear to view it as a difficult data source to monitor.

A further question ascertained whether or not authorities monitored the depletion rates of allocated sites. It may be expected that this would be carried out by a number of the authorities, as it may prove beneficial in monitoring the five year land supply. As can be seen in Table 6.21, this data has not been used widely, with only metropolitan authorities suggesting significant use. Table 6.22 illustrates that the low level of use may be due to data being problematic to collect. In comparison with some of the other indicators however (see below), the majority of responses appear to have found it either easy or straightforward.

The final indicator that was examined, and could possibly be developed from the local authorities own records, concerns planning permission 'take-up' (the time between approval and the commencement of construction). The methodology for this indicator is that the shorter the time scale, the greater the demand (see Chapter Five). Table 6.23 shows the degree to which the various authorities use the indicator.

The authorities which use this data frequently appear to have the least positive view as to how useful it is, whilst other authorities, although not using it frequently, would seem to suggest the indicator is useful. Again this low level of use is probably a result of perceived difficulties with collecting this information.

**Table 6.23 Planning Permission 'Take-Up' - Employment and Usefulness**

| | Used in the Past | | | | Used Presently | | | | Useful | | | |
|---|---|---|---|---|---|---|---|---|---|---|---|---|
| | Yes | | No | | Yes | | No | | Yes | | No | |
| | % | Nos. | % | Nos. | % | Nos. | % | Nos. | % | Nos. | % | Nos. |
| Counties | 25.6 | 11 | 65.1 | 28 | 18.6 | 8 | 72.1 | 31 | 44.2 | 19 | 27.9 | 12 |
| Metro-Authorities | 20.0 | 4 | 72.0 | 18 | 16.0 | 4 | 80.0 | 20 | 48.0 | 12 | 40.0 | 10 |
| E. Midland Districts | 30.0 | 6 | 55.5 | 11 | 30.0 | 6 | 55.5 | 11 | 35.0 | 7 | 30.0 | 6 |

**Table 6.24 Planning Permission 'Take-Up' - Ease of Use (Absolute figure is given in brackets)**

| | Very Difficult | Difficult | Straightforward but Time-consuming | Easy |
|---|---|---|---|---|
| Counties | 9.3 (4) | 27.9 (12) | 41.9 (18) | 2.3 (1) |
| Metro-Authorities | 4.0 (1) | 12.0 (3) | 68.0 (17) | 8.0 (2) |
| E.Midland Districts | - | 20.0 (4) | 55.0 (11) | - |

The majority of replies seem to only consider this data as time consuming and relatively straightforward. To successfully use this indicator, planners would have to be constantly recording the date on which development commenced. Perhaps greater use by planners of building control officers' data may go some way to alleviating this problem, although building control data is not without its critics (Gillen, 1994). In addition, it may be one of the indicators that could be improved if computer-based application filing and monitoring system were to be introduced.

*Estate Agent Data*

As changes in the housing market directly affect the business and operation of estate agency, estate agents would appear to be a useful source of market information. The survey examined a number of different information sources, the results of which are highlighted in the next section. These indicators will be of primary importance in monitoring the market for owner-occupied housing, i.e. the effective demand, rather than for 'global' housing demand.

The suggestion that changes in land and house prices indicate changes in demand is strongly dependant on neo-classical economic theory. If demand increases without a respondent increase in supply, then the price at which demand and supply reach equilibrium will increase. In a practical sense there may be a number of other factors which are responsible for changes in price for both land and houses, as one local authority pointed out;

> Caution is needed in interpretation of data, particularly in isolation from other indicators. High land prices in areas of development policy restraint typically reflect a limited land supply and interest of high income groups. It rarely reflects numerically high levels of demand in total household terms. The authority's use of these indicators has primarily figured in the preparation of specialist 'Executive' and 'Affordable' housing policy, and the representation of localised housing demand at appeals.

Clearly this data is very poorly utilised (Table 6.25), yet the table also indicates that some authorities consider it as a useful indicator. The main reason that could be adduced as to why its use does not reflect this positive support is the troublesome nature of collection and collation (Table 6.26). The price paid for any land by a developer is commercially sensitive,

186  The Formulation of Local Housing Strategies

Table 6.25  Land Prices - Employment and Usefulness

|  | Used in the Past | | | | Used Presently | | | | Useful | | | |
| --- | --- | --- | --- | --- | --- | --- | --- | --- | --- | --- | --- | --- |
|  | Yes | | No | | Yes | | No | | Yes | | No | |
|  | % | Nos. | % | Nos. | % | Nos. | % | Nos. | % | Nos. | % | Nos. |
| Counties | 18.6 | 8 | 72.1 | 31 | 11.6 | 5 | 81.4 | 35 | 39.5 | 17 | 32.6 | 14 |
| Metro-Authorities | 8.0 | 2 | 84.0 | 21 | 4.0 | 1 | 88.0 | 22 | 56.0 | 14 | 20.0 | 5 |
| E. Midland Districts | 10.0 | 2 | 60.0 | 12 | 5.0 | 1 | 65.0 | 13 | 25.0 | 5 | 35.0 | 7 |

Table 6.26  Land Prices - Ease of Use (Absolute figure is given in brackets)

|  | Very Difficult | Difficult | Straightforward but Time-consuming | Easy |
| --- | --- | --- | --- | --- |
| Counties | 44.2 (19) | 25.6 (11) | 6.9 (3) | 4.6 (2) |
| Metro-Authorities | 24.0 (6) | 44.0 (11) | 8.0 (2) | - |
| E. Midland Districts | 15.0 (3) | 35.0 (7) | 10.0 (5) | - |

Table 6.27  House Prices - Employment and Usefulness

| | Used in the Past | | | | Used Presently | | | | Useful | | | |
|---|---|---|---|---|---|---|---|---|---|---|---|---|
| | Yes | | No | | Yes | | No | | Yes | | No | |
| | % | Nos. | % | Nos. | % | Nos. | % | Nos. | % | Nos. | % | Nos. |
| Counties | 74.4 | 32 | 18.6 | 8 | 60.5 | 26 | 32.6 | 14 | 37.2 | 16 | 20.9 | 9 |
| Metro-Authorities | 56.0 | 14 | 36.0 | 9 | 40.0 | 10 | 56.0 | 14 | 52.0 | 13 | 16.0 | 4 |
| E. Midland Districts | 25.0 | 5 | 50.0 | 10 | 25.0 | 5 | 55.0 | 11 | 35.0 | 7 | 35.0 | 7 |

Table 6.28  House Prices - Ease of Use (Absolute figure is given in brackets)

| | Very Difficult | Difficult | Straightforward but Time-consuming | Easy |
|---|---|---|---|---|
| Counties | 9.3 (4) | 18.6 (8) | 28.0 (12) | 18.6 (8) |
| Metro-Authorities | 24.0 (6) | 28.0 (7) | 20.0 (5) | 16.0 (4) |
| E. Midland Districts | 5.0 (1) | 40.0 (8) | 15.0 (3) | - |

188 *The Formulation of Local Housing Strategies*

therefore it is unlikely to be readily available. However, the information may be available in a generalised form, from agencies such as the Valuation Office (see Chapter Five), an agency at least one authority said they consulted.

The monitoring of house prices was another issue examined in the questionnaire. Table 6.27 highlights the percentage of authorities which currently review house prices, as well as those that have used them in the past. In addition, the table indicates the percentage of respondents who think it is a useful indicator. The strongest adherents to the use of house prices are the county councils, yet even though they use the data, they do not appear to be strong supporters of it. One county stated;

> The multiplicity of demand indicators means that it is impossible to monitor this aspect on all fronts. The County Council has therefore concentrated on two main areas:
> - house prices
> - building land prices
> 
> The information on these topics is readily available and accessible. However it is recognised that the use of such indicators can only give a broad indication of market pressures and trends, and that it would be unwise to put to much emphasis on their use per se. However as a broad indicator across market areas, and given recognition that they are only one of many contributory factors, they have proved to be a valuable input to the monitoring process.

Table 6.28 illustrates that a higher percentage of counties appear to see this data as easy to monitor. As most of the commonly available data-sets in this field fail to reflect trends at a district level (Nicol, 1994; 1996), it is not really surprising that the metropolitan authorities and the districts find the data more problematic to obtain.

The questionnaire sought to determine the degree to which a number of specific Estate Agent-based indicators are employed. These questions examined the demand for properties on the estate agents books and the amount of interest that developed around certain types of properties. The first indicator was the volume of sales by house type and area, which should indicate the relative interest and demand for certain types of properties.

As can be seen, hardly any authorities use this data, yet the counties and the metropolitan authorities would appear to view this data as being useful. The only reason for such low rates of use must therefore be due to

Table 6.29 Volume of Sales by House Type and Area - Employment and Usefulness

|  | Used in the Past | | | | Used Presently | | | | Useful | | | |
| --- | --- | --- | --- | --- | --- | --- | --- | --- | --- | --- | --- | --- |
|  | Yes | | No | | Yes | | No | | Yes | | No | |
|  | % | Nos. | % | Nos. | % | Nos. | % | Nos. | % | Nos. | % | Nos. |
| Counties | 9.3 | 4 | 81.4 | 35 | 9.3 | 4 | 81.4 | 35 | 60.5 | 26 | 18.6 | 8 |
| Metro-Authorities | 8.0 | 2 | 84.0 | 21 | 8.0 | 2 | 88.0 | 22 | 56.0 | 14 | 32.0 | 8 |
| E. Midland Districts | 5.0 | 1 | 65.0 | 13 | - | - | 70.0 | 14 | 30.0 | 6 | 25.0 | 5 |

Table 6.30 Volume of Sales by House Type and Area - Ease of Use (Absolute figure is given in brackets)

|  | Very Difficult | Difficult | Straightforward but Time-consuming | Easy |
| --- | --- | --- | --- | --- |
| Counties | 34.9 (15) | 32.6 (14) | 13.9 (6) | 2.3 (1) |
| Metro-Authorities | 32.0 (8) | 40.0 (10) | 16.0 (4) | - |
| E. Midland Districts | 15.0 (3) | 35.0 (6) | 5.0 (1) | - |

the difficulties of data collection. Table 6.30 highlights that the majority of respondents appeared to suggest that the data was very difficult, or difficult, to monitor.

An assumption would be that those who find the data either easy or straightforward to monitor do so through surveys of estate agents. It transpires that 3 of the 6 counties who said this indicator was straightforward to use carried out surveys of estate agents (see Table 6.41) and a similar situation exists in the districts and metropolitan authorities. One county authority did say:

> That the Council did try to start arrangements with some local estate agents to monitor 'executive' house prices, but the estate agents proved uncooperative.

The next three indicators were almost totally ignored by all three tiers and as the positive response rate was so poor, they will be examined together. Table 6.31, illustrates that virtually no local authority has ever used:

1. Number of Enquiries by House Type and Area.
2. Time on the Market by House Type and Area.
3. Number of Appointments to View by House Type and Area.

(These numbers refer to the number in the second row of Table 6.31.)

This low level of usage may be due to the fact that the respondents perceive this information as being extremely difficult to collect. On average, between 67-75% of counties and metropolitan authorities thought this information would be difficult, or very difficult to obtain. The districts had a lower percentage perceiving this as a difficult indicator to monitor. However, as can be seen in Table 6.31, this is not the result of any practical experience. It may have more to do with the fact that close to one-half of respondents from the East Midlands failed to answer this question. In interviews with estate agents in Mansfield (see Chapter Five), there was a positive response to providing local planners with information, although some Agents said it would only be available in an aggregate format. As one authority stated:

Table 6.31 Use of Estate Agent Indicators (Absolute figure is given in brackets)

|  | Used in The Past | | | Used Presently | | |
|---|---|---|---|---|---|---|
|  | 1 | 2 | 3 | 1 | 2 | 3 |
| Counties | 2.3 (1) | 4.7 (2) | - | - | - | - |
| Metro-Authorities | - | - | - | - | 4.0 (1) | 4.0 (1) |
| E. Midland Districts | - | - | - | - | - | - |

Table 6.32 Usefulness of Estate Agent Indicators (Absolute figure is given in brackets)

|  | Number of Enquiries | | Time on the Market | | Appointments to View | |
|---|---|---|---|---|---|---|
|  | Useful | Not Useful | Useful | Not Useful | Useful | Not Useful |
| Counties | 32.6 (14) | 37.2 (16) | 53.5 (23) | 23.3 (10) | 23.3 (10) | 51.2 (22) |
| Metro-Authorities | 28.0 (7) | 48.0 (12) | 40.0 (10) | 40.0 (10) | 20.0 (4) | 60.0 (15) |
| E. Midland Districts | 20.0 (4) | 25.0 (5) | 25.0 (5) | 25.0 (5) | 20.0 (4) | 35.0 (7) |

The extent to which the Local Planning authority is able to gather any of this information would depend on the willingness of the local estate agents etc. to provide the data. Their involvement in Housing Studies in the past has proved useful but, on the other hand, they have been unwilling or unable to help the County Council in its preparation of the quarterly house price survey.

Yet as can be seen from Table 6.32, a percentage of authorities see this type of indicator as useful. One Welsh county highlighted a problem that may be endemic in some of these indicators:

> Indicators here need careful definition as they can be affected by the number of visitors in the area e.g. enquiries at estate agents may be affected by people on holiday.

This is obviously an important concern especially in certain areas, and it was one of the problems with these type of indicators discussed in Chapter Five.

Considering that very few authorities actually monitor these indicators, it is perhaps surprising that between one-fifth and one-third of the authorities see them as being useful. As highlighted above, estate agents (as represented by those in Mansfield) would be prepared to provide this sort of information to planners, if they were to request it.

*Housebuilder Data*

Monitoring the housebuilders themselves, in terms of how their operations progress, would seem to be justifiable. In a similar manner to the estate agents, housebuilders have to remain aware of what is affecting the housing market, as they are directly affected by changes in patterns and preferences of households, which are, in effect, their potential customers. Data gathered from bodies such as housebuilders may therefore be of importance as a monitoring tool for market housing and effective demand. With this data, there is a significant problem regarding the availability of the information, as the housebuilding industry is secretive by nature, and perceives all data to be sensitive. As the chairman of one volume housebuilder pointed out:

## The Use of Data by Local Authorities in England and Wales 193

> ...any gratuitous information provided to the planning authority may be used in evidence against us at a Local Planning Enquiry! Unfortunately planning has become an adversarial process from the viewpoint of the developer/house builder. (Response on the questionnaire sent to the Housebuilders.)

Many of these indicators were totally ignored or were only examined by a few authorities. This may be due to the fact that planners already realise that housebuilders may be unwilling to disclose such information and do not even try to obtain it. As one county explained:

> ...much depends on the accuracy of any records maintained by housebuilders and on their willingness to divulge information to planning authorities.

As can be seen in the table below very few planning authorities monitor this information. Due to the relatively poor positive response, the past and present use of the following indicators has been combined into one table, Table 6.33.

1. Ratio of Sales to Reservations.
2. Time from Completion to Sale.
3. Number of Site Reservations.
4. Sales Rates.
5. Visitor Numbers.
6. Proportion of Homes Sold Prior to Completion.

(These numbers refer to the numbers in the second row of Table 6.33)

No East Midland district has any practical experience of this data and only metropolitan authorities currently employ one of these indicators. The counties have the most experience of these data sources, yet even their experience is limited. For example, four authorities have used sales rates in the past and, of these, two continue to use the data.

Only one county has monitored the time from completion to sale, however it no longer does so. This is obviously an area where there has been little monitoring carried out. Yet this type of data would appear to have a degree of support, as can be seen in Table 6.34.

**Table 6.33** The Use of Housebuilder Indicators (Absolute figure is given in brackets)

| | Used in the Past | | | | | | Used Presently | | | | | |
|---|---|---|---|---|---|---|---|---|---|---|---|---|
| | 1 | 2 | 3 | 4 | 5 | 6 | 1 | 2 | 3 | 4 | 5 | 6 |
| Counties | - | 2.3 (1) | - | 9.3 (4) | - | - | - | - | - | 4.7 (2) | - | - |
| Metro-Authorities | - | - | - | - | - | - | 4.0 (1) | - | - | - | - | - |
| E. Midland Districts | - | - | - | - | - | - | - | - | - | - | - | - |

**Table 6.34** Housebuilder Indicators

Percentage who Perceive this Indicator as Useful (Absolute figure is given in brackets)

| | 1 | 2 | 3 | 4 | 5 | 6 |
|---|---|---|---|---|---|---|
| Counties | 20.9 (9) | 25.6 (11) | 30.2 (13) | 46.5 (20) | 18.6 (8) | 41.9 (18) |
| Metro-Authorities | 16.0 (4) | 36.0 (9) | 32.0 (8) | 40.0 (10) | 16.0 (4) | 40.0 (10) |
| E. Midland Districts | 5.0 (1) | 25.0 (5) | 20.0 (4) | 35.0 (7) | 10.0 (2) | 35.0 (6) |

The mismatch between those perceiving this data as useful, and those actually monitoring it, may be a result of the difficulties the authorities perceive with gathering this information. One Metropolitan authority pointed out that, although this type of data exists, it may not be readily available. As a result they believed that it would be very difficult to monitor this type of information. Another authority was of the opinion that:

> Co-ordinating responses of a number of participating builders and agents may not prove cost effective. Persuading local builders to participate is very difficult.

Whilst another suggested that both estate agent and housebuilder indicators:

> ...would be both difficult to obtain and unreliable for use in projecting. I do not see that such indicators would be particularly useful in making long term housing projections.

One of the authorities which has used this type of indicator did so in relation to specific sites and local areas, whilst another has only used this kind of data when it required information with which to support appeal cases. One authority was of the opinion that all of the indicators, not just the housebuilder or estate agent data, would probably be useful. However, the authority did point out that:

> ...much of the data listed could be of additional use in assessing demand, its availability cannot always be guaranteed. Not all housebuilders or District authorities monitor the data listed comprehensively and in a consistent way. Everyone has different definitions and timescales, and resources available, to carry out such detailed monitoring.

The degree of difficulty that all the authorities seem to see endemic in collecting information of this kind is comparable with that of using estate agent indicators. In the case of the counties, between 60-70% of counties stated that this data was either very difficult or difficult to obtain. For the metropolitan authorities, the proportion perceiving the data in a similar way was almost identical, whilst for the districts the figure was between 55-60%. This may, however, not appear high, given the comments that authorities made about this set of data, and the almost non-existent use of the data. However, it is low due to the fact that a significant proportion

196  *The Formulation of Local Housing Strategies*

of authorities failed to answer this question: between 25-30% of counties, 20-30% of metropolitan authorities and 40-45% of districts, failed to answer this question.

At this point, whilst it may constitute a slight deviation from the structure of the present discussion which has thus far examined the response to each question in order, it may be worthwhile highlighting the views of the housebuilders, as illustrated by the responses to their questionnaire. This allows the accessibility of housebuilder data to be placed in the context of the proceeding discussion.

Table 6.35 illustrates the percentage of respondents who would be prepared to give access to the actual data, i.e. the number of actual site reservations, sales per week, etc. As can be seen in this table, a number of housebuilders are prepared to divulge information regarding markets to the local authority. If this were to occur, some of major perceived problems with this type of data would become inapplicable, allowing these indicators to be used.

**Table 6.35 Housebuilders Prepared to Allow Access to their Data (Absolute figure is given in brackets)**

|  | Yes | No | No Answer |
|---|---|---|---|
| Time From Completion to Sale | 41.5 (22) | 13.2 (7) | 45.3 (24) |
| Site Reservations | 49.1 (26) | 15.1 (8) | 35.8 (19) |
| Sales Rates | 45.3 (24) | 15.1 (8) | 39.6 (21) |
| Number of Visitors | 41.5 (22) | 15.1 (8) | 43.4 (23) |
| Units Sold Prior to Completion | 41.5 (22) | 13.2 (7) | 45.3 (24) |

*Survey Use*

The penultimate series of questions examined the extent to which planning authorities surveyed bodies which are active in the housing market, in particular the private housing market. This part of the questionnaire would highlight the degree to which planners liase with other agencies, even if they do so in terms other than already described in this chapter. The questionnaire enquired about four different surveys:

- Estate Agents.
- Building Societies.
- Local Housebuilders.
- National Housebuilders.

**Table 6.36  Use of Surveys (Absolute figure is given in brackets)**

Estate Agents

| | Used Currently | | Used in the Past | | Building Societies — Used Currently | | Used in the Past | |
|---|---|---|---|---|---|---|---|---|
| | Yes | No | Yes | No | Yes | No | Yes | No |
| Counties | 11.6 (5) | 76.6 (33) | 32.6 (14) | 60.5 (26) | 9.3 (4) | 76.6 (33) | 25.6 (11) | 65.1 (28) |
| Metro-Authorities | 8.0 (2) | 80.0 (20) | 36.0 (9) | 52.0 (13) | 12.0 (3) | 76.0 (19) | 20.0 (5) | 64.0 (16) |
| E. Midland Districts | 25.0 (5) | 55.0 (11) | 25.0 (5) | 55.0 (11) | 10.0 (2) | 75.0 (15) | 15.0 (3) | 60.0 (12) |

Local Housebuilders

| | Used Currently | | Used in the Past | | National Housebuilders — Used Currently | | Used in the Past | |
|---|---|---|---|---|---|---|---|---|
| | Yes | No | Yes | No | Yes | No | Yes | No |
| Counties | 27.9 (12) | 60.5 (26) | 44.2 (19) | 44.2 (19) | 27.9 (12) | 60.5 (26) | 39.5 (17) | 48.8 (21) |
| Metro-Authorities | 32.0 (8) | 48.0 (12) | 44.0 (11) | 44.0 (11) | 36.0 (9) | 40.0 (10) | 48.0 (12) | 36.0 (9) |
| E. Midland Districts | 15.0 (3) | 65.0 (13) | 65.0 (13) | 15.0 (3) | 20.0 (4) | 60.0 (12) | 20.0 (4) | 60.0 (12) |

198  The Formulation of Local Housing Strategies

**Table 6.37 Usefulness of the Surveys (Absolute figure is given in brackets)**

|  | Estate Agents | | Building Societies | | Local Housebuilders | | National Housebuilders | |
|---|---|---|---|---|---|---|---|---|
|  | Yes | No | Yes | No | Yes | No | Yes | No |
| Counties | 37.2 (16) | 30.2 (13) | 30.2 (13) | 37.2 (16) | 39.5 (17) | 20.9 (9) | 44.2 (19) | 16.3 (7) |
| Metro-Authorities | 48.0 (12) | 32.0 (8) | 40.0 (10) | 28.0 (7) | 64.0 (16) | 4.0 (1) | 52.0 (13) | 16.0 (4) |
| E. Midland Districts | 30.0 (6) | 25.0 (5) | 30.0 (6) | 20.0 (4) | 30.0 (6) | 25.0 (5) | 20.0 (4) | 30.0 (6) |

**Table 6.38 Difficulties with the Surveys (Absolute figure is given in brackets)**

| | Very Difficult | Difficult | Straightforward but Time-consuming | Easy |
|---|---|---|---|---|
| **Estate Agents Surveys** | | | | |
| Counties | 9.3 (4) | 30.2 (13) | 20.9 (9) | 6.9 (3) |
| Metro-Authorities | 20.0 (5) | 24.0 (6) | 28.0 (7) | - |
| E. Midland Districts | 5.0 (1) | 15.0 (3) | 30.0 (6) | 10.0 (2) |
| **Building Societies Surveys** | | | | |
| Counties | 13.9 (6) | 30.2 (13) | 18.6 (8) | 6.9 (3) |
| Metro-Authorities | 16.0 (4) | 20.0 (4) | 28.0 (7) | - |
| E. Midland Districts | - | 30.0 (6) | 15.0 (3) | 15.0 (3) |
| **Local Housebuilder Surveys** | | | | |
| Counties | 2.3 (1) | 41.9 (18) | 13.9 (6) | 6.9 (3) |
| Metro-Authorities | 12.0 (3) | 36.0 (9) | 16.0 (4) | 4.0 (1) |
| E. Midland Districts | 5.0 (1) | 30.0 (6) | 15.0 (3) | 15.0 (3) |
| **National Housebuilder Surveys** | | | | |
| Counties | 2.3 (1) | 30.2 (13) | 20.9 (9) | 11.6 (5) |
| Metro-Authorities | 4.0 (1) | 28.0 (7) | 28.0 (7) | 4.0 (1) |
| E. Midland Districts | - | 30.0 (6) | 20.0 (4) | 15.0 (3) |

The positive responses from authorities who currently (and have in the past) conducted such surveys are given in Table 6.36. As with the other tables the actual number of responses (as opposed to the percentage) is presented in brackets.

It can be seen that the number of authorities examining this field has declined. This may be due to the fact that the surveys are developed on an ad-hoc basis, and when the questionnaire was filled in the authorities were not engaged in this type of exercise. Table 6.36 highlights that the least popular subject for surveys are the building societies. The national housebuilding companies appear to be popular survey subjects for the counties and metropolitan authorities. Surveys of estate agents appear to be popular amongst the districts, as represented by the East Midland authorities.

Many authorities seem to see these surveys as useful, particularly metropolitan authorities. The county councils seem to see surveys of national housebuilding companies as the most useful, whilst the metropolitan authorities would appear to favour the local housebuilding companies as an agency to survey. The East Midland districts favour the three surveys equally. The primary reason why so few authorities carry out this type of survey is the perceived difficulty in collection and compilation, and it is clear from Table 6.38 that a number of authorities do see these surveys as 'Very Difficult' or 'Difficult'. However, it is also clear that a significant proportion of authorities do not perceive difficulties, other than time, with the data's compilation.

*Economic Data*

The concluding section of the questionnaire examined the use of broader economic-based indicators by planning authorities. It is widely acknowledged that the private housing market depends upon the economic circumstances of would-be home-owners in order to thrive and expand. The two indicators which examined this area were affordability ratios and income estimates. In addition a question attempted to ascertain the degree to which the authorities own policies for growth are taken into account, because job and employment growth will affect the housing market, as policies which boost employment, income and prosperity alter housing preferences. Examining affordability ratios:

200  The Formulation of Local Housing Strategies

Table 6.39  Affordability Ratios - Employment and Usefulness

| | Used in the Past | | | | Used Presently | | | | Useful | | | |
|---|---|---|---|---|---|---|---|---|---|---|---|---|
| | Yes | | No | | Yes | | No | | Yes | | No | |
| | % | Nos. | % | Nos. | % | Nos. | % | Nos. | % | Nos. | % | Nos. |
| Counties | 32.6 | 14 | 58.1 | 25 | 32.6 | 14 | 60.5 | 26 | 46.5 | 20 | 27.9 | 12 |
| Metro-Authorities | 12.0 | 3 | 72.0 | 18 | 28.0 | 7 | 60.0 | 15 | 56.0 | 14 | 16.0 | 4 |
| E. Midland Districts | 10.0 | 2 | 75.0 | 15 | 15.0 | 3 | 75.0 | 15 | 35.0 | 7 | 30.0 | 6 |

Table 6.40  Affordability Ratios - Ease of Use  (Absolute figure is given in brackets)

| | Very Difficult | Difficult | Straightforward but Time-consuming | Easy |
|---|---|---|---|---|
| Counties | 27.9 (12) | 37.2 (16) | 2.3 (1) | 6.9 (3) |
| Metro-Authorities | 44.0 (11) | 24.0 (6) | 8.0 (2) | 4.0 (1) |
| E. Midland Districts | 10.0 (2) | 45.0 (9) | - | - |

As Table 6.39 shows, there is high proportion of authorities which consider this type of data as useful for monitoring housing market demand. However, the percentage of authorities that actually use this data is low, on average 18.2% in the past and 25.2% presently. If this indicator were to indicate changes in demand, an increase in the ratio should herald an increase in housing demand, particularly private housing demand. As can be seen over the early years of the 1990s, affordability was at an 'all- time' high (Housing Market Report, 1994; TSB First Time Buyers Affordability Index, 1993), yet housing transactions (a reasonable proxy for market movement and buoyancy) were low.

Clearly, this indicator illustrates the major drawback with all of these monitoring methods, because examined in isolation such data can be misleading. In the case of affordability ratios, if they are to realistically illustrate demand, the would be home-owners would also require secure income, job security, a positive view of homeownership, etc. It is, therefore, apparent that this type of indicator is difficult to use because it requires supporting data. The level of difficulty perceived with this indicator is given in the table (Table 6.40) and it is clear that the majority of the respondents found difficulty in compiling and monitoring this data.

One could argue that there is a case for the monitoring of local incomes. Not only will this data give some indication of the ability to pay for market housing, it will also highlight the need for social housing and indeed, social support services. This type of data would already be monitored by housebuilders as a means of market identification and customer profiling to achieve product targeting.

Metropolitan authorities use this data to the greatest extent and, as can be seen in the table above, are the most positive about the indicator. Both the counties and districts appear to have a limited experience with this data and also do not seem to see it as a useful source of market information. Again, this economic indicator was perceived by all three authorities as being difficult to collect and interpret. Perhaps more encouraging is the fact that although 52% of metropolitan authorities find this indicator difficult, they continue to represent the strongest advocates of income estimates.

Again the growth in housing needs studies and recognised procedures on which to conduct them may mean that this data has become more reliable, or at the very least obtainable in recent years.

The final question addressed to all authorities tried to determine the extent to which local authority economic policies were reflected by housing

**Table 6.41 Income Estimates - Employment and Usefulness**

|  | Used in the Past | | | | Used Presently | | | | Useful | | | |
|---|---|---|---|---|---|---|---|---|---|---|---|---|
|  | Yes | | No | | Yes | | No | | Yes | | No | |
|  | % | Nos. | % | Nos. | % | Nos. | % | Nos. | % | Nos. | % | Nos. |
| Counties | 20.9 | 9 | 67.4 | 29 | 16.3 | 7 | 74.4 | 32 | 34.8 | 15 | 41.9 | 18 |
| Metro-Authorities | 16.0 | 4 | 68.0 | 17 | 32.0 | 8 | 56.0 | 14 | 56.0 | 14 | 28.0 | 7 |
| E. Midland Districts | 10.0 | 2 | 75.0 | 15 | 15.0 | 3 | 75.0 | 15 | 25.0 | 5 | 40.0 | 10 |

**Table 6.42 Income Estimates - Ease of Use (Absolute figure is given in brackets)**

|  | Very Difficult | Difficult | Straightforward but Time-consuming | Easy |
|---|---|---|---|---|
| Counties | 37.2 (16) | 34.8 (15) | 2.3 (1) | 2.3 (1) |
| Metro-Authorities | 52.0 (13) | 20.0 (5) | 8.0 (4) | - |
| E. Midland Districts | 25.0 (5) | 30.0 (6) | - | - |

**Table 6.43 Reflection of Economic Policies Within Housing Policies (Absolute figure is given in brackets)**

|  | Very Difficult | Difficult | Straightforward but Time-consuming | Easy |
|---|---|---|---|---|
| Counties | 37.2 (16) | 34.8 (15) | 2.3 (1) | 2.3 (1) |
| Metro-Authorities | 52.0 (13) | 20.0 (5) | 8.0 (4) | - |
| E. Midland Districts | 25.0 (5) | 30.0 (6) | - | - |

policies. Table 6.43, highlights the answers to this question. One could argue that there is an expectation that a higher proportion of authorities, in particular metropolitan authorities, would monitor this data, because both policies are formulated by the same authority. Perhaps the reason for this is that the integration of employment, economic development and housing is not so important, when there are few options open (in terms of available space, suitable sites, etc.).

## Conclusion

This chapter has highlighted the findings of survey research which has sought to ascertain the degree to which local authorities monitored housing markets in the mid-1990s. The overall conclusion to be drawn from this is that the number of different 'types' of indicators monitored were considerable. However, there was generally more extensive use of 'internally' generated data (such as planning applications and housing start data) and less employment of data generated and made available by housebuilders or estate agents. This supports the assessment of the indicators presented in the previous chapter, where data accessibility was a criteria for assessment. Table 6.44 presents a summary of data set use and the degree to which the respondents perceived the data as useful. The empty cells are either the result of no positive response to this question (e.g. the monitoring of housebuilder data for instance) at all or indicate that the question was not directed at that tier of government (e.g. counties in the case of housing association waiting lists).

What is clear from this summary table is that certain data sets are widely monitored by local authorities. Parts of this research has already highlighted that some of the more popular data sets e.g. housing starts (used by 62.8% of counties, 68% of metropolitan authorities, and 70% of East Midland districts) and house prices (used by 60.5% of county councils, 40% of metropolitan authorities and 25% of East Midland districts), suffer from serious limitations (Nicol, 1994, 1996; Gillen, 1994b; Gillen et al., 1995). This suggests that housing strategies and housing policies produced in the mid to late-1990s may well have been based on data with considerable weaknesses. There is a case for the development of what would appear to be 'key' data sets, those which are seen to be useful by over 40% of practitioners (i.e. 5*-3* in the table). Additional work on these data

## Table 6.44 Use and Usefulness of Indicators
1- County Councils    2- Metro-Authorities    3- E. Midland Districts

| | Use The Indicator Presently | | | Used The Indicator in the Past | | | Is the Indicator Useful | | |
|---|---|---|---|---|---|---|---|---|---|
| | 1 | 2 | 3 | 1 | 2 | 3 | 1 | 2 | 3 |
| Local Authority Waiting List | ** | **** | **** | *** | **** | **** | ** | *** | *** |
| HA Waiting Lists | - | *** | ** | - | *** | ** | - | *** | *** |
| Housing Need Survey | - | ** | *** | - | ** | ** | - | **** | **** |
| Vacancy Rates | *** | ** | ** | **** | ** | ** | ** | ** | ** |
| Planning Applications | **** | **** | **** | **** | **** | **** | *** | *** | ** |
| Planning Appeals | ** | ** | ** | *** | ** | ** | ** | ** | * |
| Amendment of Planning Applications | * | * | ** | * | * | ** | * | ** | * |
| New Dwelling Starts | **** | **** | **** | **** | **** | **** | *** | *** | *** |
| Housing Density | * | ** | ** | ** | ** | ** | * | ** | ** |
| Depletion Rates for Allocated Sites | ** | ** | ** | ** | ** | ** | ** | *** | ** |
| Planning Permission Take Up | * | * | ** | ** | ** | ** | *** | *** | ** |
| Land Prices | * | * | * | * | * | * | ** | *** | ** |
| House Prices | **** | *** | ** | **** | *** | ** | ** | *** | ** |
| Volume of House Sales | * | * | * | * | * | * | *** | *** | *** |
| Number of Enquiries | - | - | - | * | - | - | ** | ** | ** |
| Time on the Market | - | * | - | * | - | - | *** | *** | ** |
| Number of Appointments to View | - | * | - | - | - | - | ** | ** | ** |
| Ratio of Sales to Reservations | - | * | - | - | - | - | ** | * | * |
| Time From Completion to Sale | - | - | - | * | - | - | ** | ** | ** |
| Number of Site Reservations | - | - | - | - | - | - | ** | ** | ** |
| Sales Rates | * | - | - | * | - | - | *** | *** | ** |
| Vistor Number | - | - | - | - | - | - | * | * | * |
| Proportion of Homes Sold Prior to Completion | - | - | - | - | - | - | *** | *** | ** |
| Estate Agents | * | * | ** | ** | ** | ** | ** | *** | ** |
| National Housebuilders | ** | ** | ** | ** | *** | ** | *** | *** | ** |
| Local Housebuilders | ** | ** | * | *** | *** | **** | ** | **** | ** |
| Building Societies | * | * | * | ** | ** | * | ** | *** | ** |
| Affordability Ratios | ** | ** | * | ** | * | * | *** | *** | ** |
| Estimates of Income | * | ** | * | ** | * | * | ** | *** | ** |

Key:    *****= 80-100%    ****=60-79%    ***=40-59%
        **=20-39%    *=0-19%

sets may ensure a commonality of approach throughout the country and provide a data set which can be monitored by the housing strategy formulators. Similarly there is an argument for revisiting this study to see if the Local Authority have developed these indicators over the last 6 years.

Table 5.7 in the previous chapter summarised the practical difficulties and advantages of many of the data sets summarised above. Therefore it may be useful to briefly compare indicators that 'scored' highly in that summation with those that have been examined in this chapter. Data sets that 'scored' three 'c' gradings or above in Table 5.7, were Planning Applications; Planning Appeals; Housing Starts; House Prices and Estimates of Income.

As can be seen in the Table 6.44, all but one of these data sets tends to be frequently employed and is seen as useful by all levels of local authority, i.e. consistently has at least three stars in a majority of categories. The exception were Estimates of Income and Planning Appeals. For instance income estimates were used infrequently, only 16.3% of counties, 32.0% of metropolitan authorities and 15% of East Midland districts replying that currently such data was employed. Perhaps most surprising was the fact that in only one case (metropolitan authorities) did income estimates register three stars (56%).

Apart from these key indicators, it would appear that a number of data sets are little used for monitoring the housing market. As was shown in the last chapter, this may be due to a number of limitations in the data, which local authorities have recognised, and ultimately felt that such data may not be worth the effort to collect. However, the survey has shown that a number of data sets have never been examined by more than a limited number of local authorities. This does not suggest a 'trial' approach, through which local authorities have found certain data sets either difficult to collect or difficult to interpret, and have therefore stopped using them for monitoring. Instead this suggests a pre-conceived idea regarding which data may be forthcoming or useful. As it has turned out, some of the data that has been used for monitoring to a very limited degree, has been shown to be problematic. However, one would suggest that, as local authorities appear to have neglected certain data sources (housebuilders and estate agents in particular), an opportunity to develop links with these other participants in the housing market has been disregarded. As highlighted in earlier chapters, such links can not only provide informal perceptions of the housing market, they can also ensure that the enablers (the local authority) and implementers (the housebuilder) of housing strategies are aware of the policies of all parties concerned.

Whilst this chapter has focused specifically on the final research question, the next chapter will take a far more holistic approach and examine all three research questions with reference to two specific case study areas; North West Leicestershire (in particular Ashby de la Zouch) and Mansfield.

# The Use of Data by Local Authorities in England and Wales 207

## Appendix 1 Non-Response Rates

| Question | Authority | Number of Respondents Who Did Not Answer Each Question | | | |
|---|---|---|---|---|---|
| | | Used in the Past | Used Presently | Useful | Ease of Use |
| Local Auth. Waiting Lists | Counties | 5 | 5 | 13 | 10 |
| | Metro Auth | 3 | 3 | 9 | 7 |
| | E.Mid | 2 | 2 | 8 | 6 |
| Housing Assoc. Waiting Lists | Counties | - | - | - | - |
| | Metro Auth | 4 | 3 | 10 | 17 |
| | E.Mid | 5 | 4 | 7 | 12 |
| Housing Need Surveys | Counties | - | - | - | - |
| | Metro Auth | 2 | 3 | 6 | 4 |
| | E.Mid | 3 | 2 | 5 | 5 |
| Vacancy Rates | Counties | 6 | 6 | 19 | 17 |
| | Metro Auth | 2 | 2 | 8 | 5 |
| | E.Mid | 5 | 5 | 7 | 5 |
| New Dwelling Starts | Counties | 2 | 3 | 17 | 12 |
| | Metro Auth | 3 | 2 | 3 | 9 |
| | E.Mid | 2 | 2 | 9 | 6 |
| Planning Applications | Counties | 3 | 3 | 17 | 10 |
| | Metro Auth | 3 | 1 | 7 | 4 |
| | E.Mid | 1 | 1 | 9 | 5 |
| Planning Appeals | Counties | 5 | 5 | 13 | 11 |
| | Metro Auth | 3 | 2 | 4 | 5 |
| | E.Mid | 5 | 5 | 9 | 7 |
| Amendment of Planning Applications | Counties | 6 | 6 | 11 | 8 |
| | Metro Auth | 2 | 1 | 5 | 4 |
| | E.Mid | 3 | 3 | 9 | 6 |
| Density of Applications | Counties | 4 | 4 | 11 | 8 |
| | Metro Auth | 2 | 1 | 4 | 4 |
| | E.Mid | 4 | 4 | 5 | 6 |
| Depletion Rates | Counties | 4 | 4 | 15 | 9 |
| | Metro Auth | 4 | 3 | 7 | 6 |
| | E.Mid | 6 | 6 | 7 | 7 |
| Planning Permission 'Take-Up' | Counties | 4 | 4 | 12 | 8 |
| | Metro Auth | 3 | 1 | 3 | 2 |
| | E.Mid | 3 | 3 | 7 | 5 |
| Land Prices | Counties | 4 | 3 | 12 | 8 |
| | Metro Auth | 2 | 2 | 6 | 6 |
| | E.Mid | 6 | 6 | 8 | 5 |

208  *The Formulation of Local Housing Strategies*

|  | Authority | Number of Respondents Who Did Not Answer Each Question | | | |
|---|---|---|---|---|---|
|  |  | Used in the Past | Question | Authority | Used in the Past |
| House Prices | Counties | 3 | 3 | 18 | 11 |
|  | Metro Auth | 2 | 1 | 8 | 3 |
|  | E.Mid | 5 | 4 | 6 | 8 |
| Volume of Sales | Counties | 4 | 4 | 9 | 7 |
|  | Metro Auth | 2 | 1 | 3 | 3 |
|  | E.Mid | 6 | 6 | 9 | 10 |
| Number of Enquiries | Counties | 7 | 6 | 13 | 10 |
|  | Metro Auth | 3 | 2 | 6 | 6 |
|  | E.Mid | 7 | 7 | 11 | 9 |
| Time on the Market | Counties | 5 | 4 | 10 | 9 |
|  | Metro Auth | 3 | 2 | 5 | 4 |
|  | E.Mid | 6 | 6 | 10 | 9 |
| Appointments to View | Counties | 5 | 4 | 11 | 10 |
|  | Metro Auth | 3 | 2 | 5 | 5 |
|  | E.Mid | 6 | 6 | 9 | 9 |
| Ratio of Sales to Reservations | Counties | 5 | 4 | 14 | 12 |
|  | Metro Auth | 3 | 2 | 7 | 6 |
|  | E.Mid | 7 | 7 | 10 | 9 |
| Time From Completion to Sale | Counties | 4 | 3 | 11 | 11 |
|  | Metro Auth | 4 | 3 | 6 | 5 |
|  | E.Mid | 6 | 6 | 7 | 8 |
| Number of Site Reservations | Counties | 4 | 4 | 15 | 13 |
|  | Metro Auth | 4 | 3 | 8 | 5 |
|  | E.Mid | 6 | 6 | 7 | 8 |
| Visitor Numbers | Counties | 5 | 4 | 13 | 13 |
|  | Metro Auth | 4 | 3 | 8 | 7 |
|  | E.Mid | 7 | 7 | 7 | 8 |
| Proportion of Homes Sold Prior to Completion | Counties | 5 | 4 | 13 | 13 |
|  | Metro Auth | 4 | 3 | 7 | 6 |
|  | E.Mid | 7 | 7 | 7 | 8 |
| Sales Rates | Counties | 3 | 2 | 13 | 11 |
|  | Metro Auth | 4 | 3 | 9 | 5 |
|  | E.Mid | 6 | 6 | 7 | 8 |
| Use of Building Society Surveys | Counties | 4 | 6 | 14 | 13 |
|  | Metro Auth | 4 | 3 | 8 | 10 |
|  | E.Mid | 5 | 3 | 10 | 8 |

## The Use of Data by Local Authorities in England and Wales 209

|  | Authority | Number of Respondents Who Did Not Answer Each Question | | | |
|---|---|---|---|---|---|
|  |  | Used in the Past | Question | Authority | Used in the Past |
| Use of Estate Agent Surveys | Counties | 3 | 5 | 14 | 14 |
|  | Metro Auth | 3 | 3 | 5 | 7 |
|  | E.Mid | 4 | 4 | 9 | 12 |
| Surveys of Local Housebuilders | Counties | 5 | 5 | 17 | 15 |
|  | Metro Auth | 3 | 5 | 8 | 8 |
|  | E.Mid | 4 | 4 | 9 | 7 |
| Surveys of National Housebuilders | Counties | 5 | 5 | 17 | 15 |
|  | Metro Auth | 4 | 6 | 8 | 9 |
|  | E.Mid | 4 | 4 | 10 | 7 |
| Affordability Ratios | Counties | 4 | 3 | 11 | 11 |
|  | Metro Auth | 4 | 3 | 7 | 5 |
|  | E.Mid | 3 | 2 | 7 | 9 |
| Income Estimates | Counties | 5 | 4 | 10 | 10 |
|  | Metro Auth | 4 | 3 | 4 | 3 |
|  | E.Mid | 3 | 2 | 5 | 9 |

# 7 Housing Strategy Development at the Local Level

**Introduction**

The early chapters of this research discussed housing markets and strategies as a concept, illustrating these theoretical discussions with an examination of the policy framework which exists in the East Midlands region and how this relates to local housing demand. Chapter Four examined the manner in which housing strategy formulation could be developed through corporate approaches to policy formulation, highlighting the degree to which some authorities involve private housebuilders and work inter-departmentally. Developing from this, Chapters Five and Six examined the manner in which local authorities monitored housing markets and the extent to which certain data sets could be utilised as a means of monitoring the housing market.

The aim of this chapter is to combine all of these questions into one integrated discussion through a detailed examination of the housing situation in Ashby and Mansfield. Initially this chapter will examine the degree to which local authorities take a corporate approach to housing policy formulation. The second section will focus upon the degree to which the local authority develops strategy in a manner which involves private housebuilders since these are the agencies responsible for the majority of new housing provision. Finally the discussion will illustrate how data may be interpreted to reflect the housing situation of a given local area. Whilst this chapter will attempt to indicate the situation in the two principal case study areas, Ashby and Mansfield, much of the discussion will revolve around North West Leicestershire and Mansfield District Councils. This is due to the fact that it is at the district council level (in these two cases) where inter-department and inter-agency working will be necessary.

## Department Co-ordination

The Councils in the two case study districts both consist of a number of different departments concerned with the differing responsibilities of government. In 1995/96 North West Leicestershire Council consisted of seven departments, including a Chief Executive and Clerks department, which has a management function over all departments. Mansfield was similarly controlled by a Chief Executive, but directly below this level there are only three divisions: Finance; Community Services and Development Services. Development Services and Community Services each consist of three 'sub' departments. Of interest to this work is the fact that in Mansfield the housing and planning departments are not only separate themselves, they are also contained within separate directorates. In North West Leicestershire this demarcation is not so apparent, as both departments, although separate, are not within different divisions as is the case with Mansfield. From this evidence one might surmise that it is easier to co-ordinate the housing and planning department in North West Leicestershire, but has this structure enabled North West Leicestershire to develop a corporate structure that is more dynamic than Mansfield?

In terms of joint working between the housing and planning departments, Mansfield would appear to have a better-developed structure. Discussion with the personnel at Mansfield indicated that a planning and housing working group exists, although they met on a project by project basis rather than at any strategic level. Officers in the planning department at Mansfield are trying to promote fuller integration at the policy formulation level. This is a course of action that has been forced upon them mainly as a result of a decline in council-owned land being available for social housing. Different priorities and a different departmental structure has meant that integration has not developed as fully as hoped. For instance, the Housing Department has been primarily focused on compulsory competitive tendering, which has meant that co-ordination has suffered. In addition the housing department is physically separate from the planning department, due to its area-based structure.

North West Leicestershire has adopted a different strategy towards integrated working. In this case it is largely based upon personal contacts between officers in the housing and planning departments, as opposed to the more formal situation that exists in Mansfield. Limitations have arisen over recent years which have tended to create a situation where the housing department has found itself pre-occupied due to the compulsory competitive tendering process.

Whilst North West Leicestershire District Council undertakes consultation and communication with those concerned with the development process within the County (see below), there has been very little cross-county or cross-regional co-operation. Formal discussions of this type took place in the late 1980s, when there was discussion regarding the fact that North West Leicestershire may have to accommodate overspill from Tamworth (in the West Midlands region). However this discussion failed to result in any form of 'concrete' expansionist housing policies and therefore no strategy to progress them. With Ashby on the perimeter of the East Midlands region, this would appear to be a significant limitation, particularly given the degree to which new homes in the district appear to cater for migrant households from other areas. It should be stressed that discussion of this type may be taking place at the strategic level, between Staffordshire and Leicestershire. This assertion is supported by the fact that NW Leicestershire has a housing allocation larger than the officers themselves believe could be created from internal demand within the District, possibly indicating that the County has recognised the commuting potential of the district, an assumption that has been borne out by Tilling's survey (see below).

With the current government structure of districts, counties and regions a situation exists where there is a facility for decisions to be made which concern migratory pressures across administrative boundaries *within* a region. This would not appear to be the case in so far as these migratory pressures cross regional boundaries. It is not suggested that integrated housing strategies will overcome this problem. However, if local authorities develop and monitor movements in the housing market successfully, the housing strategy should be in a better position to identify where new housing demand has been created. If housing strategies with sufficiently robust monitoring techniques were to be prepared by all authorities, housing strategies could be examined by neighbouring authorities. Such inter-district co-operation and information exchange may allow the local authority to be aware of the changes in neighbouring housing markets, and reappraise its own policies accordingly.

## Joint Agency Working

As discussed earlier there is a definite need for co-ordination between policy makers and policy implementers. This section will examine the manner in which joint agency working developed in the two case study areas, and will therefore elaborate on the proceeding theoretical discussion with an examination of empirical data. The discussion will initially examine the development and marketing pressures within which housebuilding companies operate in the case study areas.

It could be suggested that both districts suffer from urban deprivation and economic problems (illustrated by Mansfield having an Enterprise Zone, Development Area status (Mansfield DC, 1993) and a situation that continued into the late 1990s evidenced by a successful Single Regeneration Bid in 1998 (SRB4). North West Leicestershire on the other hand had similar difficulties in the early 1990s but it wasn't until after the field work for this research was complete that this was recognised by area based urban regeneration initiatives. The area has had two successful SRB bids in the late 1990s, one in round 5 and one in round 6 (both with South Derbyshire). This would imply that both case study areas may not be seen by housebuilders as 'ideal' areas for housebuilding (i.e. areas which benefit from a positive image allowing homes to sell quickly). Discussions with regional officers of the Housebuilder's Federation highlighted that this is the case and that there are marketing problems with developments in both case study areas, due to a negative image of the settlements that exist. Although the regional housebuilding body (HBF) indicated that both case study areas have a negative image that requires positive marketing, this does not appear to be the case at the local level in Ashby.

The officers at NW Leicestershire have been surprised by the vigorous build rate that has materialised over the last twelve months as well as the type of property that has been constructed and sold. Housebuilders in the District seem to be able to construct and sell 3-4 bedroom detached homes, despite the fact that the area may not have a well paid work-force. The officers suggest these homes may be popular and sell well because of the close proximity of the A42/M42 and the commuting potential of the district. Discussions with personnel at David Wilson Homes, the dominant builder in the area (see Table 7.1), suggests that it is the area's links with the West Midlands (it is only about 40 minutes from

214 *The Formulation of Local Housing Strategies*

Birmingham) which makes the District easier to market than Mansfield. A study of new home buyers by Tilling[1] highlighted that 52% of new home buyers had a journey to work that took in excess of twenty minutes. Such a travel time could quite legitimately place such commuters in Birmingham, Leicester, Derby or Nottingham, indicating that the new home market in Ashby may be related to large metropolitan centres outside the district, highlighting the difficulties in attempting to define a market area based upon local government boundaries (see Chapters Two and Three).

**Table 7.1 Housing Sites of Over 10 Units Built in the Ashby Area 1991-1995**

| Site | No. Built | Developer |
| --- | --- | --- |
| Off Malvern Crescent, Ashby | 45 | Bovis |
| Atkinson Road, Ashby | 20 | East Midlands HA |
| **Prior Park Road, Ashby** | 51 | **William Davies/East Midland HA** |
| **The Callis, Ashby** | 26 | **William Davies** |
| Avenue Road, Ashby | 30 | MJ Wood Development Ltd. |
| **Leicester Road, Ashby** | 68 | **David Wilson Homes** |
| **Top Street, Appleby Magna** | 23 | **David Wilson Homes** |
| **Woodcock Way, Ashby** | 22 | **David Wilson Homes** |
| Upper Packington Road, Ashby | 131 | Bloors |

**Source:** Data Supplied By North West Leicestershire District Council

In terms of actors' perceptions, it is apparent that the information provided by local housebuilders may contradict the picture of local conditions which is presented by the HBF. One would suggest that the local information would be of greater relevance for housing strategy formulation, as it may indicate needs and demands in sub-district housing markets.

Discussions with personnel at Wimpey regarding their developments in Mansfield indicated that, in 1994 and early 1995, sales were higher than expected for small, two-bed homes, often underpinned with large scale sales to housing associations. Many purchases have been from existing owner-occupiers trading down, and taking advantage of the

---

[1] Tillings work at Nottingham Trent University in 1996 highlighted the characteristics of new homebuyers in North West Leicestershire and South Derbyshire. She asked 40 occupants of new homes in Ashby a number of questions, receiving a response rate of 70%.

## Housing Strategy Development at the Local Level 215

Company's part-exchange programme. An examination of other sites indicates that smaller, less expensive units appear to be those that are being produced by housebuilders. Personnel at David Wilson Homes, a company that is just entering this housing market, indicate that it is an area dominated by new properties at the lower end of the market. This appears to suggest that Mansfield is an area where there is demand for low cost homes, whilst Ashby has more demand for larger, more expensive homes. In terms of housing strategies this may suggest the private housebuilders in Mansfield are providing homes at the margins between 'need' and 'demand', whilst housebuilding companies in North West Leicestershire may be neglecting this area of housing provision, or at least were doing so at the time of the study. Whilst in terms of this research it would be beneficial if housing provision differs due to the different co-ordination techniques pursued by North West Leicestershire and Mansfield (see below), there is not sufficient evidence to suggest this is the case. In fact as will become apparent from the next section in this chapter (housing market monitoring) the differing types of provision are more likely due to differing market conditions than local authority direction.

Between 1991-1995 there were around 1,400 units completed on large sites, i.e. those that supply ten or more dwellings, in North West Leicestershire. Of these, approximately 400 have been built in the case study area of Ashby. Table 7.1, illustrates the development, developer and number of units built in the case study area over the last five years. This indicates that two developers have been responsible for over 50% of sites in the district. If new provision is largely dominated by a small number of housebuilders, then market monitoring may prove straightforward, (in comparison to housing provision fragmented between a number of different developers). For instance, if the District Authority were to build up a connection with these 'key' local builders, a great deal of information on the new housing market could be obtained from one or two contacts, highlighting that it may not be necessary to carry out extensive surveys. As highlighted in Chapter Five, the major limitation with housebuilding companies as a data source would be the manner in which the housebuilders could manipulate the data prepared for the local authority, or fail to provide any data at all. It is therefore necessary for the housebuilding company to be accommodating and supportive to the whole monitoring process.

Housebuilding companies would appear to be prepared to fulfil such goals (see Chapter Six) at the national level. In discussion with personnel at David Wilson, it emerged that housebuilders may, in principle, be supportive of co-operating with the local authority. However, it was indicated that it may prove commercially 'difficult'. Local housebuilding companies benefit from the fact that they have significant knowledge regarding housing markets in the local areas in which they operate. If this information and knowledge were to be given to the local authority and developed into a housing strategy, it may become common knowledge and examined by competitors, with the result that a locally based company sacrifices a major advantage in the market. The alternative to such an open approach may be to develop links with key housebuilders and only use any information gathered for internal policy formulation. However this course of action creates a situation where the local authority may appear to be closely involved with one or two housebuilders. This relationship may result in the authority being criticised for unethical behaviour.

What this appears to suggest is that the use of housebuilder data, in itself not above criticism (see Chapter Five), may create a number of additional problems not yet considered. If the data were to be employed it may have only been provided on the condition that it would not become public knowledge. This would bring into question the degree to which a housing strategy, employing such data, can be examined by the public and undergo external scrutiny. The alternative to direct and implicit housebuilder involvement is to consult in a general sense through housing forums and liaison groups.

In Mansfield a housing forum met throughout the 1990s on a bi-monthly basis and consists of officers (both from the planning and housing departments), architects, tenants associations, housebuilders and estate agents. The County Council do not participate and, according to personnel interviewed, discussion between the County Council and housebuilding companies takes place on an ad-hoc basis. In Leicestershire, it is the County Council that organise the bi-annual Housebuilders' Forum, the membership of which includes officers from both the County and Districts, local housebuilders, water companies and occasionally estate agents. It could be suggested that the Mansfield approach is more localised and is seen by the HBF as being 'innovative'. The major difference between the two approaches would appear to be that the Mansfield forum takes the view of the housing market as one single entity, encompassing social and private housing and examines localised issues. The Leicestershire approach would appear to focus more specifically on the private sector and is concerned primarily with strategic issues.

Discussions with housebuilders indicates that they feel they benefit from this exercise, not only because they can present their views, but also they are able to determine the direction in which the local authority's policy is moving, allowing their own strategy to develop alongside that of the planning authority. One would suggest that as long as housebuilders perceive participation as being beneficial, they will continue to participate in such forums. Involving housebuilders in housing strategy formulation and attempting to utilise their data and perceptions on market conditions is only one factor in the development of integrated strategies. In addition there is also a need for the housing and planning departments to work closely with one another.

**Housing Market Monitoring**

Although this area has been examined in two proceeding chapters, it would be beneficial to examine the means by which the needs and demands of a housing market can be formed in a practical, rather than theoretical, sense. This section will therefore examine the data available and discuss the implications for local housing markets that can be deduced from this type of information, essentially the survey section of local housing strategies.

It would be expected that districts would have access to data generated internally (see Chapters Five and Six above) and therefore, a strategy prepared by a district would be more detailed than the examination that follows, which is based primarily on publicly available data. As both Districts employ information technology in the planning department, to 'log' and monitor planning applications and the progress of developments, it should be relatively straightforward for this type of data (planning applications, changing densities, etc.) to be monitored and employed as a means of monitoring housing markets.

To obtain an overview of the housing needs and priorities in the district, it is necessary to examine the housing tenure and housing stock of the respective districts. As can be seen in the table below, there are distinct differences in the tenure patterns of the case study districts. North West

218 *The Formulation of Local Housing Strategies*

Leicestershire has a level of owner occupation above the county and regional average. Mansfield has a level above the county average but below the regional average. The level of private renting is within one percent in both districts and they both have a lower level of private renting than the region as a whole. This is possibly due to the fact that the figures for the region contain the large metropolitan areas, where private renting tends to be higher. For instance this tenure constitutes 15.5% of the housing stock in Nottingham district (OPCS, 1992a).

**Table 7.2 Tenure of the Case Study Districts**

|  | Total Households | Owner Occupied | Private Rented or from a Housing Association or With a Job | Local Authority Rented |
|---|---|---|---|---|
| **NW Leicestershire** | 31,142 | 73.5% | 9.3% | 17.2% |
| **Mansfield** | 39,816 | 69.2% | 8.9% | 22.0% |
| **Leicestershire** | 333,547 | 72.5% | 10.7% | 16.8% |
| **Nottinghamshire** | 397,769 | 68.2% | 10.8% | 21.0% |
| **East Midlands*** | 1,596,000 | 70.2% | 11.5% | 18.3% |

**Source:** Table G, 1991 Census County Reports for Leicestershire (Part 1); Nottinghamshire (Part 1) *CSO *Focus on the East Midlands*, 1990

Mansfield District retains a high proportion of local authority rented homes in its tenure portfolio, higher than both its own county average and the regional figure. By comparison, NW Leicestershire has a level of local authority renting in excess of the county average. The Housing Departments of both authorities have to monitor their housing stock, both private and public, annually. This data is submitted to the DETR as part of the Housing Investment Program submission. Table 7.3, highlights the character of the housing market in the two case study districts, as presented in HIP submissions.

Although social housing exists in the two case study districts, a significant proportion of both local authority and housing association stock is special needs housing, for OAPs or the disabled (see Table 7.3). The net

Table 7.3 Breakdown of the Dwelling Stock *(Percentages Italicised and in Brackets)*

| NW Leicestershire | Local Authority | Housing Association | Other Public Sector | Other Private Sector | Total |
|---|---|---|---|---|---|
| Total Dwellings | 5,478 | 1,187 | 22 | 27,811 | 34,498 |
| OAP | 1,913 *(34.9)* | 229 *(19.3)* | 0 | 31 | 2,173 |
| Disabled | 44 *(0.8)* | 3 *(0.3)* | 0 | 475 | 522 |
| Unfit Dwellings | 27 *(0.5)* | 0 | 0 | 2,290 | 2,317 |
| Dwellings in Need of Renovation | 1,440 *(26.3)* | 54 *(4.6)* | 0 | | |
| Difficult to Let | 179 *(3.3)* | 10 *(0.8)* | 0 | | |
| Vacant Dwellings | 75 *(1.4)* | 37 *(3.2)* | 0 | 1,526 | 1,638 |

| Mansfield | Local Authority | Housing Association | Other Public Sector | Other Private Sector | Total |
|---|---|---|---|---|---|
| Total Dwellings | 9,004 | 1,268 | 60 | 32,555 | 42,887 |
| OAP | 3,012 *(33.5)* | 244 *(19.2)* | 0 | 116 | 3,372 |
| Disabled | 55 *(0.6)* | 9 *(0.7)* | 0 | 0 | 64 |
| Unfit Dwellings | 585 *(6.5)* | 170 *(13.4)* | 0 | 2,700 | 3,455 |
| Dwellings in Need of Renovation | 6,976 *(77.5)* | 480 *(37.9)* | 0 | | |
| Difficult to Let | 430 *(4.8)* | 0 | 0 | | |
| Vacant Dwellings | 548 *(6.1)* | 30 *(2.4)* | 0 | 1,923 | 2,501 |

Source: Section A: Dwelling Stock of NW Leicestershire and Mansfield from 'Needs Appraisal', HIP 1 for the DoE, April 1995

result of this is that, for households wishing to rent from social housing providers, a limited supply is diminished even further. In addition, the homes that are available are often in need of renovation. In the case of Mansfield, 6.5% of the local authority stock has been declared unfit, whilst a further 77.5% of the stock is in need of renovation. Although the situation is not so dramatic in North West Leicestershire, over a quarter of the stock requires a degree of renovation.

The supposition from this data is that, overall, the social housing stock in Mansfield may be less attractive to marginal homebuyers, acting as a positive incentive to join the owner occupied housing market. This is supported by the fact that housebuilding companies in Mansfield largely construct properties aimed at the lower end of the market, therefore attractive to marginal households (i.e. those on the margins between social renting and owner occupation). However, discussions with sales personnel at various sites in Mansfield suggests this may not be the case and demand for new homes is lower, for certain types of home in the area than many other similar sites in other parts of the region. Estate agents indicated similar low demand for second hand homes when they were interviewed. Whilst this may be an indication of the housing market in Mansfield being for social housing, rather than owner occupation, one would argue that it is more likely to indicate an over-provision of homes for owner occupation in the area.

In terms of the housing types that are prevalent in the District, Table 7.4 compares the make-up of the housing stock in the case study districts. Data for the county and the region are shown for comparative purposes. NW Leicestershire has a high percentage of detached properties, considerably higher than the county or regional figures. In contrast, the District has a housing stock which is under-represented in terms of terraced homes. Mansfield has similar proportions of detached and terraced homes to Nottinghamshire and to the East Midlands as a whole. Where Mansfield appears to differ from the region and county is in terms of semi-detached homes where the District appears to have an over-representation.

Although it is not wise to draw too many conclusions from such simple tables as those examined above, it may be worthwhile highlighting the implications for the housing markets and housing strategies of these areas. As North West Leicestershire has a low proportion of terraced homes in the housing stock, there is an argument that a limited choice exists for the households in these areas. The most important ramification of this is that households in these districts may have a limited choice of one of the cheaper

Table 7.4 Dwelling Types in the Case Study Areas

| | Total Dwellings | Detached | Semi-Detached | Terraced | Purpose Built Flat | Converted Accommodation |
|---|---|---|---|---|---|---|
| NW Leicestershire | 32,337 | 35.5% | 37.0% | 21.3% | 5.5% | 0.7% |
| Mansfield | 41,579 | 24.3% | 42.8% | 24.2% | 7.7% | 0.9% |
| Leicestershire | 349,873 | 26.2% | 37.2% | 25.8% | 9.0% | 1.6% |
| Nottinghamshire | 413,743 | 27.7% | 35.6% | 24.8% | 10.2% | 1.6% |
| East Midlands* | 1,634,000 | 29.2% | 35.5% | 25.3% | 8.4% | 1.5% |

Source: Table H, 1991 Census County Reports for Leicestershire (Part 1) and Nottinghamshire (Part 1) DoE, 1995d

housing options, namely terraced homes. Examining house prices, for example, indicates that the cheaper homes are usually terraced properties and this can be seen by examining any of the commonly-cited house price series. For instance in the first quarter of 1995, terraced homes in the UK were 21.6% cheaper than the average house price, while detached homes were 67% more expensive (Halifax House Price Index). The logical conclusion from this is that the housing market of NW Leicestershire is more constrained for the marginal home buyer, than is the case in Mansfield, as it has a higher proportion of the more expensive house types.

Not only does NW Leicestershire have fewer terraced properties, but those that do exist in the District, (demonstrated by Ashby in Figure 7.3) are also more expensive than those traded in Mansfield. It should be noted that these figures, because they refer to small geographical areas, are based on small sample sizes, a problem that is particularly noticeable in the case of Ashby, where insufficient data is available to plot some quarters. This said, in general Ashby's prices are between £5,000-£10,000 more expensive than those in Mansfield. Can the population of this area afford to pay such high house prices? As these house prices are based on applications for mortgages accepted by the Halifax, one would have to suggest that, these house prices are affordable. Yet this area of affordability and income is worth examining further as it may allow housing strategies to estimate levels of housing need.

The preceding discussion has indicated what assumptions can be made regarding the housing markets of the two districts from data that is readily available. Yet the questionnaire study examined in Chapter Six (completed by both planning departments) does indicate that both case study councils monitor the housing market more directly. One of the questions concerned the use of affordability data, i.e. data such as the TSB's affordability index for first time buyers, and the Housing Market Report's affordability data. Neither case study district answered positively to having employed affordability ratios, but planning officers at Mansfield are of the opinion that it would be a useful data source if the difficulties in collating the data could be overcome. Similarly, neither District has tried to estimate the average income levels in their areas. The only income data that has been obtained by NW Leicestershire is through a housing need survey. NW Leicestershire has carried out its own housing survey (see below) and one part of this questionnaire concerned the annual income of a household. Of the 489 who responded to this questionnaire, 29% did not answer this question. Of those that did, 14% had a household income below £6,000;

Housing Strategy Development at the Local Level 223

**Figure 7.1 Comparison of Terraced House Prices in the Case Study Areas**

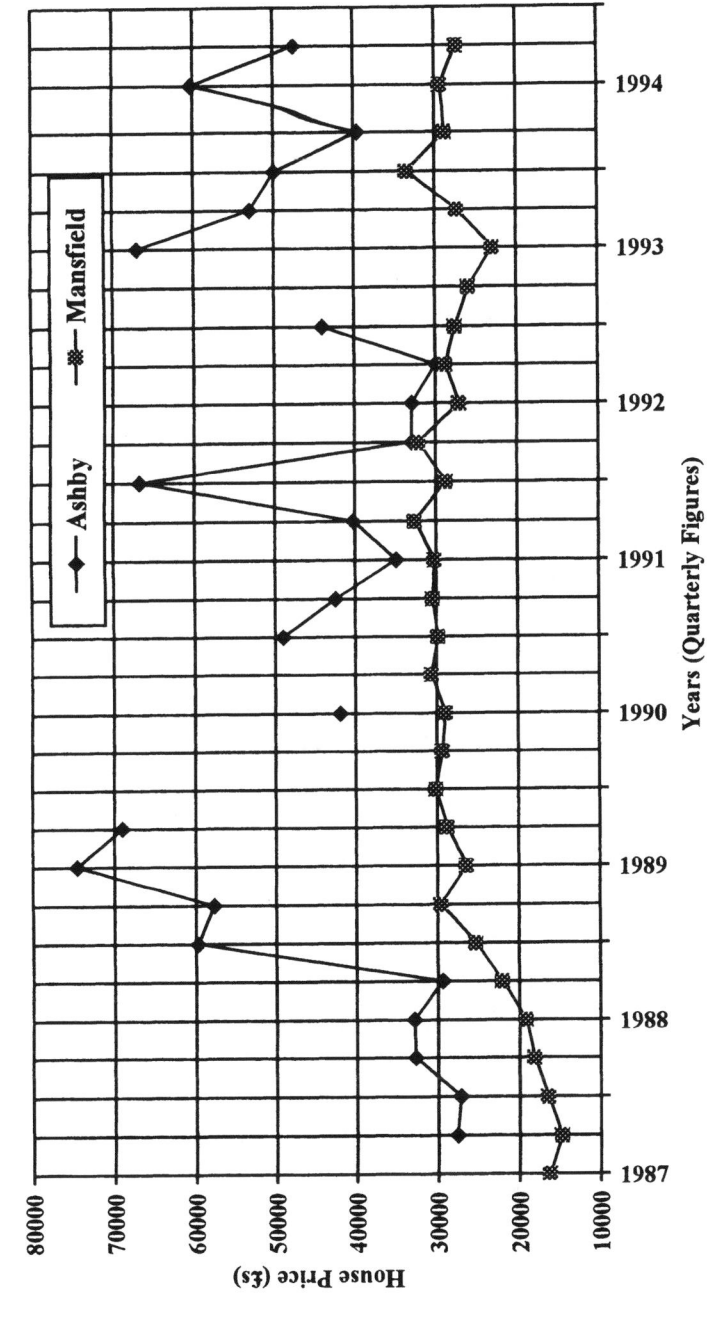

Source: Halifax Data

224  *The Formulation of Local Housing Strategies*

**Figure 7.2  Semi-Detached House Prices in the Case Study Areas**

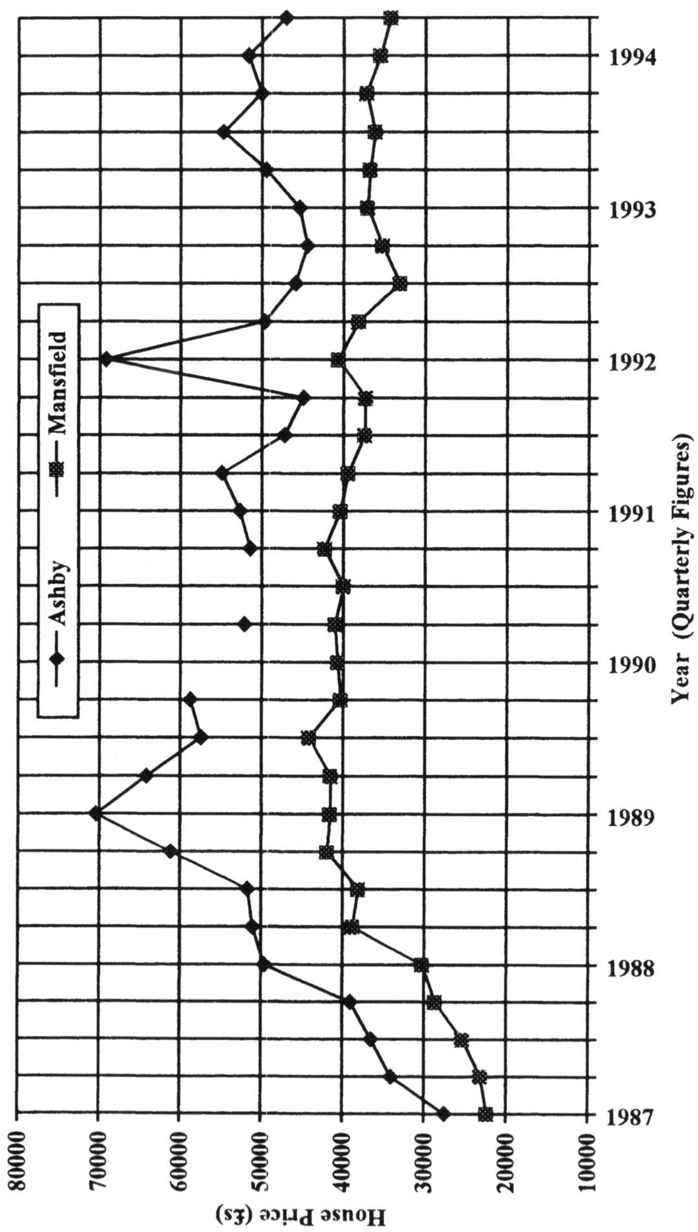

Source: Halifax Data

13% between £6,000-£9,999; 15% between £10,000-£14,999 and the remaining 29% earned more than £15,000. When compared with the national gross average annual income of £18,205 (Table 27, CSO, 1992) it would appear that North West Leicestershire is a district where incomes were at a low level.

One alternative method of determining income characteristics is to make assumptions based upon the type of employment that dominates in an area. For instance North West Leicestershire planners see the most common type of employment in the district as B8, storage and distribution (DoE, 1987). According to the Transport and General Workers Union (TandGWU) the average wage for employees in this type of work, warehouse or storekeepers, in July 1995 was between £200-£250 per week, (data supplied by the TandGWU in August 1995). This level of weekly wage would result in an annual salary of between £10,400-£13,000 per annum. Employing this figure in a similar manner to that which is illustrated in Table 5.2, NW Leicestershire can be seen as having a larger mismatch between affordable homes and incomes. For instance if an average income in the District for an employee of one of the distribution warehouses is around £12,000 then, on a 90% mortgage, a house of around £30,300 could be purchased. It can be seen from the house price figure above (Figure 7.3) that even terraced homes in Ashby are unobtainable on this income. Whilst Figure 7.4, indicates that semi-detached homes in Ashby are on average priced £15,000- £20,000 higher. As this equates to 37% of the housing stock in the district it may clearly limit the chances for the lower paid sections of the population. This may clearly indicate a need for a housing strategy to enable more affordable or low-cost home ownership.

*Housing Need Surveys*

As mentioned already North West Leicestershire has conducted a housing need survey, a method of developing information that has not been undertaken by Mansfield. In January 1991, NW Leicestershire sent 34,000 survey forms to every household in the District. By September, 8,007 completed forms had been returned. Discounting vacant properties, this gave a response rate of 24.6%. This low response rate conceals the fact that different parishes in the district responded differently to the questionnaire. The less populous parishes tended to have a lower response rate than the urban centres, simply because there are less people in these parts of the

226  *The Formulation of Local Housing Strategies*

district. The main problem is that the low number of responses from villages and other rural parts of the district may mean that the survey cannot be relied upon for 'exceptional' housing need developments. The officers at North West Leicestershire realise this and are of the opinion that the survey was beneficial in providing an overview of the District, and if any detailed study is required to justify the 'exceptional' developments, then a detailed locally-based survey will be employed. In addition, to enable future housing surveys to be carried out, the elected members have to sanction funding, and they will only do this if it can be demonstrated that there is a need for the survey.

The planners in North West Leicestershire were of the opinion that the questionnaire was not particularly beneficial for them, which they attributed to the fact that the Housing Department, as the leader of the survey, drafted the questionnaire, so that the form of the responses were not particularly helpful. One major difficulty was that three departments provided the funding for the study, and all three had to obtain approval from their own committees for the expenditure, further complicating the matter and delaying the process. This illustrates that practical difficulties of departmentalism can affect even the successful monitoring of housing markets, let alone the implementation of housing strategies. This view of housing need surveys in practice should be compared with the results apparent from the questionnaire survey, where housing need surveys were seen to be a 4* rated in terms of usefulness (Table 6.44). This demand indicator has been singled out because one would argue that such direct market monitoring has increased in importance with the introduction of Circulars 13/96, 6/98 and with a good practice guide having been prepared and published (Bramley, Pawson and Parker, 2000).

**Conclusion**

This chapter has focused the discussion more directly on the situation at the local level. It has developed the data examined in earlier chapters and attempted to arrive at some conclusions regarding local housing markets. Broadly it has examined three focus areas:

- Department co-ordination, essentially the integration of planning and housing departments.

## Housing Strategy Development at the Local Level 227

- Joint agency working, better integration between policy formulation and policy implementation.
- Housing market monitoring and the findings that can be reached from analysing housing data.

This chapter has examined these themes in a practical context, namely the situation in the two case study areas. This therefore developed the themes examined in the proceeding chapter which focused more directly on the results of the questionnaire survey.

It has been shown in this Chapter that the two case study authorities take a different approach as to the degree to which the housing and planning departments develop policy and work in a corporate manner in terms of housing. The officers at Mansfield appear to accept the need for greater strategic integration and a joint working group exists in the District. The approach taken by North West Leicestershire is less formalised, largely relying upon individual and personal relationships between the officers themselves rather than more formal links. Both authorities indicated that differences in the management of the planning and housing departments (decentralisation and compulsory competitive tendering) created difficulties in physically integrating both the priorities of the departments and the working practices. In North West Leicestershire, the practical difficulties created by local government bureaucracy and departmentalism resulted in the housing needs survey producing disappointing results for the planning department.

The second area concerned the integration of policy formulation and implementation, namely the manner in which the local authority co-ordinate with housebuilding companies in an attempt to ensure housing policies and strategies are realised. The interviews with housebuilders and the local authority indicated that both case study authorities enjoyed good working relationships, both with the housebuilders representative agencies (HBF) and the housebuilding companies themselves. Interviews and discussions found that it may be problematic to try and attain information from selected 'key' housebuilding companies. Firstly, key housebuilding companies would be those with the best knowledge of the local housing market. As pointed out by one housebuilder, this expert local knowledge may be the factor that allows such housebuilders to operate effectively in the local housing market. As a result, housebuilders may be unwilling to provide such information in a form that could be of benefit to their competitors. Such a close relationship with one or two key housebuilders may also be problematic for the local authority. It may, for instance, result in the local authority leaving itself open to accusations of bias when it comes to dealing with applications from these 'key' housebuilders.

This chapter has shown that both authorities participate in housing forums, although they involve slightly different agencies and would appear to focus on slightly different areas of the housing market. The forum in North West Leicestershire is organised by the County and tends to be a specific arena for discussion on strategic housing maters. The Mansfield forum is organised by the district council themselves and would appear to examine more detailed areas than that of Leicestershire. It is encouraging that both case study authorities participate in housing forums, as it appears from the questionnaire (see Chapter Six) that a significant number of authorities are not involved in such a process. It could be suggested that as these 'discussion' groups, are attended by a number of different agencies, it may allow the local authority to gain information regarding the housing market, whilst still appearing to be disassociated from the housebuilding companies. The housebuilding companies themselves would appear to be willing to participate in such forums as they can gain an insight into the local authorities future strategies (see above).

The third area examined in this chapter concerned the data that can be utilised for monitoring housing markets. As mentioned in the earlier chapters, one would expect the local authorities themselves to be in a position to monitor and disaggregate data to a greater degree than is possible for a study such as this. Notwithstanding this fact, this research has still been able to examine the housing market and develop some conclusions regarding the likely needs and demands for housing provision in the two case study districts. To summarise, it would appear that North West Leicestershire has a housing market dominated by more expensive properties and having a relatively limited social housing stock. Mansfield has a housing stock which has a greater number of cheaper properties, and higher numbers of social homes to rent. From an examination of income estimates, this chapter highlighted that the work force of both districts could not be described as well paid, and this may create significant problems in the Ashby area, due to the higher house prices. In the examination of Ashby, it was possible to highlight the results of a new house purchaser survey, which indicated that a high percentage of respondents commuted to work. This suggested that the housing market may be supported by households with a primary income earned in another area, casting doubt on the usefulness of local income based housing demand and need estimates.

The examination of 'real data' in this chapter (in addition to the theoretical discussion of Chapter Five) underlined the fact that some monitoring may be problematic due to small data sets upon which to base any conclusions. Data generated by movements in the housing market such as transactions, house prices, etc., would therefore appear to be more useful when the housing market is buoyant, and data sets are large. Uncertainty caused by 'missing' data (Figures 7.3 and 7.4) may mean that local housing strategies fall back upon data which implies certain housing market pressures (levels of unemployment, income levels, etc.) and the perceptions of those who are working in the housing market (housebuilders and estate agents for instance). Of these, it would appear that the first type are used, as they are contained within local plans and structure plans, although, as stressed in Chapter Six, it is apparent that economic policy is directly reflected in housing policy in fewer authorities than one might expect.

This chapter has attempted to examine, in practical terms, the concepts that have been discussed elsewhere in this research. It is clear that both case-study districts have attempted different approaches towards housing market monitoring and housing strategy preparation. Perhaps the most significant conclusion that can be drawn from this local focus, concerns attitudes. At the local level it would appear that a number of other concerns, far more mundane than is apparent from a desk-top study, hamper the development of integrated housing strategies which involve housebuilders. These more mundane uncertainties range from questions of funding for needs-based housing research to uncertainty regarding the security of employment, through programs such as compulsory competitive tendering. One would suggest that the onset of local government reorganisation may create further uncertainties, especially with regard to the technical treatment of housing market areas. These are significant problems that will have to be examined, as it is ultimately the enthusiasm of the officers that will result in a housing strategy being developed.

# 8 Concluding Comments

**Introduction**

This research has examined the formulation of local authority housing strategies, through the employment of empirical questionnaire surveys, interviews and a review of relevant literature. This chapter will present and discuss the conclusions that can be drawn from this project whilst indicating areas where future research could be directed. In addition it is important to reconsider how the methodology, identified in Chapter One, progressed, including any areas which did not develop as initially expected. First it is worthwhile reiterating the aims and objectives of this study.

**Overview**

As stated in Chapter One the objective of this study was to critically examine the formulation of local authority housing strategies. This was to be achieved through the resolution of three research questions;

1. To what degree do local authorities operate in a fashion that allows policies to be integrated and co-ordinated?
2. To what extent are private housebuilding companies, as the main implementers of housing policy, involved in the development of housing strategies?
3. To what extent do local authorities employ relevant data as a means of monitoring the housing market?

Initial work indicated that the majority of new dwellings continue to be supplied by the private sector and it was seen that it would be interesting to examine the manner in which local authorities, and in particular the planning department, can influence this supply. It then became apparent that there exists within a local authority structure a system for developing a strategy which impacts upon the housing production of private housebuilding companies. As this housing strategy has been largely prepared by the housing department, it became clear that there would be a need to examine the manner in which the two departments co-ordinated and developed policy. These areas had been examined in the past and calls have been made for the fuller integration of housing and planning documents as well as greater involvement of private housebuilders in the development of policy and identification of land (DoE, 1977b; 1979; Carter, Brown and Abbot, 1991a, 1991b; Audit Commission, 1992; Cole and Goodchild; 1993, DoE, 1995c).

At this stage a research field had developed and this focused directly upon formulation of housing strategies. However to form a strategy, local authorities would have to be in a position to prioritise the housing needs and demands of an area, an objective that requires a knowledge of the housing market (in the widest sense). Whilst Chapters Two and Three could be seen as providing a contextual background to the discussion Chapter Four investigated housing strategy formulation more directly, and in doing so focused specifically on the first two research questions. This chapter progressed the discussion through presenting results from the empirical surveys. Essentially it examined three different aspects of integrated housing strategy formulation approaches.

Firstly, the relationship between central and local government. One conclusion that could be drawn from this discussion was that, initially, central government perceived the local authority, through the housing department, as being the implementer of a housing policy and a housing strategy. However, for the last 20 years it has become increasingly the case that direct provision of housing by the local authority, the most direct way of ensuring a housing strategy is implemented, has become increasingly less important. This has been apparent with the focus of the housing strategy programme becoming one of financial management, rather than an instrument for directing future housing supply.

Secondly, the discussion focused upon the degree to which local authority departments, particularly the housing and planning departments, co-ordinate their housing policies. This is clearly an area that is of crucial importance for the development of integrated housing strategies, forms a specific research question and it is an area that had been examined in a number of DoE publications in the mid-1990s (DoE, 1995b and 1995c). The chapter argued that departmental structure has led the housing department to be primarily concerned with social rented homes, whilst the planning department has found itself dealing with speculative housebuilders and the owner occupied sector. This is a generalisation, yet it illustrates that the two departments tended to become divided in terms of the tenures of the housing market with which they are primarily concerned.

Such tenure-based approaches to housing policy is clearly more of a hindrance than a help. For instance, in terms of demand, households may move from tenure to tenure throughout their housing history, taking advantage of the different attributes of each tenure, yet does the present view of the housing market reflect this? Creating an integrated housing strategy, within which local authority departments interact more fully, may help overcome these tenure based attitudes. Such an approach is necessary due to the growth of both 'hybrid' tenures, such as shared ownership, and planning policies which seek to achieve social housing from private speculative housing, through planning gain. These steps will have meant that both departments will be working closer with one another, and the logical step is for this to develop into policies and strategies. It was shown through the presentation of the results of the empirical research that the majority of local authorities do prepare integrated housing strategies, although almost without exception the housing department plays the dominant role in the development of such documents. This is again, perhaps, to be expected, as the strategy could well be seen as being an expansion of the HIP policy documents. Yet this may limit the development of the housing strategy, as the planning department may be better placed to involve housebuilding companies in the process.

The third area examined in Chapter Four concerned the working relationship between the local authority and the implementers of policy, namely housebuilding companies (research question two). The discussion highlighted the ways in which planning authorities and housebuilding companies have worked with one another in the past, through joint land availability studies and similar working groups. There was little evidence of housebuilding companies developing links and connections with the housing department and it was suggested that housebuilders would only

Concluding Comments 233

take an interest in HIPs if they are involved in building homes on a contract basis. As strategy preparation is largely led by the housing department this indicates that there may be difficulties in ensuring housebuilding companies are involved in the process. This tends to demonstrate that if integrated housing strategies were to develop from the strategic statement of HIPs, it is necessary for the personnel in the planning department to become increasingly involved with their colleagues in the housing department, to ensure that the former's knowledge of housebuilders is effectively employed. The empirical research indicated that a number of authorities organised housing liaison groups where the housebuilding companies (as well as other interested parties) discussed housing issues with the local authority. One would suggest that this forum could be developed to form a discussion group upon which housing strategy formulation could be based.

This chapter was the first to introduce the results of the questionnaire surveys which were to increasingly play an important part in the following chapters. What had not yet been examined was the means by which housing strategies would be formulated and based upon the needs and demands of local housing markets, and this was achieved in the following chapters.

Chapter Five critically examined the data that could be employed by local authorities as part of a program of housing market monitoring. The data examined ranged from that which is available from commercial organisations, such as building society house price series, to information that the local authority already collects, such as housing waiting lists. In an attempt to illustrate the strengths and weaknesses of each data set, a grading system was employed, and the results were illustrated in Table 5.7. The examination found that no single data set could be presented as an 'ideal' means of monitoring housing markets. In fact, the indications are that all the data sets examined possess one or more limitations. The question of availability was seen to be a major problem with certain data sets, particularly those that relied on private agencies (such as housebuilders or estate agents) to provide the data. This led directly to the second problem with data sets, and this was the degree to which they could be manipulated to illustrate trends in the housing market that may not be occurring. It would appear that the data sets most open to manipulation are those which are developed from actions that require minimal financial commitment, for instance planning enquiries. The final, and perhaps most significant limitation, concerns the degree to which a data set accurately indicates housing market demand. This was based upon the assertion that certain data sets may indicate factors other than changes in housing demand. Although work published since the research for this book was completed has developed part of this area (Maclennan et al., 1998) there are still points made in this chapter and the following one that are not covered elsewhere. For instance although Maclennans work is useful as it focuses on local housing systems, the document is only a 'best practice guide' and is not statutory guidance. As a result Scottish Homes have decided not to undertake any national surveys into it's use amongst there own managers, never mind the housing strategists elsewhere. As a result the research in this book goes further, as it presents the results of a study into the use of alternative market monitoring data as well as illustrating how they could be used to develop a housing strategy for two case study areas. In addition there does not appear to be any guidance comparable to that of Scottish Homes for those currently working south of the border.

Chapter Six presented the results of the empirical survey that sought to resolve a number of different questions, among them the use of data sets. Questionnaires were sent to all metropolitan authorities and county councils and all districts in the East Midlands. The response rates were high and one would argue that this should support the assertion that the results are representative of housing market monitoring and strategy integration at a local level. Broadly speaking these questionnaires examined three areas;

- the level of inter-department working as regards housing strategies;
- the co-operation between the council and outside agencies; and
- the use of data by local authorities and the degree to which they have found it useful.

On the whole, it would appear that a wide number of different data sets are monitored by local authorities, with different perceptions regarding the levels of usefulness. As one would expect, the more frequently employed data would appear to be that which the authority can obtain easily, either through their own records or from some other source. The least popular means of monitoring housing markets tended to be those that required the co-operation of housebuilders or estate agents and the data sets produced by these agencies, also tend to be those that had a low 'grading' in Chapter Five, yet it was shown that this type of data was perceived as being useful by a number of authorities and may therefore justify some additional research.

Questions concerning the involvement of outside agencies in the formulation of housing strategies examined two specific areas:

- Firstly the degree to which a body such as a housing liaison group is established by the authority, and the agencies that attend, or are members of, such forums. The replies to these questions indicated that such a forum existed in between a third and a half of respondent authorities and on average four different agencies attended. This is arguably a smaller percentage than may have been expected, given that such groups have been encouraged by a number of studies and DoE circulars.
- The second question concerned the use of surveys of housebuilding companies; estate agents and building societies as a means of gauging opinion on the housing market. Overall, surveys of housebuilding companies appeared to be the most popular, with very little work being carried out with respect to estate agents and the lenders. This may have changed slightly latterly with the development of methods to formulate housing need studies.

It was common for many of the respondents to highlight the fact that they had significant doubts regarding the extent to which housebuilding companies would be prepared to provide information regarding levels of sales, reservations, etc. This was seen to be a valid concern. Therefore it was necessary to determine the degree to which housebuilders would be prepared to give information to the planners. The response to this questionnaire was lower than those sent to the local authorities, so the results may not be as reliable. However, the survey did show that of those that responded, a clear majority were prepared to allow access to their data.

Each of Chapters One through to Six had examined specific areas of housing strategy formulation in an attempt to develop the discussion logically through the research questions. It was clear however that the research questions may be answered more directly through an examination of each research question as represented by the case study districts, and this was the objective of the penultimate chapter, Chapter Seven.

Chapter Seven examined housing market monitoring and housing strategy development at the local level, highlighting the situation that exists in the two case study areas. Although data from the case study areas had been examined in earlier chapters (where the discussion of data sets were illustrated through using Ashby and Mansfield as examples) Chapter Seven took a more direct approach, comparing the experiences and practices of the two districts in terms of the three research questions namely:

- Integration of policy development within the local authority.
- The degree to which the local authority consulted with other agencies, particularly private housebuilding companies.
- What conclusions can be drawn from an examination of housing market data?

The examination of these areas indicated that there was significant differences between the approaches adopted in the two areas, differences that will be looked at in turn.

In terms of corporate working within the local authority, the district councils took significantly different approaches. In Mansfield an internal planning and housing working group exists, suggesting the process of policy co-ordination was formalised. In contrast, the authority responsible for housing policy in Ashby relied upon officer contacts for policy co-ordination between the housing and planning departments. The approach at North West Leicestershire appears to be more informal than that applied by Mansfield.

Both authorities indicated that corporate working was problematic and this was seen to be due, primarily, to the following reasons;

1. At the time of the study both housing departments had recently undergone compulsory competitive tendering, creating a situation where the housing department has been preoccupied with different priorities. The result of this is that it may be difficult to free resources at the same time to work on policy development together.
2. Simple geography can often create practical problems for attempts at joint department working. Housing services are often

provided through decentralised area offices. This can result in housing and planning officers being physically separate, making it difficult to consult one another regularly.
3. As both departments are directed by different district council committees and both have their own dedicated budgets, there may be problems in funding joint projects. This was seen to be a limitation in the case of a housing need survey conducted in NW Leicestershire.

In terms of working with other agencies, in particular private housebuilding companies, both authorities had again taken slightly different approaches. In the case of North West Leicestershire a forum organised by the county council met twice a year. The membership of this forum suggests that it is focused towards strategic issues, rather than more specific local housing matters. The Mansfield forum meets with greater regularity and is organised by the District Council itself. The membership of this forum would appear to suggest that it differs from the Leicestershire body in two respects. Firstly it examines both social housing and private market housing, an integrated approach that is lacking in the Leicestershire forum. Secondly, the forum would appear to focus on local issues to a far greater degree than that of Leicestershire.

The alternative to forum discussions is to gain information directly from agencies such as housebuilding companies. Discussion with one of the most active local housebuilders would suggest that housebuilding companies may support such data gathering methods, a conclusion supported by the survey of housebuilding companies that was examined in Chapter Six. However there may be limitations to this approach which may seriously question its usefulness. These limitations, discussed in Chapter Seven, coupled to the problems with the private housebuilder data that could be monitored (discussed in Chapter Five) suggest that forum discussions may be the most useful method of gaining information from agencies outside the local authority, and in particular housebuilders. Again, this is not an innovative suggestion, but it can be seen from the questionnaire results that it may have become less of a priority for many authorities. If forums are to be encouraged as a means through which the local authority can gauge market demand and build links with the implemeters of policy then one would suggest they should be developed to become more like the forum in existence in Mansfield. Local preference would decide the membership of such forums, but clearly it should involve, the local planning and housing departments, housebuilders (to provide information on new supply), estate agents (providing information on the demand for both second hand properties and those to rent privately) and housing associations (to highlight social housing demand).

Chapter Seven also examined the data that may be employed as a means of monitoring housing markets. The discussion illustrated that significant data is available at either a district, or more local level. Moreover, in examining the data it became clear that a number of different agencies could provide an insight into the local housing market and the profile of the resident households. An analysis of this data indicated that the housing markets of the two areas were experiencing different housing demands and needs. What was apparent was that if the present research could obtain such information, then so could the local authority. The local authority would be expected to be able to supplement the data considered in this chapter with data it can (or does) collect itself.

An interesting conclusion from the case studies was the degree to which the housing market does not reflect the local authority boundary. In the case of Ashby, the local housing market would appear to cross the boundary into the West Midlands, reflecting the fact that Ashby is part of the Burton travel-to-work area. This was also inferred from examining the housing market of Ashby from the perspective of new home buyers, indicating that travel-to-work distances were such that cross-district migration may be common place. In terms of housing market monitoring, this may undermine the relevancy of income data and income estimates, as these would largely be based upon the resident district population, and do little to estimate the income of neighbouring households, who may be the groups most likely to purchase new homes. What it does suggest is a need for greater cross-district, cross-county, or even cross-regional co-operation and co-ordination.

One question that remains to be asked is the degree to which the case studies can be seen as representative of the situation elsewhere. The situation in Ashby would appear to be less than innovative in terms of the methods the district council employ in trying to develop housing strategies. Mansfield appears to be rather more inventive, developing both internal connections between departments and a locally based external liaison group. One might suggest that the case studies would therefore represent a pro-active authority (Mansfield) and a rather inactive authority (North

West Leicestershire), in addition to the criteria which formed the basis for case study selection. Other authorities could be expected to have developed policy in a manner similar to one of these two approaches or, if not, then somewhere between the two.

## Re-engagement With Contemporary Research Discussions and Policy Debates

The research that was carried out for this work was concluded by 1996. At the time it appeared as though there was renewed interest in the development of integrated housing strategies. For instance the DoE increasingly encouraged the housing strategy section of HIPs to develop and reflect the contribution that can be made by the private sector. As highlighted in 1995, there was a view that:

> Local authorities should take a strategic approach to addressing housing needs and service delivery, and are expected to develop, and keep under review, a housing strategy. In addressing the full range of housing activities and programmes, authorities should consider their role both as landlord and enabler, with policies and programmes to encourage support and assist the activity of others. (DoE, 1995c, p. 1)

This government encouragement developed from discussion that had been ongoing since the start of the 1990s (Carter, Brown and Abbot, 1991a, 1991b; Audit Commission, 1992; DoE, 1993d, 1995b, 1995c; Goodlad, 1992,1994). Whilst there were also calls from the Royal Town Planning Institute and the Rural Development Commission for more enhanced housing strategies to meet housing needs more effectively (Planning Week, 1996; RDC, 1996). Similarly academic work has also highlighted the need for better quality data with which housing markets may be monitored as well as focusing upon the interrelationship between planning policies and housing markets (for instance Bramley, 1996 and Bramley's submission to the House of Commons Select Committee, HoC, 1996).

However in the intervening 5 years it appears as if only parts of integrated housing strategy development has moved forward. For instance the realisation that greater research is required has thus far only been reflected through greater support for housing need surveys. Similarly the acceptance that greater corporate and inter agency working is required has thus far focused strongly on the providers, and to a degree the users, of social housing. There are clearly some exceptions, such as the Scottish Homes published guidance, but it is difficult to estimate how far this is used, either by the organisations own offices or more importantly by local authorities in general.

There is a possibility that the development of housing strategies may now stagnate, in a similar way to the situation that occurred in the 1970s when HIPs became focused on financial and social housing issues. One would argue that over the last 5 years the concept of an integrated housing strategy, that may have blossomed out of the studies and directions issued in the mid-1990s has been pruned, with the most politically palatable and possibly straightforward sections being adopted, whilst the remainder, has been left to wither.

**Findings**

Perhaps the principal finding of this research is that the housing market should be examined as a single entity, with all different tenures, house types, housing providers, housing demands, examined as part of an integrated approach; both internally (between departments) and externally (between local authorities and housebuilding companies, housing associations, etc.). Maybe this is easier said than done given that policy, direct provision, support networks and social norms all focus on certain parts, often not even trying to understand the impacts changes in one component may have on the other sectors of the housing 'market'.

If a single entity approach were to be accepted, it follows that the local authority would have to develop a means of effectively monitoring local housing markets. This illustrates the three research questions that have underpinned this research.

*Internal Inter-Department Collaboration*

Such a comprehensive approach appears to occur in a very fragmented way (both internal and external links). At their best, local authorities' housing and planning departments co-ordinate and integrate their policies (creating an 'internal consensus'). Yet the results of the surveys in this research have shown that a number of local authorities fall short of such innovative and integrated approaches. Perhaps this is far from surprising, given the difficulties of collaboration. One would suggest that the structure of many local government departments does not facilitate such collaboration. In addition, the pressures placed on authorities throughout the 1990s (ranging from compulsory competitive tendering to re-organisation) created a climate of uncertainty.

As shown by the survey results, integrated housing strategies are prepared by the majority of local authorities. However, the lead role is taken by the housing department in almost all cases. As the housing department usually takes the lead role, it might be suggested that housing strategies are, consequently, closer to the strategic document of the HIP submission, which has been shown by earlier work to be viewed negatively by housebuilders. If this is the case, then there is a need for the housing strategy process to be more fully developed, more in line with the type of 'new' strategy called for over recent years, if only to involve the agency of implementation (in the majority of cases housebuilding companies) more directly.

Mansfield and North West Leicestershire were seen to employ differing methods of co-ordination. In North West Leicestershire it was shown that the officers contacted one another on an informal basis to discuss issues of interest if and when required. In Mansfield, interdepartmental communication was far more formal, with regular meetings being held. Whether one technique is significantly better than the other was not established. However, one would argue that it is *likely* Mansfield is closer to integrating housing policy formulation because the formal working group approach may create joint working, which would mean both housing and planning policies could be developed fully aware of the needs and demands of the other department. Although Mansfield had not undertaken a housing needs survey, one would suggest that if this were to be undertaken (as has been the case in North West Leicestershire), the results would be of great practical utility. This assertion is made due to the joint working group being in a position to develop the survey jointly, which was not the case in North West Leicestershire, where the housing needs survey was of little use to the planning department.

It may transpire that recently issued best practice guidance examining housing need studies may encourage greater collaboration. It would be interesting to compare the conclusion of this book with future research which could examine the situation in 2005 for example.

## External Inter-Agency Collaboration

As shown in this research, external collaboration between local authorities and housebuilding companies has been problematic, possibly due to the fact that housebuilding companies have had a combative relationship with local authorities in the past. It was shown that, through joint land studies, planning departments have had experience of co-operating and working with private housebuilding companies. It would follow that these forums may develop to allow discussion on the housing market to be undertaken. One would suggest that since the advent of sections 54a and 106 of the 1991 Act, closer working has become more important for the housebuilding company and should, in the future, improve understanding. The internal collaboration between departments, if it is to result in one single published document regarding a districts' housing policy, should ensure that housebuilding companies are aware of all the objectives that an authority would wish to see achieved within its housing market.

In terms of external connections, the questionnaire indicated that some of the most proactive local authorities would appear to involve housebuilders and housing associations in consultations and discussions at a pre-policy stage. At best local authorities consult widely and survey a number of different participants in the housing market, however a number of authorities do not meet 'best practice'.

Although housebuilding companies, constructing for private owner occupation, are responsible for in excess of 80% of housing starts, it is important to realise that most properties traded in the housing market are second-hand. It is therefore crucial for the authority preparing the housing strategy to work with agencies, such as estate agents, to gain an insight into the needs and demands within the second hand housing market. In addition, estate agents can provide detail regarding private rented homes, arguably the housing market's most flexible tenure. The use of estate agents as a means of gathering data is very limited, but it is essential for the housing strategy to gain as much insight into the housing market if it is to present a range of policies which reconcile the global demand for housing with cost and environmental constraints. Similarly, one would suggest that there should be consideration by the local authority of a greater involvement of building societies and banks, in an attempt to illustrate the economic circumstances of an area's households. This last point is worth reiterating, as a number of banks and building societies have recently become increasingly proactive in the housing market, illustrated by the number of mortgage rescue units which have been established, and tend to work alongside local authorities in such circumstances.

One issue that may well increase in importance over the next five or ten years is inter-authority working. The research illustrated that housing markets do not respect administrative boundaries, and cross district/county/regional commuting could create significant difficulties in determining demand from indicators based on the administrative area. As re-organisation has created a local government structure which may have little in the way of hierarchical co-ordination, it may become increasingly difficult for markets to be determined and monitored. To overcome this type of problem, it would be useful for the authorities to establish frameworks for inter-authority working as part of the re-organisation process. Perhaps this would legitimately lead to an increased role for the Government regional offices, to act as a co-ordinator. In the East Midlands, steps have already been taken to increase the degree to which the different authorities co-ordinate with one another. In place of the existing regional forum, officers developed a regional association. Yet more will have to be done to develop inter-regional links to increase understanding of the processes involved in inter-regional commuting and migration, of a type seen in Ashby. Even the proposal for more regional autonomy through the devolution to the English regions would not overcome this issue.

*Data Monitoring by Local Authorities*

This research has examined a number of data sets that could be employed to monitor changes in housing demand. Clearly a number of data sets would not appear to be reliable indicators of housing demand, as they are likely to be effected by other factors in the economy or changes in consumer preference. The number of possible data sets are eroded further when one considers that certain data may not be available or may be open to manipulation. The net result of this is that few data sets may be of sufficient 'quality' or produced frequently enough and disaggregated to a useful geographical level to be of benefit. In practical terms, it was suggested that some of the data that is frequently employed by local authorities may not be of a 'quality' to be relied upon. This suggests that there is a need for better data upon which to base housing strategies. It was shown that in Scotland the legal registering of house purchase, the Sasines, provides an invaluable data base of trends and movements in owner occupation. This can be used to chart migration patterns (perhaps the most uncertain part of household projections) as well as giving an accurate and extensive house price data base. In England and Wales the Land Registry have developed and now (2001) produce a similar data set. However, it is uncertain whether or not, legally, researchers in England and Wales could use this data to monitor migration. Other data sets exist which provide considerable data on house purchase and house purchasers, for instance the DoE 5% series. At the moment the sample is too small to be a major data source for the development of housing policy, yet it should not be ignored.

This research has illustrated that a housing market can be seen to be a different concept for different agencies. It can range from a term used to describe the process of achieving housing goals, to a term that describes a geographical area, creating a problem in so far as different agencies may refer to different definitions of a 'housing market'. One would suggest that a housing strategy prepared by a local authority, an agency which is geographically focused on an administrative area rather than a housing market, will be a compromise. The manner in which the geographical view of housing markets cross district, county, regional and in some cases national, boundaries, result in authorities being unable to fully influence and reflect all the factors that create housing demand within their boundaries. However, this is not to say that housing strategies should be ignored. One would suggest that, as they develop, neighbouring strategies should become equally supportive. For instance, North West Leicestershire, in examining the housing situation in Ashby, would be able to consult with the neighbouring authorities to establish the manner in which changes in neighbouring housing demands may affect the situation in Ashby.

Overall the questionnaire-based sections of the research would seem to suggest four key conclusions:

- Local authorities tend to use a number of key data sets, but rarely examine other relevant indicators that may be useful.
- A number of authorities do co-ordinate with other agencies at a rudimentary level, yet overall there appears to be limited regular formal consultation.

- Many housebuilding companies would appear to be willing to provide information regarding local housing markets.
- Housing strategies are prepared, but on the whole they are prepared under the auspices of the housing department, suggesting that they may be biased towards a social housing document, based on HIP submissions.

In addition to a situation where housing strategies ensure that a local authority looks to other authorities for indications of factors that may, or may not, affect its housing strategy, these documents would serve another purpose. The development of integrated housing strategies will require local authorities to examine the housing market as an authority, rather than in terms of departments. One would suggest, therefore, that housing strategies should be seen as a means of overcoming the tenurally-based view of the housing market, that appears to predominate currently. This would ensure that policy and housing provision becomes more responsive to the practicalities of housing choice and housing provision, which has increasingly become less clear with the margins that exist between 'categories' becoming less distinct.

## Final Remarks

This work has examined a number of different areas, ranging from an analysis of the housing market to the national policy as it relates to housing strategies. Each of these areas could provide a research topic in itself, yet it was thought necessary to combine these areas to provide an integrated approach. When the research commenced, the expectation was that integrated housing strategies would be prepared by a number of authorities (proved to be the case); that a number of different agencies would be involved (rather less than may have been anticipated); and a number of data sets would be used (apart from a few exceptional authorities this did not really prove to be the case).

What is necessary to ensure that housing strategies develop into the next millennium is commitment, support and encouragement. The commitment of the local authorities to produce integrated housing strategies; the support of external agencies to contribute and develop such

## 246  *The Formulation of Local Housing Strategies*

strategies; and perhaps more fundamentally the encouragement of central government to ensure innovative strategic plans are supported and local authorities are not discouraged from producing strategies based upon extensive data monitoring and multi-agency involvement. It is perhaps the last of these requirements that may prove the most difficult to achieve.

# Bibliography

Acres, J. (1993) 'Leicestershire Exploits New System', *EM Spectrum*, June.
Association of District Councils (1989) *Meeting Housing Needs: A Report on Research for the Association of District Councils*, ADC.
Association of Metropolitan Authorities (1987) *Local Housing Strategies*, AMA, London.
Audit Commission (1992) *Developing Local Authority Housing Strategies*, HMSO, London.
Audit Commission Update (1998) *Developing Local Authority Housing Strategies*, HMSO, London.
Ball, M. and Kirwan, R. (1977) 'Accessibility and Supply Constraints in an Urban Housing Market', *Urban Studies*, Vol. 14, No. 3, pp. 11-32.
Ball, M. (1983) *Housing Policy and Economic Power*, UP, London.
Ball, M. (1996) *Housing and Construction: A Troubled Relationship*, Policy Press/Joseph Rowntree Foundation, York.
Barkham, R. and Geltner, D. (1995) 'Owner-Occupied Houses versus Commercial Property in the UK: A Suggestion for Promoting Home Affordability and Investment Opportunities', *Cutting Edge '95*, Conference, Aberdeen.
Barlow, J. (1990) *Who Plans Berkshire? The Housing Market, House Price inflation and Developers*, Working Paper 72, CURR, University of Sussex.
Barlow, J. and King, A. (1992) 'The State, the Market and Competitive Strategy. The Housebuilding Industry in Britain, France and Sweden', *Environment and Planning A*, Vol. 24.
Barlow, J., Cocks, R. and Parker, M. (1994) *Planning for Affordable Housing*, DoE/HMSO, London.
Barnett, P.R. and Lowe, S. (1990) 'Measuring Housing Need to the Provision of Social Housing', *Housing Studies*, Vol. 5, pp. 184-194.
Barrett, S. and Healey, P. (1985) *Land Policy Problems and Alternatives*, Gower, Aldershot.
Bateman, T. (1993) 'A Private Sector Perspective', *Planning for the 21st Century Conference*, 21 November 1993.
Bell, J. (1988) *Doing Your Research Project*, Open University Press, Milton Keynes.
Berry, F. (1974) *Housing The Great British Failure*, Charles Knight.
Bibby, P. and Shepard, J. (1993) *Housing Land Availability: The Analysis of PS3 Statistics on Land With Outstanding Planning Permission*, DoE/HMSO, London.
Birchall, J. (Ed) (1992) *Housing Policy in the 1990s*, Routledge, London.

Black, J. and Stafford, D.C. (1988) *Housing Policy and Finance*, Croom Helm, London.
Blincoe, W.F. (1987) 'Demand Attention: Why Development Plans Need to Take Account of Market Demand', *The Planner*, Vol. 73, No. 11, pp. 37-38.
Boulton, R. (1993) 'Draft EM Regional Guidance Eagerly Awaited', *EM Spectrum*, June.
Bramley, G. (1989) *Meeting Housing Needs*, Association of District Councils.
Bramley, G. (1991) *Bridging the Affordability Gap in 1990 - An Update of Research on Housing Access and Affordability*, Housebuilders Federation and Association of District Councils.
Bramley, G. (1993) 'The Impact of Land Use Planning and Tax Subsidies on the Supply and Price of Housing in Britain', *Urban Studies*, Vol. 30, No. 1, pp. 5-30.
Bramley, G. (1994a) *Housing Supply: The Effects of Differing Land Use Controls and Expectations on Private Housebuilding*, Housing Economics Seminar, Glasgow, 28-30th March 1994.
Bramley, G. (1994b) 'The Enabling Role for Local Housing Authorities', *Implementing Housing Policy*, (Eds) Malpass, P. and Means, R., OUP.
Bramley, G. (1996) *Steering the Housing Market: New Building and the Changing Planning System*, Policy Press/Joseph Rowntree Foundation.
Bramley, G. and Watkins, C. (1996) *Steering the Housing Market. New Building and the Changing Planning System*, Policy Press/Joseph Rowntree Foundation.
Bramley, G., Bartlett, W. and Lambert, C. (1995) *Planning, the Market and Private Housebuilding*, UCL Press, London.
Bramley, G., Leather, P. and Murie, A. (1979) *Housing Strategies and Investment Programmes*, SAUS Working Paper No. 7, Bristol.
Bramley, G., Pawson, H. and Parker, J. (2000) *Local Housing Needs Assessment: A Guide to Good Practice*, DETR, London.
Bramley, G., Bartlett, W., Franklin, A. and Lambert, C. (1990) *Housing Finance and the Housing Market in Bristol*, Joseph Rowntree Foundation, York.
Breheny, M. (1993) 'Fragile Regional Planning', *The Planner*, January, pp. 10-12.
Breheny, M. (1995) 'The Housing Numbers Game – Again', *Town and Country Planning*, July 1995.
Brooke, R. (1989) *Managing The Enabling Authority*, Longman, Harlow.
Brooke, R. and Fordham, R. (1993) 'A Survey of Surveys', *Housing*, July, p. 59.
Brotherton, D. I. (1982) 'Development Pressures and Control in the National Parks. 1966-1981', *Town Planning Review*, No. 53, pp. 439-59.
Bruton, M. and Nicholson, D. (1987) *Local Planning in Practice*, Hutchinson, London.
Buchanan, C.D. (1963) *Traffic in Towns (Buchanan Report)*, HMSO, London.
Cairncross, F. (1992) 'The Influence of the Recession', in *British Social Attitudes: 9th Report*, Dartmouth Publishing, Aldershot.
Cambell, R. (1975) *Population Trends*, No. 5, OPCS, HMSO, London.

Cambridge Econometrics/North Ireland Economic Research Centre (1988) *Regional Economic Prospects*, Cambridge.
Cambridge Econometrics (1994) *Regional Economic Prospects: Analysis and Forecasts to 2005*, Cambridge.
Cambridge Econometrics (1995) *Regional Economic Prospects: Analysis and Forecasts to 2005*, Cambridge.
Cambridge Econometrics (1996) *Regional Economic Prospects: Analysis and Forecasts to 2005*, Cambridge.
Cardoso, A. and Short, J.R. (1983) 'Forms of Housing Production: Initial Formulations', *Environment and Planning A*, No. 15, pp. 917-928.
Carter, N. and Brown, T. (1990) *The Relationship Between Expenditure-Based Plans and Development Plans; Working Paper No.1*, Leicester Polytechnic School of the Built Environment.
Carter, N., Brown, T. and Abbot, T. (1991a) *The Relationship Between Expenditure-Based Plans and Development Plans; Summary Report*, Leicester Polytechnic School of the Built Environment.
Carter, N., Brown, T. and Abbot, T. (1991b) *The Relationship Between Expenditure-Based Plans and Development Plans; Final Report*, Leicester Polytechnic School of the Built Environment.
Champion, A.G. and Green, A.E. (1975) *In Search of Britains Booming Towns*, CURDS Discussion Paper 72, University of Newcastle upon Tyne.
Champion, A.G. and Green, A.E. (1987) 'The Booming Towns of Britain: The Geography of Economic Performance in the 1980s', *Geography*, Vol. 72, pp. 97-108.
Champion, T. (1993) *Population Matters: The Local Dimension*, PCP, London.
Champion, T. and Brunsdon, C. (1988) *The Variation of House Prices Between Local Labour Market Areas. A Preliminary Analysis of Building Society Data*, CURDS Discussion Paper 90, University of Newcastle upon Tyne.
Charles, S. (1977) *Housing Economics*, Macmillan, Basingstoke.
Cherry, A.H. (1993) 'Social Housing the Housebuilders' View', *Housebuilder*, July/August 1993, pp. 18-19.
Cheshire County Council (1986) *Housing Demand in Cheshire, A Study of Possible Indicators*, Chester.
Chiddick, D. (1987) 'The Need for New Housing', *The Planner*, Vol. 73, No. 2, pp. 33-35.
Chiddick, D. and Dobson, M. (1986) 'Land for Housing; Circular Arguments', *The Planner*, March.
Church, J. (Ed.) (1993) *Regional Trends 28*, CSO, HMSO, London.
Clapham, D. (1996) 'Housing and the Economy: Broadening Comparative Housing Research', *Urban Studies*, Vol. 33, Nos. 4-5, pp. 631-647.
Clark, D.M. (1990) *Affordable Rural Housing. Challenge for the Nineties*, ACRE/RDC, Cirencester.

CML/BSA (1994) *Housing Finance*, Statistical Summary, August and November.
CML/BSA (1995) *Housing Finance*, Statistical Summary, November.
CML/BSA (1996) *Housing Finance*, February.
Coates, D. (1996) 'High Court Confirms Housebuilders Worst Fears Over Plan Led System', *Housebuilder*, June.
Coles, A. (1991) 'Changing Attitudes to Owner Occupation', *Housing Finance*, No. 11, CML.
Coles, A. and Taylor, B. (1993) 'Trends in Tenure Preferences', *Housing Finance*, No. 19, CML.
Cole, I. and Goodchild, B. (1993) *Local Housing Strategies in England*, CRESR Working Paper 26, Sheffield Hallam University, School of Urban and Regional Studies.
Constable, M. (1987) *Village Homes for Village People*, NACRT.
Coombes, M. (1995) 'The LS and Travel to Work Areas', *OPCS Longitudinal Study*, Issue 12.
Coopers and Lybrand Associates (1985a) *Land Use Planning and the Housing Market, Analysis of Structure Plans and Supporting Documantation*, Phase I Working Paper, London.
Coopers and Lybrand Associates (1985b) *Land Use Planning and the Housing Market, The Case Study's*, Phase II Working Paper, London.
Coopers and Lybrand Associates (1985c) *Land Use Planning and The Housing Market, Summary Report*, DoE, London.
Coopers and Lybrand Associates (1987) *Land Use Planning and Indicators of Housing Demand*, London.
Corner, I. (1994) *Household Projection Methods*, Paper prepared on behalf of the DoE for LUDCARPS Technical Meeting on Household Projections, Feb. 1994.
Council of Mortgage Lenders (2000) *Housing Finance*, No. 45 February.
Council of Mortgage Lenders (2001) *Housing Finance*, No. 49, February.
Crabtree, D. (1993) 'Leicestershire Revises SP Housing Figures', *EM Spectrum*, June.
Crofton, B. (1977) 'Housing Investment Programmes', *Housing Review*, July-August, pp. 83-86.
Crook, T., Hughes, J. and Kemp, P. (1995) *The Supply of Privately Rented Housing*, Housing Research Findings, No. 139, Joseph Rowntree Foundation, York.
Crook, T., Kemp, P., Anderson, I. and Bowman, S. (1991) *Tax Incentives and the Revival of Private Renting*, Cloister Press, York.
CSO (1992) *Family Spending. A Report on the 1991 Family Expenditure Survey*, GSS, HMSO, London.
CSO (1993) *Social Trends 23*, GSS, HMSO, London.
CSO (1995) *Focus on the East Midlands*, GSS, HMSO, London.
Cuddy, A. and Hollingsworth, M. (1985) 'The Review Process in Land Availability Studies: Bargaining Positions for Builders and Planners', in Barrett, S. and

Healey, P. (Eds) *Land Policy Problems and Alternatives*, pp. 160-178, Gower, Aldershot.
Cullingworth, J.B. (1976) 'Housing Priorities and Inflation', *Housing Review*, January/February 1976, pp. 5-7.
Cullingworth, J.B. (1979) *Essays on Housing Policy. The British Scene*, George Allen and Unwin.
Cullingworth, J.B. and Nadin, V. (1994) *Town and Country Planning in Britain*, Routledge, London.
CURS (1980) *The Role of the Local Authority in Land Programming and the Process of Private Residential Development*, Residential Memorandum 80.
Darke, J. and Darke, R. (1979) *Who Needs Housing?*, Macmillan, Basingstoke.
Dent, M. (1991) 'Unitary Development Plans', *The Planner*, TCPSS Proceedings, December, pp. 93-95.
Department of Employment (1984) 'Revised Travel to Work Areas', *Employment Gazette*, September.
Department of the Environment (1970) *Land Availability for Housing*, Circular 10/70.
Department of the Environment (1972) *Land Availability for Housing*, Circular 102/72.
Department of the Environment (1973) *Land Availability for Housing*, Circular 22/73.
Department of the Environment (1975) *Statistics of Land without Standing Planning Permission*, Circular 32/75.
Department of the Environment (1977a) *Housing Capital Expenditure: Arrangements for the Financial Year 1977/78*, Circular 18/77.
Department of the Environment (1977b) *Housing Strategies and Investment Programmes: Arrangements for 1978/79*, Circular 63/77.
Department of the Environment (1977c) *The Assessment of Housing Requirements*, Housing Services Advisory Group.
Department of the Environment (1977d) *Housing Policy: A Consultative Document*, HMSO, London.
Department of the Environment (1978a) *Housing Strategies and Investment Programmes for Local Authorities in England: Arrangements for 1979/80*, Circular 38/78.
Department of the Environment (1978b) *Private Sector Land Requirements and Supply*, Circular 44/78.
Department of the Environment (1979) *Study of the Availability of Private Housebuilding Land in Greater Manchester*, London.
Department of the Environment (1984) *Land for Housing*, Circular 15/84.
Department of the Environment (1987a) *Housing the Governments Proposals*, HMSO, London.

Department of the Environment (1987b) *Change of Use of Buildings and Other Land*, Town and Country Planning (use Classes) Order 1987, Circular 13/87.
Department of the Environment (1988) *Land For Housing*, Planning Policy Guidance 3, HMSO, London.
Department of the Environment (1989) *The Future of Development Plans* (CM569), HMSO, London.
Department of the Environment (1991a) *Household Projections England 1989-2011*, HMSO, London.
Department of the Environment (1991b) *Housing and Construction Statistics 1980-1990: Great Britain*, HMSO, London.
Department of the Environment (1991c) *Housing Land Availability*, Planning Research Programme, HMSO, London.
Department of the Environment (1991d) *Annual Report 1991*, HMSO, London.
Department of the Environment (1991e) *Evaluating the Low Cost Rural Housing Initiative*, Planning Research Programme, HMSO, London.
Department of the Environment (1991f) *Planning for Affordable Housing*, Circular 7/91.
Department of the Environment (1992a) *Housing*, Planning Policy Guidance 3, HMSO, London.
Department of the Environment (1992b) *Development Plans and Regional Planning Guidance*, Planning Policy Guidance 12, HMSO, London.
Department of the Environment (1992c) *Planning Policy and Regional Guidance*, HMSO, London.
Department of the Environment (1992d) *The Relationship Between House Prices and Land Supply*, HMSO, London.
Department of the Environment (1992e) *Development Control Statistics: England 1990/91*, GSS, HMSO, London.
Department of the Environment (1993a) *Housing and Construction Statistics 1982-1992*, HMSO, London.
Department of the Environment (1993b) *Housing Land Availability: The Analysis of PS3 Statistics on Land With Outstanding Planning Permission*, HMSO, London.
Department of the Environment (1993c) *Housing and Construction Statistics, Great Britain*, September Quarter Part 1, HMSO, London.
Department of the Environment (1993d) *Letter to all Chief Executive's Officers of Local Housing Authorities in England*, 11/2/93.
Department of the Environment (1993e) *Development Control Statistics: England 1991/92*, DoE, London.
Department of the Environment (1994a) *Regional Planning Guidance for the East Midlands Region*, RPG8, East Midlands Regional Office.
Department of the Environment (1994b) *Local Housing Statistics*, No.110, HMSO, London.

Department of the Environment (1995a) *Projections of Households in England to 2016*, HMSO, London.
Department of the Environment (1995b) *The Housing Investment Programme: A Review of the Present Process*, Capita Management Consultancy.
Department of the Environment (1995c) *Housing Strategies Guidance for Local Authorities on the Preparation of Housing Strategies*, London.
Department of the Environment (1995d) *Development Control Statistics: England 1993/94*, DoE, London.
Department of the Environment (1996) *Housing Need. The Governments Response to The Second Report From The House of Commons Select Committee on the Environment*, London.
Desborough, J. and Ingham, J. (1988) 'Under Pressure', *Building*, pp. 24-25, London.
DETR (1998) *Planning and Affordable Housing*, Circular 6/98.
DETR (2000) *Conversion and Redevelopment: Processes and Potential*, Llewelyn-Davies, University of Westminster, Urban Investment Partnership and Nottingham Trent University, London.
DETR (2000b) *Housing*, PPG 3 (Revised), London.
DETR (2000c) *Monitoring the Delivery of Housing Through the Planning System: A Good Practice Guide*, TSO, London.
Doak, A.J. (1988) 'Demand Indicators and Local Housing Markets-Reflections From Practice', *University of Manchester Seminar-Housing Market Demand and Planning Policy-Local Impacts and Issues*, 5$^{th}$ May 1988.
Doak, A.J., Henderson, B. and Nadin, V. (1987) 'Joint Housing Studies: Where Do We Go From Here?', *Planning*, 706, pp. 6-7.
Doak, A.J., Nadin, V. and Wood, C. (1990) *Housing Markets and the Planning System*, unpublished draft chapters.
Doling, J. and Ford, J. (1991) 'The Changing Face of Home Ownership: Building Societies and Household Investment Strategies', *Policy and Politics*, Vol. 19, No. 2, pp. 109-118.
Donnison, D.K. (1967) *The Government of Housing*, Pelican.
Donnison, D. and Maclennan, D. (1985) 'What Should We Do About Housing?', *New Society*, 11th April, pp. 43-46.
Donnison, D. and Maclennan, D. (1991) *The Housing Service of the Future*, Institute of Housing/Longman, Harlow.
Dorling, D. (1991) *The Demand for Housing in Britain*, North East Regional Research Laboratory Research Report, 91/8.
Dunmore, K. (1992) *Planning For Affordable Housing. A Practical Guide*, Institute of Housing/Housebuilders Federation.
Dyer, S. (1993) *Local Authority Housing Waiting Lists in Scotland*, Scottish Office Central Research Unit, Edinburgh.
Eddison, T. (1973) *Local Government Management and Corporate Planning*, Leonard Hill Books, London.

Eldridge, B. (1994) *Housing Finance*, No. 21, BSA/CML, London.
Ellis, G., Maktelow, I., Speakman, J. and Stowell, P. (1990) *Prime Numbers. An Analysis of Serplan and Strategic Housing Provision in the South East*, University of Reading (mimeo).
Elworthy, D. (1992) 'Preparing a District Local Plan', *The Planner*, TCPSS Proceedings, November, pp. 72-74.
Ennis, F. (1995) 'Planning Obligations and Developers: Cost and Benefits', paper delivered at the *Cutting Edge '95*, Aberdeen.
Evans, A.W. (1978) *Estimating House Prices and their Movement from Valuation Office Data*, DoE/DoT Research Report 25, London.
Faludi, A. (1973) *Planning Theory*, Pergamon.
Field, B. and McGregor, B. (1987) *Forecasting Techniques for Urban and Regional Planning*, UCL Press, London.
Findlay, J. and Bourke, A. (1988) *Joint Housing Land Availability Studies - The Greater Manchester Experience*, Greater Manchester Research and Information Planning Unit.
Fleming, M.C. and Nellis, J.G. (1990) 'The Rise and Fall of House Prices: Causes, Consequences and Prospects', *Nat West Bank Quarterly Review*, November 1990.
Fleming, M.C. and Nellis, J.G. (1993) Unpublished Internal Report, Department of the Environment Housing Data Statistics Division, 2 Marsham Street London, SW1P 3EB.
Foot, M. (1973) *Anuerin Bevan*, Dowis Poynter, London.
Ford, J. and Wilcox, S. (1992) *Reducing Mortgage Arrears and Possessions*, Joseph Rowntree Foundation, York.
Forrest, R. and Murie, A. (1983) 'Residualisation and Council Housing: Aspects of the Changing Social Relations of Housing Tenure', *Journal of Social Policy*, 12(4), pp. 453-468.
Forrest, R., Murie, A. and Williams, P. (1990) *Home Ownership: Differentiation and Fragmentation*, Unwin Hyman, London.
Forrest, R., Leather, P., Gordon, D. and Pantazis, C. (1995) 'The Future of Home Ownership', *Housing Finance*, No. 27, August.
Foster, S. (1993) *Missing the Target*, Shelter, London.
Fothergill, S. and Beatty, C. (1996) 'Labour Market Adjustment in Areas of Chronic Industrial Decline: The Case of the UK Coalfields', *Regional Studies*, 30 (7), pp. 627-640.
Foulkes, A. and Woodhead, K. (1986) 'Cheap - But How Effective? House Price Monitoring from Newspaper Advertisements', *BURISA*, 73, April.
Fraser, R. (1991) *Working Together in The 1990s*, Institute of Housing.
Freeke, J. (1993) *Local Plan Practice and Migration Data: A Glasgow Case Study*, Strathclyde University, Glasgow.
Fulton, S. (1993) *UK Housing*, Yamaichi, London.

Gentle, C., Dorling, D. and Cornford, J. (1994) 'Negative Equity and British Housing in the 1990s: Cause and Effect', *Urban Studies*, Vol. 31, pp. 181-199.

Gerald Eve/Department of Land Economy, Cambridge University (1992) *The Relationship Between House Prices and Land Supply*, DoE Planning Research Programme.

Gibbs, K. and More, A. (1991) 'Choking Growth', *New Statesman and Society*, 7th June 1991.

Gillen, M. (1994a) *The Volume Housebuilders. Identification and Taxonomy*, Centre for Residential Development Working Paper No. 2, Nottingham Trent University.

Gillen, M. (1994b) *Housebuilding Starts and Completions: Robustness, Trends and Market Share*, Centre for Residential Development Working Paper No. 8, Nottingham Trent University.

Gillen, M., Nicol, C. and Tilling, S.A. (1995) *Market Monitoring and the Employment of Data: The Experience of Planning Authorities*, Centre for Residential Development Working Paper No. 18, Nottingham Trent University.

Gillingwater, D. (1992) 'Regional Strategy for East Midlands', *Town Planning Review* 63 (4), pp. 422-425.

Godfree, S. (1978) 'Housing Needs, Housing Plans and HIPs' *Housing Review*, March-April 1978, pp. 40-42.

Goodlad, R. (1992) *The Housing Authority as an Enabler*, Longman/Institute of Housing, Coventry.

Goodlad, R. (1994) 'Conceptualising "Enabling": The Housing Role of Local Authorities', *Local Government Studies*, Vol. 20, pp. 570-587.

Gordon, I. (1990) 'Inter District Migration in Great Britain 1980-81', *Environment and Planning A*, Vol. 20, pp. 907-24.

Goss, S. and Blackaby, B. (1998) *Designing Local Housing Strategies. A Good Practice Guide*, CIH/LGA, Coventry.

Government Statistical Service (1995) *New Earnings Survey*, London, HMSO.

Greenwood, R. and Stewart, J.D. (1974) *Corporate Planning in English Local Government: An Analysis with Readings 1967-72*, Institute of Local Government Studies.

Guillou, N.J.H. (1990) *Assessing Local Housing Requirements: A Study With Reference to Planning Practice*, PhD Thesis, Nottingham Polytechnic.

Hall, P., Thomas, R., Gracey, H. and Derwett, R. (1973) *The Containment of Urban England*, Vols 1 and 2, Allen and Unwin.

Hambleton, R. (1988) 'Policy Planning Reconsidered', *The Planner*, November 1988, pp. 12-15.

Hamnett, C. (1993) 'The Spatial Impact of the British Home Ownership Market Slump 1989-91', *Area*, Vol. 25, No. 3, pp. 217-227.

Hamnett, C. and Randolph, B. (1988) *Cities, Housing and Profits: Flat Break-up and The Decline of Private Renting*, Hutchinson Educational.

Hamnett, C., Harmer, M. and Williams, P. (1991) *Safe as Houses. Housing Inheritance in Britain*, Paul Chapman Publishing, London.
Hampshire County Council (1988) *Market Demand For Housing in Hampshire*, Planning Department, Winchester.
Hampshire County Council (1990) *Market Demand For Housing in Hampshire*, Planning Department, Winchester.
Harvey, J. (1993) *Modern Economics: An Introduction for Business and Professional Students*, Macmillan, Basingstoke.
Henley Centre (1994) *Local Futures 94*, The Henley Centre, London.
Hills, J. (1991) *Unravelling Housing Finance. Subsidies, Benefits and Taxation*, Oxford University Press.
HMSO (1985) *Lifting the Burden*, White Paper, London.
Hole, W. and Brindley, T. (1983) 'Housing Strategies in Practice-Problems and Opportunities', *Local Government Studies*, May/June, pp. 31-34.
Holmans, A. (1995) *Housing Demand and Need in England, 1991-2011*, Joseph Rowntree Foundation, York.
Holmans, A., Kiddle, C. and Whitehead, C. (2000) *Housing Need in the South East and London: An Update*, Cambridge Housing and Planning Research, Research Report 111, University of Cambridge.
Home, R.K. (1985) 'Forecasting Housing Land Requirements', *Land Development Studies*, Vol. 2.
Hooper, A. (1979) 'Land Availability', *Journal of Planning and Environmental Law*, pp. 752-756.
Hooper, A. (1980) 'Land for Private House Building', *Journal of Planning and Environmental Law*, pp. 795-806.
Hooper, A. (1985) 'Land Availability Studies and Private Housebuilding', in Barrett, S. and Healey, P. (Eds) *Land Policy Problems and Alternatives*, pp. 106-127.
Hooper, A. (1992) *Bumping Along the Bottom? The Semi-Detached Housing Market*, Inaugural Professorial Lecture, Nottingham Trent University.
Hooper, A. (1994) *Land Holding by the Housebuilding Industry*, Centre for Residential Development Working Paper No. 7.
Hooper, A. and Nicol, C. (2000) 'Design Practice and Volume Production in Speculative Housebuilding', *Construction Management and Economics*, 18, pp. 295-310.
Hooper, A., Pinch, P. and Rogers, S. (1988) 'Housing Land Availability: Circular Advice, Circular Arguments and Circular Methods', *Journal of Planning and Environmental Law*, April, pp. 225-239.
Houlihan, B. (1983) 'The Professionalisation of Housing Policy Making', *Public Administration Bulletin*, Vol. 41, March, pp. 14-31.
House of Commons (1996) *Housing Need*, House of Commons Environment Committee 2nd Report.
Housebuilders Federation (1994) *Housing Market Report*, August.

Housebuilders Federation (1995a) *Housing Market Report*, March.
Housebuilders Federation (1995b) *Housing Market Report*, July.
Housebuilders Federation (1996) *Housing Market Report*, April.
Housing Monitoring Team (1980a) *New Housebuilding and Housing Strategies: A Report of The Public/Private Sector Housing Forum*, CURS, Research Memorandum 82.
Housing Monitoring Team (1980b) *The Housing Market a Conceptual Framework*, CURS.
Housing Services Advisory Group (1977) *The Assessment of Housing Requirements: Case Studies*, DoE, London.
Hughes, G.A. (1989) *Land Supply, Planning and Private Housebuilding: A Review*, Working Paper 81, SAUS, Bristol.
Hutton, W. (1996) *The State We're In*, Vintage.
Institute of Housing (1990) *Housing Allocations: Report of a Survey of Local Authority's in England and Wales*, IoH, Coventry.
Jackson, A., Morrison, N. and Royce, C. (1994) *The Supply of Land for Housing. Changing Local Authority Mechanisms*, University of Cambridge, Department of Land Economy, DP42.
Johnston, R.J. (1987) 'A note on housing tenure and voting in Britain 1983', *Housing Studies*, 2(2), pp. 112-121.
Joint Land Requirements Committee (1983) *Is There Sufficient Housing Land For the 1980s?*, Housing Research Foundation.
Joint Land Requirements Committee (1984) *Housing and Land 1984-1991: 1992-2000*, Housing Research Foundation.
Kearns, A. and Maclennan, D. (1991) 'Public finance for housing in Britain', in Donnison, D. and Maclennan, D. (Eds) *The Housing Service of the Future*, IOH/Longman, Harlow.
Keogh, G. (1989) *A Review of House and Land Price Data in the UK*, University of Reading Research Papers in Land Management, Development and Environment Policy No. 2.
Khan, F. (1990) *House Purchaser Survey - An Aid to Plan Monitoring*, University of Strathclyde.
King, D. (1984) *Forecasting Local Housing Requirements. A Renewal of Interest in the Demographic Approach?*, Chelmer Working Papers in Environmental Policy No. 2, Chelmsford.
King, D. (1986) *Proposals for Major Extensions of CPHM Re: Market Demand Forecasting*, CPHM Working Note 2.
King, D. (1987a) 'Grasping the Nettles in the Numbers Game', *Planning*, No.747, pp. 10-11.
King, D. (1987b) 'Housing: Local Vacancy Rates', *BURISA*, No. 78, pp. 8-11.
King, D. (1991) *'The Demographic Bulldozer' - Myth or Reality*, HBF, London.

King, D. (1993) 'Demography and Housebuilding Needs: A Critique of the Demographic Bulldozer Scenario' in Champion, T. (Ed.) *Population Matters, The Local Dimension*, PCP, London.

Kirk, B. and Shucksmith, M. (1990) *Rural Housing Market Studies. A Summary*, Scottish Homes Research Report Number 13, Edinburgh.

Kirkby, K., Finch, H. and Wood, D. (1988) *The Organisation of Housing Management in English Local Authorities*, DoE/HMSO, London.

Kleinman, M. and Whitehead, C. (1989) 'The Market for New Housing in the 1990s', in Cross, D.T. and Whitehead, C.M.E. (Eds) *Development and Planning 1989*, Newbury Policy Journals.

Kleinman, M. (1991) *Social Housing in the 1980s and 1990s. Past Experience and Future Needs*, Discussion Paper 32, University of Cambridge Department of Land Economy.

Kleinman, M. and Roberts, E. (1991) *The Acceptable Face of Social Housing*, Discussion Paper 29, University of Cambridge, Department of Land Economy.

Lambert, C. (1990) *New Housebuilding and the Development Industry in the Bristol Area*, Working Paper 86, SAUS, Bristol.

Lavender, S.P. (1990) *Economics for Builders and Surveyors*, Longman, Harlow.

Leach, S. et al. (1983) 'Uses and Abuses of Policy Planning Systems', *Local Government Studies*, Jan/Feb.

Lee, J. and Robinson, W. (1990) 'The fall in the savings ratio: the role of housing', *Fiscal Studies*, 11, pp. 36-52.

Lee-Steere, G. (1989) 'The Need for Affordable Rural Housing', *Housing and Planning Review*, Vol. 44, No. 2.

Leicestershire CC (1994) *Structure Plan 1991-2006*, County Hall, Leicester.

Leicestershire CC (1996) *Unemployment Bulletin*, May, County Hall, Leicester.

Lichfield, N. (1990) 'Dialogue in Development Planning: The Changing Dimension', in Trench, S. and Oc, T. (Eds) *Current Issues in Planning*.

Lipsey, R.G. (1979) *An Introduction to Positive Economics*, Wiedenfeld and Nicolson, London.

Littler, S., Tewdwr-Jones, M., Fisk, M. and Essex, S. (1994) *Housing Planning and the Development Process*, Paper to the Housing Studies Association, SAUS, Bristol.

Lloyd, M.G. and Rowan Robinson, J. (1992) 'Review of strategic planning guidance in Scotland', *Journal of Environmental Planning and Management*, 35, pp. 93-99.

Lowndes, V. and Stoker, G. (1992) 'Evaluation of Neighbourhood Decentralisation', *Policy and Politics*, Vol. 20, No. 9, pp. 47-61.

Maclennan, D. (1977) 'Some Thoughts on the Nature and Purpose of House Price Studies', *Urban Studies*, 14, pp. 59-71.

Maclennan, D. (1982) *Housing Economics*, Longman, Harlow.

Maclennan, D. (1991) 'Extending the Strategic Role', pp. 185-211 in Donnison, D. and Maclennan, D (Eds) *The Housing Service of the Future*, IOH/Longman, Harlow.

Maclennan, D. and Gibb, K. (1993a) *Housing Policy and Economic Recovery*, Joseph Rowntree Foundation, York.

Maclennan, D. and Gibb, K. (1993b) 'Political Economy, Applied Welfare Economics and Housing in the UK', in Bains, N. and Whyues, D. (Eds), *Current Issues in the Economics of Welfare*, Macmillan, Basingstoke.

Maclennan, D. and Gibb, K (Eds) (1993c) *Housing Finance and Subsidies in Britain*, Avebury, Aldershot.

Maclennan, D., Gibb, K. and More, A. (1990) *Paying for Britains Housing*, Joseph Rowntree Foundation, York.

Maclennan, D., Gibb, K. and More, A. (1993) 'Housing finance, subsidies and the economy: agenda for the nineties', in Maclennan, D. and Gibb, K. (Eds), *Housing Finance and Subsidies in Britain*, Avebury, Aldershot.

Maclennan, D., Gibb, K. and More, A. (1994) 'Housing Systems, Regions and the National Economy', *Economic Modelling*, 11(2), pp. 228-237.

Maclennan, D., Munro, M. and Wood, G. (1987) 'Housing Choices and the Structure of Housing Markets', in Turner, B., Kemeny, J. and Lindqvist, L. (Eds) *Between State and Market Housing in the Post Industrial Era*, Almqvist and Wiksell, Stockholm.

Maclennan, D., More, A., O'Sullivan, A. and Young, G. (1998) *Local Housing System Analysis Best Practice Guide*, Scottish Homes, Edinburgh.

Malpass, P (1986) 'From Complacency to Crisis', in Malpass, P. (Ed.) *The Housing Crisis*, Croom Helm.

Malpass, P. (1990) *Reshaping Houing Policy. Subsidies, Rents and Residulisation*, Routledge, London.

Malpass, P. (1992) 'Housing policy and the disabling of local authorities', in Birchall, J. (Ed.) *Housing Policy in the 1990s*, Routledge, London.

Malpass, P. (1994) 'Housing policy and the housing system since 1979', in Malpass, P. and Means, R. (Eds), *Implementing Housing Policy*, Open University Press, Milton Keynes.

Malpass, P. and Murie, A. (1994) *Housing Policy and Practice*, Macmillan, Basingstoke.

Mansfield District Council (1993) *Consultative Draft Local Plan*, Civic Centre, Mansfield.

Mansfield District Council (1995) *Economic Development Strategy 1995/96*, Civic Centre, Mansfield.

Mansfield Regeneration Partnership (1994) *The Demand Strategy*, Submission to the East Midlands Government Office Under the Single Regeneration Bid.

Mansley, N., Moore, B., Nicholls, D., Rhodes, J. and Tyler, P. (1992) *Cambridge Economic Review: Volume 2*, PA Cambridge Economic Consultants Ltd/Department of Land Economy, University of Cambridge.
McClenaghan, J. (1991) 'Local Plans: Planning for the Next Property Boom', *Estates Gazette*, 9121, pp. 76-77.
McClenaghan, J. and Blatchford, C. (1993) 'Development Plan Slippage', *The Planner*, February, pp. 29-30.
McGregor, A. and Ross, A. (1995) 'Master or Servant? The Changing Role of the Development Planning System', *Town Planning Review*, Vol. 66, No. 1.
McNamara and Healey, P. (1984) 'The Limitations of Development Control Data in Planning Research: A Comment on Ian Brotherton's Recent Study', *Town Planning Review*, No. 55, pp. 91-101.
Means, R. (1994) 'Perspectives on implementation', in *Implementing Housing Policy*, (Eds) Malpass, P. and Means, R., Open University Press, Milton Keynes.
Merrett, S. (1979) *State Housing in Britain*, RKP, London.
Merrett, S. (1982) *Owner Occupation in Britain* (with Fred Grey), RKP, London.
Merrett, S. (1992) *Towards the Renaissance of Private Rental Housing*, Institute for Public Policy Research, London.
Miles, D. (1992a) 'Housing and the Wider Economy in the Short and Long Run', *National Institute Economic Review*, February, pp. 64-78.
Miles, D. (1992b) 'Housing Markets, Consumption and Financial Liberalisation in the Major Economies', *European Economic Review*, 36, pp. 1093-1136.
Minay, C.L.W. (1992) 'Developing Regional Planning Guidance in England and Wales. A Review Symposium', *Town Planning Review*, Vol. 63, No. 4, pp. 415-434.
Ministry of Housing and Local Government (1945) *Housing*, Cmnd 6609.
Ministry of Housing and Local Government (1965) *Housing Programme*, Circular 21/65, April 1965.
Monk, S. (1991) *Planning, Land Supply and House Prices*, Discussion Paper 33, University of Cambridge, Department of Land Economy.
Monk, S., Pearce, B. and Whitehead, C. (1991) *Planning Land Supply and House Prices; A Literature Review*, Monograph 21, University of Cambridge, Department of Land Economy.
Montgomery, J. and Thornley, A. (1990) *Radical Planning Initiatives*, Gower, Aldershot.
Moor, N. (1993) 'All Change in The Shires', *HouseBuilder*, July/August 1993, pp. 2-3.
Moor, N. (1996) 'Time for a System Overhaul', *Building*, February, pp. 28-29.
Morrell, J. (1992) *Business Forecasts for the Housing Market to 1997*, James Morrell Associates.
Morris, J. (1980) 'The Rise and Fall of Local Housing Strategies?', *Housing Review*, Vol. 29, No. 2, pp. 50-53.

Morris, J. (1991) 'Housing Land Availability', *The Planner*, TCPSS Proceedings, p. 58.
Morris, J. and Winn, M. (1990) *Housing and Social Inequality*, Shipman, London.
Muellbauer, J. (1990) 'The housing market and the UK economy: problems and opportunities', in Ermisch, J. (Ed.) *Housing and the National Economy*, NIESR, Avebury.
Munro, M. (1986) *Testing for Segmentation in the Glasgow Private Housing Market*, Centre for Housing Research Discussion Paper No. 8, University of Glasgow.
Murie, A. (1978) 'Estimating Housing Needs Technique or Mystique', *Housing Review*, May-June, pp. 54-58.
Murie, A. (1983) *Housing Inequality and Deprivation*, Heinemann, London.
Murie, A. and Leather, P. (1977a) 'HIPs: Some Issues', *Housing Review*, July-August, pp. 88-90.
Murie, A. and Leather, P. (1977b) 'Developments in Housing Strategies', *The Planner*, November 1977, pp. 167-169.
Murie, A., Niner, P. and Watson, C. (1976) *Housing Policy and The Housing System*, Allen and Unwin.
Murphy, M. and Berrington, A. (1993) 'Household Change in the 1980s: A Review', *Population Trends*, No.73, pp. 18-26, OPCS, London.
National Federation of Housing Associations (1990) *Paying for Rented Housing*, Research Report 12, London.
National Federation of Housing Associations (1991) *Review of Low Cost Homeownership*, Tony Shepard and Associates for the NFHA, London.
National Housing Forum (1989) *Housing Needs in The 1990s; An Interim Assessment*, National Housing Forum.
Needleman, L. (1965) *The Economics of Housing*, Staples Press.
Neutze, M. (1987) 'The Supply of Land For a Particular Use', *Urban Studies*, 24, pp. 379-388.
Newton, J. (1992) 'Housing Caught in the Web', *Municipal Journal*, April, pp. 16.
NHBC (1993) *Private Housebuilding Statistics*, Quarter 3.
Nicol, C. (1991) *Rural Housing: A Crisis in Search of a Solution*, unpublished Degree Dissertation, Department of Planning and Housing, Heriot-Watt University.
Nicol, C. (1994) *House Price Series: Interpretation, Compatibility and Applications*, Centre for Residential Development Working Paper No. 4, The Nottingham Trent University.
Nicol, C. (1995) *East Midlands: Trends, Prospects and the Implications for Housebuilders*, Centre for Residential Development Working Paper No. 9, The Nottingham Trent University.
Nicol, C. (1996) 'Interpretation and compatibility of house-price series', *Environment and Planning A*, Vol. 28, pp. 119-133.
Niner, P. (1989) *Housing Needs in the 1990s*, Housing Forum.

North West Leicestershire D.C. (1993) *Consultation Draft Local Plan Written Statement*, Coalville.
Nottinghamshire County Council (1982) *National Dwelling and Housing Survey Data for Nottinghamshire*, Monitoring Note Three.
Nottinghamshire County Council (1994a) *Nottinghamshire Structure Plan Review Deposit Draft*, County Hall Nottingham.
Nottinghamshire County Council (1994b) *Nottinghamshire Structure Plan Review. Technical Report 1: Population and Housing*, County Hall, Nottingham.
Nottinghamshire County Council (1994c) *Nottinghamshire Structure Plan Review. Technical Report 2: The Economy*, County Hall, Nottingham.
Nuffield Foundation (1986) *Town and Country Planning: The Report of a Committee of Enquiry*, The Foundation, London.
OPCS (1992a) *1991 Census County Report Nottinghamshire (Part 1)*, HMSO, London.
OPCS (1992b) *1991 Census County Report Leicestershire (Part 1)*, HMSO, London.
OPCS (1993a) *1991 Based National Population Projections*, Series PP2, No. 18, HMSO, London.
OPCS (1993b) *Census Report for Great Britain (Part 1) Volume 1 of 3*, HMSO, London.
OPCS (1994) *1993 Based Population Projections for Local Authority Areas in England*, PP3 94/1, OPCS, London.
OPCS/GRO(S) (1992) *1991 Census Definitions Great Britain*, HMSO, London.
Orchard, K. (1992) *The Role of the Market Researcher within Wimpey Homes Holdings*, Wimpey Homes PLC/The Nottingham Trent University.
Page, D. (1993) *Building for Communities: A Study of New Housing Association Estates*, Joseph Rowntree Foundation, York.
Pannell, B. and Champion, D. (1992) 'The New Survey of Mortgage Lenders', *Housing Finance*, No. 16, p. 20.
Pearce, B. and Wilcox, S. (1991) *Homeownership Taxation and the Economy*, Joseph Rowntree Foundation, York.
PIEDA (1985) *Housing Demand in Scotland*, PIEDA, Edinburgh.
PIEDA (1995) *Strategic Use of Local Authority Housing Plans*, Scottish Homes Working Paper, Edinburgh.
Planning (1993) *Leicestershire Gets No Respite From Housebuilders Over Plan*, No. 1016, Ambit Publications.
Planning (1994a) *Leicestershire Landmark Plan Sticks to its Guns on Housing*, No. 1951, Ambit Publications.
Planning (1994b) *Landmark or Black Mark for Self-Approval Regime*, No. 1052, Ambit Publications.
Planning (1994c) *Berkshire Rejects Panel Calls for Higher Housing Allocation*, No. 1069, Ambit Publications.

Planning (1995a) *Government Sticks to Regional Suggestion for Housing Target*, No. 1115, Ambit Publications.
Planning (1995b) *Rising Household Projections Lined Up for More Controversy*, No. 1109, Ambit Publications.
Planning Week (1996) *RTPI News*, 28th March 1996.
Plowden Report (1967) *Children and Their Primary Schools*, Central Advisory Committee for Education, HMSO, London.
Randolph, B. (1995) 'The Shared Ownership Market: A Review of Provision and Prospects', *Housing Finance*, No. 27, pp. 30-32, BSA/CML.
Ratcliffe, J. (1985) *An Introduction to Town and Country Planning*, The Built Environment, Hutchinson.
Reid, B. (1995) 'Interorganisational Networks and the Delivery of Local Housing Services', *Housing Studies*, Vol. 10, No. 2, pp. 133-149.
Roger Tym and Partners (1984) *Housing Demand in Greater Manchester*, Housing Research Foundation.
Roger Tym and Partners (1988) *South Warwickshire Housing Study*, Technical Paper Four, London.
Royal Institution of Chartered Surveyors (1986) *Housing The Next Decade*, RICS.
Rural Development Commission (1996) *Rural Needs in Local Authority Housing Strategies*, Salisbury.
Rydin, Y. (1983) *Housebuilders as an Interest Group: The Issue of Residential Land Use Availability*, Geography Discussion Papers New Series No. 6, L.S.E.
Rydin, Y. (1985) 'Residential Development and The Planning System', *Progress in Planning*, Vol. 24, p. 69.
Rydin, Y. (1986) *Housing Land Policy*, Gower, Aldershot.
Rydin, Y. (1988) 'Joint Housing Studies: Housebuilders, Planners and the Availability of Land', *Local Government Study*, March/April, No. 14, pp. 69-90.
Saul, S. (1989) 'New Homes, New Work Patterns', *Housebuilder*, Vol. 48, No. 11, pp. 30-32.
Saunders, P. (1990) *A Nation of Home Owners*, Unwin Hyman.
Saunders, P. and Harris, C. (1988) *Home Ownership and Capital Gains*, University of Sussex Working Paper 64.
Scottish Development Department (1975) *Housing Needs and Strategies*, Circular 100/1975.
Scottish Development Department (1977) *Scottish Housing Handbook 1: Assessing Housing Requirements*, HMSO, Edinburgh.
Scottish Homes (1993) *Local Market Analysis and Planning in Scottish Homes. A Best Practice Guide*, Edinburgh.
Secretary of State for Scotland (1977) *Scottish Housing - A Consultative Document*, HMSO, Edinburgh.
Seebohm Report (1968) *Report of the Committee on Local Authority and Other Allied Personal Social Services*, CMND 3703, HMSO, London.

Shaw, C. (1993) '1991 Based National Population Projections for the UK and Constituent Countries', *Population Trends*, No. 72, pp. 45-50, Summer.
Shoemaker, A.C. (1987) 'Housing Needs Assessments: A Procedural Guide', *Journal of Housing*, pp. 25-29.
Short, J., Fleming, S. and Witt, S. (1986) *Housebuilding, Planning and Community Action*, Routledge and Kegan Paul, London.
Simpson, S. (1993) 'Measuring and Coping With Local Under Enumeration in the 1991 Census', paper presented to *The British Society of Population Studies Conference*, Research on the 1991 Census, University of Newcastle-upon-Tyne, 13th-15th September.
Smith, M.E.H. (1989) *Guide to Housing*, Housing Centre Trust.
Smith, R. (1988) 'Housing Policy, The Local Economy and Social Life Styles: The Case of Nottingham', *International Conference on Housing, Policy and Urban Innovation*, University of Amsterdam, 28th June to 1st July 1988.
Smyth, H. (1982) *Land Banking, Land Availability and Planning for Private Housebuilding*, School of Advanced Urban Studies, University of Bristol.
Solesbury, W. (1974) *Policy in Urban Planning*, Urban and Regional Planning Series, Vol. 8, Pergamon Press.
Stafford, D. (1978) *The Economics of Housing Policy*, Croom Helm.
Stewart, J.D. (1971) *Management in Local Government: A Viewpoint*, Charles Knight and Co., London.
Stewart, J. (1994) *Housing Market Report*, October, HBF.
Thomas, R. (1994) *The Housing Market in the Late 1990s: What Kind of Recovery*, UBS Global Research, UBS, London.
Thornley, A. (1981) *Thatcherism and Town Planning*, Planning Studies No. 12, Polytechnic of Central London: School of Environment Planning Unit.
Thornley, A. (1991) *Urban Planning Under Thatcherism: The Challenge of the Market*, Routledge, London.
Tilling, S.A. (1994) *Household Projections: Best Guess or Statistical Exactitude?* Centre for Residential Development Working Paper No. 6, The Nottingham Trent University.
Tilling, S.A. (1995a) *British Households: An Analysis of 1991 Census Findings*, Centre for Residential Development Working Paper No. 11, The Nottingham Trent University.
Tilling, S.A. (1995b) *Demographic Forecasting: The Local Dimension. A Case Study of The East Midlands Region*, Centre for Residential Development Working Paper No. 12, The Nottingham Trent University.
Turnbull, G.K., Glascock, J.L. and Sirmans, C.F. (1991) 'Uncertain Income and Housing Price and Location Choice', *Journal of Regional Science*, No. 31, November, pp. 417-33.
Urban Task Force (1999) *Towards an Urban Renaissance*, E. and F.N. Spon, London.

Valuation Office Agency (1995) *Property Market Report: Spring*, Inland Revenue, London.
Van Zijl, V. (1993a) 'Read the Need', *Housing*, July, pp. 56-57.
Van Zijl, V. (1993b) *A Guide to Local Housing Needs Assessments*, David Couttie Associates Ltd./ IoH Coventry.
Wakeford, R. (1993) 'Planning policy guidance. What's the use?', *Housing and Planning Review*, April/May.
Waley, S. (1987) 'Understanding Wonders of the Housing Market', Letter in *Planning*, No. 742, p. 2.
Watson, C. and Crofton, B. (1977) 'Housing Plans-Housing Investment Programmes', *Housing Review*, July/August, pp. 80-90.
Watson, C.J., Niner, P., Vale, G.R. and Smith, B.M.D. (1973) *Estimating Local Housing Needs: A Case Study and Discussion of Methods*, Centre for Urban and Regional Studies Occasional Paper No. 24, University of Birmingham.
Watson, C., Forrest, R., Groves, R., Jarman, R. and Williams, P. (1979) 'Housing Investment Programmes and the Private Sector', *Local Government Studies*, Vol. 28, No. 5, pp. 41-52.
Wells, M. (1996) 'Finding Holes in the Affordable Fence', *Planning Week*, 11th April 1996, pp. 14-15.
Welsh Office (1998) *Local Authority Housing Strategies and Operational Plans 1999-2000*, Welsh Office, Housing Department, Cardiff.
White, P. (1986) 'Land Availability, Land Banking and the Price of Land for Housing: A Review of Recent Debates', *Land Development Study*, May, pp. 101-111.
Whitehead, C.M.E. and Kleinman, M.P. (1992) *Housing Needs and Demands in the 1990s* University of Cambridge Department of Land Economy.
Wilcox, S. (1990) *The Need For Social Rented Housing in England in the 1990s*, Institute of Housing, Coventry.
Wilcox, S. (1994) *Housing Finance Review 1994/95*, Joseph Rowntree Foundation, York.
Wilcox, S. (1998) *Housing Finance Review 1998/99*, Joseph Rowntree Foundation, York.
Williams, G. (1989) 'Monitoring Housing Market Demand in Local Plans', *The Planner*, January, pp. 11-14.
Williams, N.J. and Twine, F.E. (1991) *A Research Guide to the Register of Sasines and the Land Register in Scotland*, Scottish Homes, Edinburgh.
Wilson L.A. (1992) *House Purchasers Survey: An Aid to Planning Monitoring*, Strathclyde University.
Wiltshire County Council (1981) *Housing Market Survey 1981*, Trowbridge.
Wiltshire County Council (1993) *Housing Market Survey 1992*, Trowbridge.
Wriglesworth, J. and Villiers, R. (1994a) *Housing Market Monitoring*, p. 11, UBS Global Research, London.

Wriglesworth, J. and Villiers, R. (1994b) *The Housing Market in the late 1990s: What Kind of Recovery?*, UBS Global Research, London.

Wylie, P. (1994) *Housing Demand Assessment: Towards an Improved Approach*, Unpublished MSc Thesis, Strathclyde University.

9781138263871